This important collection of essays offers a sustained philosophical examination of fundamental questions raised by multicultural education in primary and secondary schools. The essays focus on both theory and policy. They discuss the relation between culture and identity, the role of reason in bridging cultural divisions, and the civic implications of multiculturalism in the teaching of history and literature. Several of the essays examine aspects of multicultural policies in California and New York, as well as the curriculum guidelines promulgated by the National Council for the Social Studies.

Although there exists an extensive literature on multiculturalism in the primary and secondary schools, it remains largely unknown outside professional circles. Moreover, it offers no philosophically sophisticated treatments of multicultural education's pivotal concepts and commitments. This volume, which carefully addresses the philosophical issues surrounding multicultural education, will be welcomed by philosophers and historians of education, sociologists, professional educators and policymakers, other academics, journalists, and the reading public.

Public education in a multicultural society

Cambridge Studies in Philosophy and Public Policy

General Editor: Douglas MacLean

The purpose of this series is to publish the most innovative and up-to-date research into the values and concepts that underlie major aspects of public policy. Hitherto most research in this field has been empirical. This series is primarily conceptual and normative; that is, it investigates the structure of arguments and the nature of values relevant to the formation, justification, and criticism of public policy. At the same time it is informed by empirical considerations, addressing specific issues, general policy concerns, and the methods of policy analysis and their applications.

The books in the series are inherently interdisciplinary and include anthologies as well as monographs. They are of particular interest to philosophers, political and social scientists, economists, policy analysts, and those involved in public administration and environmental policy.

Mark Sagoff: *The Economy of the Earth*
Henry Shue (ed.): *Nuclear Deterrence and Moral Restraint*
Judith Lichtenberg (ed.): *Democracy and the Mass Media*
William Galston: *Liberal Purposes*
Elaine Draper: *Risky Business*
R. G. Frey and Christopher W. Morris: *Violence, Terrorism, and Justice*
Douglas Husak: *Drugs and Rights*
Ferdinand Schoeman: *Privacy and Social Freedom*
Dan Brock: *Life and Death*
Paul B. Thompson: *The Ethics of Trade and Aid*
Steven P. Lee: *Morality, Prudence & Nuclear Weapons*
Jeremy Waldron: *Liberal Rights*
Bernard E. Rollin: *The Frankenstein Syndrome*
Robert E. Goodwin: *Utilitarianism as a Public Philosophy*

education in a
ultural society

Policy, theory, critique

Edited by

ROBERT K. FULLINWIDER

University of Maryland, College Park

CAMBRIDGE
UNIVERSITY PRESS

Published by the Press Syndicate of the University of Cambridge
The Pitt Building, Trumpington Street, Cambridge CB2 1RP
40 West 20th Street, New York, NY 10011-4211, USA
10 Stamford Road, Oakleigh, Melbourne 3166, Australia

First published 1996

Printed in the United States of America

Library of Congress Cataloging-in-Publication Data
Public education in a multicultural society : policy, theory, critique/
[edited by] Robert K. Fullinwider.
p.   cm. – (Cambridge studies in philosophy and public policy)
Includes index.
ISBN 0-521-49624-1. – ISBN 0-521-49958-5 (pbk.)
1. Multicultural education – United States.   2. Multiculturalism–United States.
3. Multiculturalism – Study and teaching – United States.   I. Fullinwider,
Robert K., 1942–   .   II. Series.
LC1099.383   1995
370.19'6'0973 – dc20   95-7766
                                                                   CIP

A catalog record for this book is available from the British Library.

ISBN 0-521-49624-1 Hardback
ISBN 0-521-49958-5 Paperback

Contents

Contents

Contributors

K. Anthony Appiah is Professor of Afro-American Studies and Philosophy at Harvard University. A coeditor of *Transition*, he is the author, most recently, of *In My Father's House: Africa in the Philosophy of Culture* (Oxford University Press, 1992).

Lawrence A. Blum, Professor of Philosophy at University of Massachusetts-Boston, is the author of *Moral Perception and Particularity* (Cambridge University Press, 1993).

Arthur Evenchik is Editor at the Institute for Philosophy and Public Policy. He formerly taught writing and literature at the Illinois Mathematics and Science Academy and continues to teach each summer with the Center for Academically Talented Youth at Johns Hopkins University.

Amy Gutmann directs the University Center for Human Values at Princeton and is the author of *Democratic Education* (Princeton University Press, 1987).

Robert K. Fullinwider directs the Program in Civic and Moral Education at the Institute for Philosophy and Public Policy and writes on moral learning, multiculturalism, and politics.

Susan Khin Zaw teaches at the Open University (Great Britain) and writes on practical reason and moral deliberation.

Gary B. Nash is Professor of History at UCLA and co-director of the Center for History in the Schools. He is an author of *A More Perfect Union*, *A Message of Ancient Days*, and *Across the Centuries* in the Houghton Mifflin Social Studies series designed to meet California's history/social science and multicultural education standards.

Gilbert T. Sewall directs the American Textbook Council. He is a former instructor of history at Phillips Academy, Andover, and education editor at *Newsweek* magazine. He is the author of *Necessary Lessons: Decline and Renewal in American Schools* (Free Press, 1983).

Sandra Stotsky is Research Associate at the Harvard Graduate School of Education and Director of the Institute on Writing, Reading, and Civic Education. She edited and contributed to *Connecting Civic Education & Language Education* (Teachers College Press, 1991).

Jeremy Waldron is Professor of Law, Jurisprudence, and Social Policy in the School of Law, University of California, Berkeley, and the author of *The Right to Private Property* (Oxford University Press, 1988) and *Liberal Rights: Collected Papers 1981–1991* (Cambridge University Press, 1993).

Preface

The chapters in this book evolved from a Working Group on Multicultural Education that met twice in Washington, D.C., during 1991–92. Several members wrote papers discussed at the two meetings, then revised and rewrote them. Other members of the Working Group who did not write papers were nevertheless valuable interlocutors and commentators and helped improve all the papers. Those members (and their affiliations in 1991–92) were Peggy Altoff, Maryland Department of Education; Samuel Banks, Thomas DeLaine, and Jesse Gladden, Baltimore City School System; Richard Wilson, Montgomery County (Maryland) School System; John Fonte, U.S. Department of Education; John Bremer, *The World & I* magazine; Louis Harlan, Department of History, University of Maryland; Jorge Klor de Alva, Anthropology, Princeton University; and William Galston, Institute for Philosophy and Public Policy, University of Maryland.

The Working Group discussed multicultural education in the context of the public school, not the college or university. Although there is considerable overlap in the debates about curriculum on our campuses and curriculum in our public schools, the issues are not always the same. The public schools educate children, rather than adults; they possess a distinctive civic mission; and they must be responsive to community and parental interests. The movement for multicultural education in the schools has an earlier origin than the multicultural reforms on the campuses, with a distinct history and supporting literature. Although the chapters in this book are quite pertinent to contemporary controversies in colleges and universities, their starting points are multicultural policies and challenges in the elementary and secondary school.

"Diversity" is the watchword in multicultural education, and the Working Group exhibited a number of diversities of its own. It contained members whose nations of origin are Ghana, Burma, Mexico, and New Zealand; members from different regions of the United States; members younger and older; members more and less sympathetic to multicultural education; members with practical involvement in multicultural policies; and members with only theoretical interest.

In other ways, the Group reflected uniformities: all of the chapter writers but one are academics, and although the academic disciplines represented include history, literature, and education, philosophy heavily predominates. Moreover, partly as a result of accidents and drop-outs from the Group, the contributions don't span as wide a range of political views as they might in another volume. It was never the aim in composing the Group, however, to represent every opinion. The leading goal was to convene a group of individuals who would not retreat behind their already well-fortified barricades to lob grenades at one another but who would engage in a lively give-and-take from which all would learn something. The Working Group discussions succeeded in this regard, and all the chapters are better for that success.

All the chapters are markedly better, as well, as a result of the painstaking editorial work of Arthur Evenchik, Editor at the Institute for Philosophy and Public Policy and contributor of a chapter of his own. Thanks are also owed to Carroll Linkins and Teresa Chandler of the Institute for helping to organize the Working Group meetings and for providing research assistance.

The Working Group and this consequent volume are projects of the Institute's Program in Civic and Moral Education. The object of the Program is to deepen understanding of moral character and civic virtue, and to explore the best institutional means for their generation. The Program gratefully acknowledges the support it has had from the University of Maryland, the Spencer Foundation, and the Bradley Foundation.

Though written originally for the Working Group, Sandra Stotsky's "Multicultural Literature and Civic Education: A Problematic Relationship with Possibilities" was adapted and condensed for publication as "The Changing Literature Curriculum in K–12," *Academic Questions*, vol. 7, copyright 1993–94, and is here used with permission. The first third of Gary Nash's contribution, "Multiculturalism and History: Historical Perspectives and Present Prospects," borrows from his essay, "The Great Multicultural Debate," *Contention*, vol. 1, copyright 1992, and is likewise used with permission.

RKF

PART I

Introduction and critique

Chapter 1

Multicultural education: concepts, policies, and controversies

ROBERT K. FULLINWIDER

A good school takes children of different ages, temperaments, interests, and abilities and over time brings them to a common level of achievement. It does so in two ways. First, it adjusts its own structure and mode of teaching to the characteristics of the students. For example, it groups younger students together to give them preparatory instruction older students don't need. It gives extra instruction to slower learners. It offers art for students interested in drawing and shop for those interested in building.

Second, a good school requires the students to adjust to it. Whatever their ages, temperaments, interests, and abilities, the school expects the students to work hard, eschew cheating, and treat each other and their teachers with respect and courtesy.

There seems nothing at all controversial about this description of the rudiments of good schooling. Yet we can generate from it educational proposals that spark considerable dissent. Suppose that a school's students differ "culturally." They don't speak the same languages; in their folkways and customs, they are alien to each other and to their teachers; their religious views put them at odds with some of the school's expectations. Then the good school must adjust itself "culturally" to the students, and it must overcome "cultural" barriers to the students' adjusting to it. Here is the germinal idea of *multicultural education*. Multicultural education is what good schools do in the face of extensive "cultural" differences among students and teachers. Multicultural education is what good schools do to assure that "cultural" factors don't get in the way of equal educational opportunity and high student achievement.[1]

Whence, then, comes the controversy? Controversy arises, first, from different ways educators use the idea of "culture." Consider the range of the concept. Is gender "culture"? Is class, ethnicity, race, religion, disability, sexual preference, or age? All of these have been

3

counted as carriers or marks of culture by some multiculturalists.[2] Consider the import of describing something as "cultural." Does the word simply refer to a repertoire of habits and beliefs common to a particular group, or does it also valorize those habits and beliefs, implying some idea of "cultural equality"?[3] Consider membership in a "cultural" group. Is each of us a member of one and only one "culture"?[4] How do we draw the boundaries? What is the significance of overlapping membership?

Controversy likewise arises over how schools should change to assure that "cultural" factors do not impede equal opportunity and high achievement for some students.[5] Do schools currently stack the deck against members of some "cultural" groups by imposing curricular content that ignores or implicitly devalues them?[6] By measuring them against norms appropriate only to other "cultural" groups?[7] By providing them with teachers unable to understand and adjust to their "cultural" differences?[8] We can imagine the wide spectrum of claims offered in answer.

Thus, the germinal idea of multicultural education opens the door to a series of basic questions about schooling – what to teach? how to teach? who to teach whom? – whose answers cannot help but mirror the political struggles of the larger society, with its racial tensions, ethnic hostilities, religious conflicts, class divisions, gender grievances, and ideological cleavages. The classroom becomes an arena where larger cultural and political contests play themselves out. Almost any form of multicultural education will generate quarrels.

THE NEW YORK CONTROVERSY

We can catch some of the flavor of contemporary multicultural quarrels by considering the recent controversy over New York State's multicultural reform efforts. In 1989, a task force established by the Commissioner of Education to review how well New York schools provided "quality education in a pluralistic society" submitted a report called *A Curriculum of Inclusion*. According to the report, New York schools were "contributing to the miseducation of all young people through a systematic bias toward European culture and its derivatives." European culture, the report said, had assumed the place of "master of the house," seated at the head of the educational dinner table looking down at his other cultural guests, who had been invited "through his beneficence." To replace this objectionable state of affairs the report proposed that "all curricular materials be prepared on the basis of multicultural contributions to all aspects of our society." Such a change would supply Native American, Puerto Rican/Latino, Asian-American, and African-American children with greater "self-esteem," and give children from European cultures "a less arrogant perspective."[9]

The report prompted a public retort from a self-styled "Committee of Scholars in Defense of History," whose members included Diane Ravitch, Arthur Schlesinger, Jr., Michael Kammen, Richard Sennett, Frances FitzGerald, James MacGregor Burns, and David Garrow. The Committee charged that *A Curriculum of Inclusion* "contemptuously dismisses the Western tradition" and transforms the teaching of history into "a form of social and psychological therapy whose function is to raise the self-esteem of children from minority groups." The Committee asserted its "belief in a pluralistic interpretation of American history" and its "support for such shamefully neglected fields as the history of women, of immigration and of minorities," but rejected the task force's "reduction of history to ethnic cheerleading."[10]

These strong words prepared the ground for greater public attention to the report of a subsequent panel of scholars and educators reviewing the New York social studies curriculum. When the panel released its report, *One Nation, Many Peoples: A Declaration of Cultural Interdependence*, in June 1991, the *New York Times* featured front-page stories several days running.[11] The widely publicized dissent of Arthur Schlesinger, Jr., one of the panel's consultants, soon augmented by his best-selling book, *The Disuniting of America: Reflections on a Multicultural Society*,[12] written principally in response to *A Curriculum of Inclusion*, helped to fix the public impression of New York's multicultural policies.

Schlesinger detected in *A Curriculum of Inclusion* and in other quarters a "cult of ethnicity" in education. "Of course history should be taught from a variety of perspectives," he allowed; and students "need to learn much more about other races, other cultures, other continents." But the "cult of ethnicity" goes too far.

> The new ethnic gospel rejects the unifying vision of individuals from all nations melted into a new race. Its underlying philosophy is that America is not a nation of individuals at all but a nation of groups, that ethnicity is the defining experience of most Americans.

The "militants of ethnicity," according to Schlesinger, want the schools to protect, strengthen, celebrate, and perpetuate ethnic identity. He worried that if each ethnic and racial community is "taught to cherish its own apartness from the rest," the American melting pot may "give way to the Tower of Babel."[13]

The "militants of ethnicity" who drew most of his attention in *The Disuniting of America* are proponents of "Afrocentric" curricula, whose ideology Schlesinger sees stamped on *A Curriculum of Inclusion*.[14] Afrocentric curricula proceed on the idea that each group should be taught its "appropriate" culture – European culture for Euro-Americans, African culture for African-Americans.[15] Among those promoting Afrocentric schools for American blacks, examples are readily available of the "separatism" Schlesinger writes to warn us away from.

However, neither Schlesinger, nor the Committee of Scholars in Defense of History, nor the authors of *A Curriculum of Inclusion*, reject the germinal idea of multicultural education offered above. Rather, from that idea they proceed in very different directions. For one side, equal educational opportunity requires knocking European "arrogance" down a peg or two. For the other, "ethnic cheerleading" threatens the integrity of the school curriculum and the cohesion of the nation. The germinal idea clearly doesn't contain or forestall controversy. Still, recourse to it might force contending positions better to isolate their differences and describe how they stand in relation to one another.

BACKGROUND

The attention that greeted *One Nation, Many Peoples* in 1991 had a certain peculiarity about it: New York was revisiting a policy already on its books for twenty years.[16] By 1991, more than half the states had adopted some policy or other to implement multiculturalism, and numerous school systems had established some version of a multicultural curriculum.[17]

The New York report didn't formulate the aims and means of multicultural education out of thin air. Rather, it drew upon an extensive body of educational theory. A comprehensive bibliography of materials on multicultural education would likely list as many as a hundred books and several hundred articles and essays.[18] Indeed, one 1986 contribution was already calling the debate "interminable."[19]

This literature – and the movements it supports – arose in response to certain social, political, and educational changes in the United States, Canada, Great Britain, and Australia during the period 1965–90.[20] In the United States, the Civil Rights Movement had by 1965 broken down the barriers of de jure racial segregation, beginning a process that confronted school systems with the challenges of integrating students from different racial and social backgrounds. Overlying this development, extensive immigration from Asia, Central America, the Caribbean, and Mexico added to the mix of students in American classrooms. In many districts, the family backgrounds and economic resources of students varied widely. Students from very poor families, previously segregated schools, or schools in other lands were often underprepared in comparison to other students, and classrooms were filling with students whose first, and often only, language was Korean, Chinese, Vietnamese, Spanish, Creole, or Japanese. Moreover, student populations exhibited a wider and more challenging range of religious diversity than ever before.

Immigration wrought similar changes in classrooms in Great Britain, Canada, and Australia. In all these countries as well as the United States, teachers, administrators, and theorists grappled with the problem of minority student underachievement and sought ways to understand and overcome it. Added to the challenges of immigration and desegregation were three other factors. First, in all these countries, the feminist movement forced comprehensive reconsideration of how the capabilities and opportunities of women and girls were to be conceived. Second, in Canada, cultural nationalism in Quebec emerged as a strong political force. Finally, in the United States, Canada, and Australia, policies toward native or aboriginal populations came under review and were substantially reformed. In each case, these developments put pressure on classroom practices.

In the United States, an early impetus to multicultural education was provided by the Ethnic Heritages Act of 1972, which lent federal support to educational efforts to stimulate greater awareness of cultural variety in America.[21] At about the same time, professional organizations and accrediting bodies began encouraging practical implementation of multiculturalism. The American Association of Colleges for Teacher Education developed a position on multicultural education in its 1969 publication, *Teachers for a Real World*,[22] and its 1972 report, "No One Model American."[23] In 1976, the National Council for the Social Studies (NCSS), the professional association of social studies teachers, published "Curriculum Guidelines for Multiethnic Education"[24] and in 1977 the Teacher Corps in conjunction with the Association of Teacher Educators published a set of materials for multicultural teaching.[25] In 1979, the National Council for Accreditation of Teacher Education established a requirement that all teacher training institutions include some instruction in multicultural education.[26]

I rehearse these matters to show that the idea of multicultural education has been developing for quite some time, and in many different settings, not just the United States. I mention Australia, Canada, and Great Britain because the existing literature on multicultural education reflects considerable reciprocal influence between theorists and policies in those countries and theorists and policies here.[27]

POLICY

How is multicultural education desirable and how is it undesirable as an element of educational policy? To answer that question, we need

7

to know what policies are in dispute. Four important documents are worth considering closely, since they reflect the policies of two of the most populous states – California and New York – and of NCSS, the largest professional organization of teachers in the United States most directly involved in multicultural education. These are (1) the 1991 report of the New York social studies review committee, *One Nation, Many Peoples: A Declaration of Cultural Interdependence*, which laid the basis for, and was partly incorporated in, (2) *Understanding Diversity*, the policy statement adopted by the New York State Board of Regents in July 1991;[28] (3) the California History–Social Science Framework, adopted in 1987;[29] and (4) the NCSS Curriculum Guidelines for Multi-cultural Education, issued in 1991, which revised the Council's 1976 guidelines on ethnic studies.[30]

The California History–Social Science Framework, largely the work of Diane Ravitch (subsequently Assistant Secretary of Education) and Charlotte Crabtree (director of UCLA's National Center for History in the Schools), is significant for the way it restores the study of world and national history to the K-12 curriculum, with formal classes starting in grade four. It also makes "a multicultural perspective" a basic component of the historical studies it establishes.

The NCSS Curriculum Guidelines were written by James Banks, one of the pioneering and most influential theorists of multicultural education. For that reason, these Guidelines represent a canonical version of the multicultural approach to education policy.

Do these documents exhibit the "new ethnic gospel" that worried Arthur Schlesinger? Do they reject "the unifying vision of individuals from all nations melted into a new race"? Do they teach each group to "cherish its apartness from the rest" at the risk of national disunity?

None of these charges would be laid against the California Framework, so I will put it aside to consider two more contentious documents, *One Nation, Many Peoples* and the NCSS Curriculum Guidelines. Let us start with *One Nation*. There is certainly a sense in which it rejects "a unifying vision" of individuals "melted into a new race." It specifically rejects "assimilation" in favor of "pluralism." (This rejection is a fundamental theme of multicultural education. I discuss it further below.) But in rejecting assimilation, what *One Nation* rejects is "assimilation to an Anglo-American model" (xi).[31] It rejects the idea of a "new race" if individuals must relinquish their non-Christian religions, their non-English languages, and their non-British folkways to be a part of it. "Many people in the United States today are no longer comfortable with the requirement, common in the past, that they shed their specific cultural differences in order to be considered Americans," declares *One Nation*. But to reject this particular "unifying vision" is not to reject unity itself; such a vision is simply unneces-

sary in educating "citizens who value this country's ideals and participate in its polity and economy" (4). The pluralism that *One Nation*
favors over assimilation is not a rejection of "American identity" but
"a more tolerant, inclusive, and realistic vision" of it. This latter identity will remain "committed to the democratic principles of the nation
and the nation-building in which all Americans are engaged" (xi).

Schooling that starts from the premise of pluralism will "respond
to the joint imperatives of educating toward citizenship in a common
polity while respecting and taking account of continuing distinctiveness" (4). It will invite students "to search for the commonalities
between their own cultures and those of others" (11). While honoring
the "diverse and pluralistic elements in our nation," it will give "special attention" to "those values, characteristics, and traditions which
we share in common" (1) and to "the common concerns, achievements and aspirations that are the source of national unity" (7). Students of whatever background "must learn the significance of our
democratic rights and principles and the importance of playing an
active role in preserving them and extending them to everyone" (7).

An evangelist of the "cult of ethnicity" would not find *One Nation*
an ideal vehicle for spreading the gospel. A document that refers to
our "common national culture" (11), encourages students "continually" to ask "What holds us together as a nation?" and proposes that
schooling "continually" emphasize the "full and equal humanity of all
persons" (9), seems a poor medium for imparting the view that America is not a nation of individuals and that "apartness from the rest" is
more important than any "unifying vision." This doesn't mean that
One Nation's understandings of race and ethnicity are fully satisfactory, or that there are no tensions between its commitments to diversity and its commitments to unity. But before we note further *One
Nation*'s tensions, let us turn first to look at the NCSS Curriculum
Guidelines.

Do *they* promote the "cult of ethnicity"? Here is what the Guidelines declare: a "democratic society protects and provides opportunities for ethnic and cultural diversity at the same time having
overarching values ·· such as equality, justice, and human dignity –
that all groups accept and respect" (276).[32] A multicultural education
will emphasize pluralism, but a "pluralism . . . within the context of
national unity" (284). These declarations certainly don't give much
aid and comfort to the new ethnic gospel. Indeed, if anything the
Guidelines may seem to err too much on the unity side. They insist
on "the right of ethnic groups to socialize their young" into their own
cultural practices but only "so long as such practices are consistent
with human dignity and democratic ideals. . . . [M]embers of ethnic
groups have both the right and the responsibility to accept U.S. dem-

9

ocratic values and to help shape the significant institutions of the larger society" (277). Applied literally to groups and associations in general, the constraints and responsibilities imposed here by the Guidelines may imply that the Amish, for example, who disengage from involvement with the institutions of the larger society, don't warrant the full tolerance demanded by an appropriate pluralism.

Do the Guidelines teach that "ethnicity is the defining experience of most Americans"? Ethnicity is important "in the lives of many citizens," the Guidelines tell us (275); membership in ethnic groups "can provide [individuals] a sense of belonging, of shared traditions, of interdependence of fate" (277). Even so, the

> degree of individuals' ethnic attachments and affiliations var[ies] great-ly. The beliefs and behaviors of some individuals are heavily influenced by their ethnic culture or cultures; others maintain only some ethnic be-liefs and behavioral characteristics; still others try to reject or lose, or are simply unaware of, their ethnic origins. . . . For many persons, then, ethnic criteria may be irrelevant for purposes of self-identification. . . . Although a democratic society can and should protect the right to ethnic identification, it cannot insist upon it. To do so would violate individual freedom of choice. To confine individuals to any form of affiliation violates the principles of liberty. (278)

Multicultural education not only helps students "*affirm* their commu-nity cultures" but "helps to *free* them from cultural boundaries, allow-ing them to create and maintain a civic community that works for the common good" (274; emphases added).

The Guidelines encourage and support "diversity," to be sure, but explicitly subordinate it to unity (284). They describe individual liber-ty of association and self-definition as the ideal (278, 283). On both scores, the Guidelines explicitly subscribe to, rather than reject, the educational aims Schlesinger thinks proper in our schools.

Still, there is a tension within the Guidelines between avowed aims and programmatic proposals. If ethnicity is important in America, as the Guidelines insist, then schools ought to give it due place, both in what and how they teach and in how they organize themselves. But "due place" doesn't immediately cash out into determinate, uniform programs. Because of the great variability in the meaning of ethnicity, in its larger social effects, and in its effects on individual students – a variability the Guidelines acknowledge on several occasions – and because of the importance of other things besides ethnicity, schools should exercise discretion and flexibility in the way they take eth-nicity into account. Elsewhere, however, the Guidelines seem insis-tent on making ethnicity a pervasive and constant organizing princi-ple both for curriculum and school organization. Ethnic and cultural diversity should "permeate the total school environment," the Guidelines recommend at one point (279). "A school's staff should reflect the ethnic and cultural diversity within the United States," they recommend at another (280). But why should the staff of a high school in North Dakota, say, reflect the ethnic diversity in the United States rather than the diversity in its own community? And what does "permeate the total school environment" mean?

The injunction to "permeate the total environment" might be read innocently as pointing up the need to address ethnicity not only in the school's classrooms but in its extracurricular activities and functions as well. Schools should see to it, for example, that some students are not informally debarred from the cheerleading squad because of their color or family background and that counsellors don't assume certain kinds of students are incapable of advanced academic work (280). Less innocently, the injunction may require the whole curriculum to be organized around ethnicity. This less innocent idea is suggested by the Guidelines' claim that "[p]ersonal ethnic identity is *essential* to the sense of understanding and the feeling of personal well-being that promote intergroup and international understanding." As a consequence, "multicultural education should *stress* the process of self-identification" (278; emphases added).

But how can personal ethnic identification be essential to anything if "for many persons . . . ethnic criteria may be irrelevant for purposes of self-identification" (278)? If throughout its curriculum and activities a school continually stresses "the process of self-identification" in terms of ethnicity, how has it honored the liberty of students not to identify themselves ethnically? Has it not, rather, established a regime of "compulsory ethnicity"?

Such a worry is reinforced when the Guidelines add that "[s]tudents should be helped to develop accurate self-identities" (281). The idea of "accurate self-identities" suggests that identity is some real feature of the student that she can be mistaken about. Multicultural education will set her straight, correct her mistake. This suggestion, however, stands at odds with the idea of self-definition implied in other parts of the Guidelines: a student's identity is just what she makes it. Her identity isn't fixed but fluid, drawing from a variety of sources and influences.

There are, then, aspects of the Guidelines that seem to put ethnicity at the very center of schooling even though at other places the Guidelines concede that ethnicity has varying importance for people. A similar problem arises in *One Nation*. The multicultural education described in it likewise may amount to "compulsory ethnicity" if its insistence that the curriculum "continually encourage students to ask themselves . . . Who am I?" requires students to answer in terms of ethnicity (9). Neither *One Nation* nor the Guidelines leaves the matter fully clear and uncontroversial. How we construe the documents will depend upon our individual sifting and weighing of all the qualifications and elaborations we find in them.

Whether readers find the Guidelines and *One Nation* worrisome or not, the Committee of Scholars in Defense of History, exercised by the first New York report, and other such forces of vigilance among us, should take some solace at the policy on multiculturalism actually adopted in New York State. In the proposals he put before the Board of Regents, the Commissioner of Education, Thomas Sobol, emphatically itemized what he was *not* recommending: trashing the traditions of the West; an Afrocentric curriculum; ethnic cheerleading and separatism; distorting history; a curriculum of self-esteem; or a study of American history based on ethnicity or culture alone.[33]

MULTICULTURAL THEMES

As we read the various policy documents, our likely sticking points will not be the general values, aims, or intentions they express but the specific mind-sets particular educators might bring to interpreting and implementing those values, aims, and intentions. We may all accede to the proposition that students should be presented with a realistic view of American history (Guidelines, 282), but my realism may be your panegyric and another's denunciation. We may agree that curricula should be language-sensitive (*One Nation*, 19), but find ourselves all over the map about acceptable and unacceptable terms and descriptions in schoolbooks and classrooms.[34] We may all believe that students should learn that "difference does not necessarily imply inferiority" (Guidelines, 283), yet quarrel vigorously about the value and acceptability of particular "differences." Thus, in reading the policy statements, we may be more concerned about the lacunae we find there than about anything they actually say.

The extensive literature on multicultural education can fill in some of the lacunae. For the most part, however, the literature leaves many of the crucial questions unaddressed, or deals with them in unsatisfactory ways.

For example, a leading theme in multiculturalism is the preference for "pluralism" over "assimilation,"[35] a motif sounded at the very beginning of *One Nation*. What is the purported contrast? Multicultural theorists typically characterize assimilation as an extreme pole on a continuum of adaptations that culturally different groups might make to a dominant culture. Assimilation means "complete abandonment" of cultural differences;[36] it means a new cultural group giving up its identity and "adopt[ing] totally" the identity of the dominant group;[37] it means an ethnic minority being wholly absorbed into the dominant culture, no longer distinct as a separate group.[38] The other extreme pole on this continuum would represent some sort of cultural separatism, in which cultural groups retain most of their original differences and interact with other groups only for purposes of impersonal economic exchange or political bargaining.[39]

Now, few contemporary Americans would endorse either extreme as an ideal. They, like the multiculturalists, would opt for some midpoint on the continuum. But because the extremes are so far apart, and the points on the continuum so many, simply declaring for *some* mix of assimilation/separatism leaves all the interesting and controversial questions still up in the air.[40] What guides us to one point on the continuum rather than another? What cultural characteristics might we legitimately expect groups to modify or abandon as they are integrated into the larger society?

One Nation rejects the need for ethnically different people to "shed their specific cultural differences" but then immediately describes them "busily adapting to" American ideals (xi). If, however, the "specific cultural differences" in question happen to center on ideals at odds with American ideals, then this busy adapting will necessarily demand some shedding of cultural differences.

There are certainly many "specific differences" that both *One Nation* and the NCSS Guidelines do expect individuals to shed. Just as the Guidelines extend to ethnic groups the right to socialize their young into their own customs only so long as the customs conform to "human dignity and democratic ideals" (277), they likewise instruct the multicultural educator that "ethnic groups' behaviors should be honored as long as they are not inconsistent with major school and societal goals" (280). By this standard, a rather considerable amount of ethnic "shedding" might be called for, depending on how the "major school and societal goals" get specified. Even apart from this potentially repressive standard, no multiculturalist suggests that immigrants to the United States should be encouraged to retain, for example, their native forms of criminality, their virulent hostility to other ethnic groups, or their rejection of peaceful means of adjudication and redress of grievances.

Thus, the crucial question about assimilation/adaptation is, *Which adaptations are reasonable to expect of ethnic groups, and which unreasonable?* For the multiculturalist, the word "assimilation" just stands for the *unreasonable* extreme end of the continuum of adaptations, whatever it is. Thus, the multiculturalist slogan, "pluralism, not assimilation," instead of being instructive, simply encapsulates an empty tautology: culturally different groups needn't give up characteristics that needn't be given up. The real question remains, *What characteristics need to be given up?*

A similar problem infects a second multicultural theme that also serves as a slogan, namely, that students must learn to appreciate and respect cultural diversity.[41] Taken without qualifications – qualifications surely implicit in *One Nation's* injunction that multicultural education should teach respect for common values as well as distinctive ways of life – the slogan seems to recommend an undesirable mindlessness rather than a desirable broad-mindedness. Surely students should learn to respect what is *respectable* and learn to appreciate what is *worthy of appreciation*; and this learning would seem as apposite in ethnic and cultural matters as in any other. But multiculturalists don't press very far beyond the slogan. As with assimilation, they leave the real question unaddressed: *What standards of discrimination should we use to identify the respectable and the worthy in matters of culture?* Multiculturalists remain content to offer the slogan without pressing further largely because they fear that taking stands on the worthy and the respectable in matters of culture opens them to the charge they dislike most, the charge of ethnocentrism. Certainly our history affords no shortage of instances of cultural conceit, boastfulness, and arrogance, and certainly a complex and interesting story needs to be told about ethnocentrism. But the story will be bogus if it proceeds via the suppression of critical judgment. In promoting broad-mindedness and generosity of judgment, multiculturalism must avoid a vacuous relativism.

Consider a third multicultural slogan. When the NCSS Guidelines propose that students must learn that "difference doesn't necessarily mean inferiority" (283), they tap into a central theme in the multicultural literature: *difference, not deficit.*[42] As I indicated earlier, a principal concern of educators in the 1960s and 1970s was how to understand and overcome minority student underachievement. The typical response of educators was to identify and focus on *deficiencies* in minority students. Their impoverished, often broken home environments left them less well prepared for school than other students, went the diagnosis. The solution: various forms of early intervention and remediation.[43]

However well conceived this response might have been, in practice it has frequently resulted in large proportions of African-American and Hispanic children being designated as mentally retarded or relegated to classes for slow learners. Black and Hispanic social scientists, educators, and parents protested vigorously that the problem was not the children but the schools, which were unprepared to adapt to the new students in their classrooms. An egregious example: schools that tested Spanish-speaking children in English and counted their low performances as signs of mental retardation. Thus was born a counter-movement: schools should count their students' cultural experiences and backgrounds as *strengths*, not weaknesses; the school should adjust to the child.

As with the other multicultural slogans, "difference, not deficit" serves as a valuable political prophylactic in a certain kind of environment. In a world where a thoughtless intolerance rules the day, the injunction to "respect and appreciate diversity" points us in the right direction. In a world where a mindless conformism oppresses those who don't fit in, "pluralism, not assimilation" delivers a cogent lesson. In a world where too many children have been victimized by too many unfair educational measurements, "difference, not deficit" prompts a salutary bias: *always* question the measure first rather than the child. Where there is underperformance, don't assume the child must change; assume the school must change.

Still, we cannot erect any of these slogans, including "difference, not deficit," into mechanical rules. For, as I noted at the outset of this chapter, a good school requires children to adjust to it in some respects just as it adjusts itself to its students. In a good school there are genuinely valuable subjects to be learned and fully reasonable rules to be followed. Not every prevailing educational standard or school procedure should be changed because it presents difficulties for some "culturally different" children; and some characteristics, whatever their origins, may truly be deficiencies or liabilities. Not every difference is a deficiency, but neither is every difference *not* a deficiency. The crucial question here, as with the other multicultural slogans, concerns the grounds for discriminating between the good and the bad, the justified and the unjustified: *By what independent criteria should we select or reject educational measures and procedures?*

Finally, consider an aspect of "culture" greatly underdeveloped in the multicultural literature: religion. Although religion almost always appears on the list of "differences" that multiculturalists address, it seldom receives any substantial discussion. Multiculturalist texts containing long chapters on how to deal with race, ethnicity, or gender in the classroom omit instruction on religious differences.[44] Yet these differences are surely among the most important and profound the school will encounter. Indeed, the multiculturalist understanding of ethnicity itself must remain pretty shallow if it doesn't take account of the distinct religious observances and beliefs that anchor many of the customs and folkways of different ethnic groups, especially those that have to do with the organization of the family and the treatment of the sexes. Learning how to approach and discuss religious differences constitutes a central challenge to the schools. One of the strengths of the California History–Social Science Framework lies in the emphasis it places on learning about religion.[45]

One reason religion gets only nominal attention in the multicultural literature lies in a preference expressed in the formative peri-od of multicultural theorizing. Writing in 1977, James Banks observed that although culture is a broad notion, "[p]olicy considerations sug-gest that we limit the boundaries of multicultural education at least to the extent that the focus . . . will be on those groups which are vic-tims of discrimination because of their unique cultural characteris-tics."[46] *Oppression* early became the triggering factor for multicultural education, and in the thoroughly secular perspectives from which most multiculturalists write, religious oppression doesn't show up as an ongoing American problem in the way that racial, ethnic, or gen-der oppression does.[47]

Yet, religious considerations lie as close to the identities of many Americans as their ethnic or racial backgrounds; and religious divi-sion fuels many contemporary political struggles. A multiculturalism genuinely dedicated to pluralism needs to engage religious differ-ences directly and effectively.

CONCLUSION

Democratic institutions do not work by default. Their operations re-quire a citizenry with particular habits of mind and particular commit-ments. These habits of mind and commitments constitute the *political culture* that students must be educated to value and sustain. This civic dimension of multicultural education sets the scene for the chapters that follow in this book.

Jeremy Waldron and Anthony Appiah take up the general connec-tion between culture and identity. The word "culture," they suggest, often carries too much freight in multicultural education, standing variously for society, affinity group, linguistic community, worldview, civilization, and the like. Waldron contrasts a "One Person: One Cul-ture" model to a "One Person: Many Fragments" model, arguing that individual identity typically borrows from a wide array of hetero-geneous "cultural" materials. Looking at society and education from the "One Person: Many Fragments" perspective may incline us to be less concerned about "cultural integrity" and less "hung up on the issue of what it is to acquaint students fully and faithfully with a variety of cultures in the classroom." Similarly, Appiah wants to put into question the idea that public schools should teach each child "its" culture, partly because such teaching actually creates and entrenches the cultural differences it purports only to be mirroring.

Multiculturalism offers the ideal of citizens working together in a common polity while retaining their memberships in distinct cultural communities that accord one another mutual respect. But what underwrites this mutual respect in the face of cultural conflict, especially when this conflict is transferred to the political realm? Is there a culture-neutral Reason to which individuals can appeal in order to resolve conflict? Or does the resort to Reason paradoxically contain within it the seed of dogmatism and coercion? These are the issues Susan Khin Zaw takes up in her chapter, as she gives an account of Reason's practical application that avoids both intolerance and relativism.

Amy Gutmann's contribution starts from multiculturalism's combined ideal. What kind of education does justice to both civic unity and cultural diversity? She describes two inadequate responses, the one too universalist in its approach, the other too particularist. She applies her conception of an appropriate democratic education to a case of religious controversy in the schools.

Lawrence Blum's chapter closely examines the California Framework to see whether it offers a satisfactory conception of citizenship to support antiracist education, whose aims he distinguishes from education for cultural respect. He also looks at the approach of *One Nation, Many Peoples*. Gilbert Sewall, in his chapter, finds in some multicultural sources a distinct anti-Western bias. He dwells on the views expressed in *A Curriculum of Inclusion* and on the influential materials produced in the 1970s by the Council on Interracial Books for Children.

The California Framework, the NCSS Guidelines, and *One Nation, Many Peoples* all take for granted that civic education is centered in the social studies, whose core subject is history. Many multicultural quarrels involve charges about accuracy and distortion in history texts, and about exclusion and inclusion. Two chapters in this book look at teaching history. Gary Nash's chapter describes the great changes that have already taken place in historical scholarship in the last three decades, as well as the changes in the history taught in the classroom. My own chapter gives a sympathetic account of "patriotic history," history taught with a moral and political aim.

Finally, Sandra Stotsky elsewhere has done much to encourage the idea that not just the social studies but the literature curriculum serves civic education.[48] Here, in the context of that idea, she raises a series of questions for appraising changes in the literature curriculum to make it more multicultural. Arthur Evenchik, who has taught literature to high school students, examines theories of civic education and literary pluralism that emerged at the turn of the century. He suggests that neither theory fully recognizes the "moral, aesthetic, and intellectual dimensions of the reading experience," and that the teacher of literature must maintain a certain detachment from both.

NOTES

1. James A. Banks, "Multicultural Education: Characteristics and Goals," in *Multicultural Education: Issues and Perspectives*, ed. James A. Banks and Cherry A. McGee Banks (Boston: Allyn & Bacon, 1992), p. 2 ("Multicultural education incorporates the idea that all students – regardless of their gender and social class, and their ethnic, racial, or cultural characteristics – should have an equal opportunity to learn in school").
2. Christine E. Sleeter and Carl A. Grant, *Making Choices for Multicultural Education: Five Approaches to Race, Class, and Gender* (New York: Merrill, 1994), p. vi; Pamela L. Tiedt and Iris M. Tiedt, *Multicultural Teaching: A Handbook of Activities, Information, and Resources*, 3d ed. (Boston: Allyn & Bacon, 1990), p. 3.
3. Charles Payne, "The Integration of Multicultural Education into the General Preparation of Teachers," in *Multiculturalism in Contemporary Education, Viewpoints in Teaching and Learning* 56, ed. Donna M. Gollnick and Philip C. Chinn (Winter 1980), pp. 80–2; Donna M. Gollnick and Philip C. Chinn, *Multicultural Education in a Pluralistic Society*, 2d ed. (Columbus, Ohio: Charles E. Merrill, 1986), p. 13.
4. Banks, "Multicultural Education: Characteristics and Goals," pp. 13–4.
5. Ibid., p. 1 ("Another important idea in multicultural education is that some students, because of these characteristics, have a better chance to learn in schools as they are currently structured than do students who belong to other groups or have different cultural characteristics").
6. Geneva Gay, "Ethnic Minorities and Educational Equality," in *Multicultural Education: Issues and Perspectives*, ed. Banks and Banks, p. 183; James A. Banks, "Integrating the Curriculum with Ethnic Content: Approaches and Guidelines," in *Multicultural Education: Issues and Perspectives*, ed. Banks and Banks, p. 190; Louis Cohen and Lawrence Manion, *Multicultural Classrooms: Perspectives for Teachers* (London: Croom Helm, 1983), pp. 180–3.
7. Gollnick and Chinn, *Multicultural Education in a Pluralistic Society*, pp. 156–8; Geneva Gay, "Curriculum for Multicultural Teacher Education," in *Pluralism and the American Teacher: Issues and Case Studies*, ed. Frank H. Klassen and Donna M. Gollnick (Washington, D.C.: American Association of Colleges for Teacher Education, 1977), pp. 55–6; James A. Banks, *Multiethnic Education: Theory and Practice*, 2d ed. (Boston: Allyn & Bacon, 1988), p. 212; Jane Mercer, "Alternative Paradigms for Assessment in a Pluralistic Society," in *Multicultural Education: Issues and Perspectives*, ed. Banks and Banks, pp. 289ff.
8. Peter Murrell, "Afrocentric Immersion: Academic and Personal Development of African American Males in Public Schools," in *Freedom's Plow: Teaching in a Multicultural Classroom*, ed. Theresa Perry and James Fraser (New York: Routledge, 1993), pp. 255 ("public schooling, as it is presently constituted, is *congenitally incapable* of providing developmentally appropriate and culturally responsive education for children of color"), 241 ("the predominantly white middle-class teacher corps cannot create or

maintain the same ties with the African American children as they do with mainstream children").

9. Report of the Commissioner's Task Force on Minorities: Equity and Excellence, *A Curriculum of Inclusion*, July 1989 (typescript), pp. 2, iii, iv; see also 37–8.

10. *New York Times*, August 12, 1990, p. E7; originally published in *Newsday*, June 29, 1990, p. 28.

11. New York State Social Studies Review and Development Committee, *One Nation, Many Peoples: A Declaration of Cultural Interdependence* (Albany: New York State Education Department, June 1991).

12. Arthur M. Schlesinger, Jr., *The Disuniting of America: Reflections on a Multicultural Society* (New York: W. W. Norton, 1992). Originally published by Whittle Direct Books, Knoxville, Tenn., 1991.

13. Ibid., pp. 15, 16, 17, 18.

14. Ibid., p. 69. A principal drafter of *A Curriculum of Inclusion* was Leonard Jeffries, the controversial chair of the black studies program at CCNY, most widely known for his teachings about the "ice people" (whites) and the "sun people" (Africans), and for his anti-Semitic diatribes.

15. See Molefi Kete Asante, *Afrocentricity: The Theory of Social Change* (Buffalo, N.Y.: Amulefi, 1980); Molefi Kete Asante, *The Afrocentric Idea* (Philadelphia: Temple University Press, 1987); Portland Public Schools, *African American Baseline Essays* (Portland, Oreg.: 1987).

16. *Understanding Diversity*, Commissioner of Education Thomas Sobol to the New York State Board of Regents, July 12, 1991 (typescript), p. 4.

17. See Robert Crumpton, "Policy Analysis of State Multicultural Education Programs," in *Research and Multicultural Education: From the Margins to the Mainstream*, ed. Carl A. Grant (Washington, D.C.: Falmer Press, 1992), p. 246.

18. Some of the most important works, apart from those referred to in earlier notes, include R. K. Arora and C. G. Duncan, *Multicultural Education: Toward Good Practice* (London: Routledge & Kegan Paul, 1986); James A. Banks, *An Introduction to Multicultural Education* (Boston: Allyn & Bacon, 1994); James A. Banks and James Lynch, eds., *Multicultural Education in Western Societies* (New York: Praeger, 1986); Christine I. Bennett, *Comprehensive Multicultural Education: Theory and Practice*, 2d ed. (Boston: Allyn & Bacon, 1990); Brian Bullivant, *Race, Ethnicity, and the Curriculum* (Melbourne: Macmillan, 1981); Brian Crittenden, *Cultural Pluralism and Common Curriculum* (Melbourne: Melbourne University Press, 1982); Carl Grant, ed., *Research and Multicultural Education: From the Margins to the Mainstream* (Washington, D.C.: Falmer Press, 1992); Carl Grant and Christine Sleeter, *Turning On Learning: Five Approaches for Multicultural Teaching Plans for Race, Class, Gender, and Disability* (Columbus, Ohio: Merrill, 1989); Frances Kendall, *Diversity in the Classroom: A Multicultural Approach to the Education of Young Children* (New York: Teachers College Press, 1983); James Lynch, *Multicultural Education: Principles and Practice* (London: Routledge & Kegan Paul, 1986); James Lynch, *Multicultural Education in a Global Society* (London: Falmer Press, 1990); Patricia G. Ramsey, *Teaching and Learning in a Diverse World: Multicultural Education for Young*

Children (New York: Teachers College Press, 1897); Robert C. Serow, *Schooling for Social Diversity: An Analysis of Policy and Practice* (New York: Teachers College Press, 1983); and Christine E. Sleeter, ed., *Empowerment Through Multicultural Education* (Albany, N.Y.: SUNY Press, 1991). See also Gale S. Auletta and Terry Jones, "Reconstituting the Inner Circle," *American Behavioral Scientist* 34 (November/December 1990): 137–52; William M. King, "Challenges Across the Curriculum: Broadening the Bases of How Knowledge Is Produced," *American Behavioral Scientist* 34 (November/December 1990): 165–80; Michael R. Olneck, "The Recurring Dream: Symbolism and Ideology in Intercultural and Multicultural Education," *American Journal of Education* 98 (February 1990): 147–74; Richard Pratte, "Multicultural Education: Four Normative Arguments," *Educational Theory* 33 (1983): 21–32; Diane Ravitch, "Multiculturalism," *American Scholar* 59 (Summer 1990): 337–54; and Philip Walking, "Multicultural Education," in *Handbook of Educational Ideas and Practices*, ed. Noel Entwistle (London: Routledge, 1990). See also the works referred to in subsequent notes.

19. Sohan Modgil et al., eds., *Multicultural Education: The Interminable Debate* (London: Falmer Press, 1986).

20. I limit my discussion here to the literature in English. Other countries, including many European nations, developed their own forms of multiculturalism during this period.

21. Public Law 92–318 (June 23, 1972); 20 USC 821. The purpose of the Act was to "provide assistance designed to afford students opportunity to learn about the nature of their own cultural heritage, and to study the contributions of the cultural heritages of other ethnic groups in the Nation."

22. B. Othannel Smith, et al., *Teachers for a Real World* (Washington, D.C.: American Association of Colleges for Teacher Education, 1969).

23. "No One Model American," in *Educational Comment*, ed. Thomas R. Lopez (Toledo, Ohio: University of Toledo College of Education, 1979).

24. National Council for the Social Studies, "Curriculum Guidelines for Multiethnic Education," *Social Education* 40 (1976): 386ff.

25. Milton J. Gold, Carl Grant, and Harry Rivlin, eds., *In Praise of Diversity: A Resource Book for Multicultural Education* (Washington, D.C.: Teacher Corps/Association of Teacher Educators, 1977).

26. See Donna M. Gollnick and Philip C. Chinn, eds., *Multiculturalism in Contemporary Education*, a special issue of *Viewpoints in Teaching and Learning* 56 (1980).

27. Among the most influential writers have been James Banks and Carl Grant (United States), James Lynch (Great Britain), and Brian Bullivant (Australia).

28. *Understanding Diversity*, Thomas Sobol to the Board of Regents, July 12, 1991 (typescript). Thus, there were *three* "New York reports." The first, *A Curriculum of Inclusion*, badly written and certainly meriting something like the reaction of the Committee of Scholars in Defense of History, preceded the second, *One Nation, Many Peoples*, but otherwise had no impact on New York policy. The third, *Understanding Diversity*, formally

setting New York policy, incorporated the substance of *One Nation, Many Peoples* as well as some key dissents published to it.

29. *History-Social Science Framework for California Public Schools* (Sacramento: California State Department of Education, 1988).

30. NCSS, "Curriculum Guidelines for Multicultural Education," *Social Education* 55 (September 1992): 274–94.

31. *One Nation, Many Peoples.* Page references given in parentheses in the text.

32. NCSS Guidelines. Page references given in parentheses in the text.

33. Addendum to Thomas Sobol, *Understanding Diversity*, p. 2.

34. For example, *One Nation* proposes that the word "slave" be dropped from textbooks in favor of "enslaved persons." Its reason: the word "slave" suggests that being a slave was "one's role or status, similar to that of gardener, cook, or carpenter" (p. 20). Using "enslaved persons" is better, according to *One Nation*, because doing so "would call forth the essential humanity of those enslaved, helping students to understand from the beginning the true meaning of slavery (in contrast to the sentimental pictures of contented slaves, still found in some texts)." But of course, "slave" *did* define a role or status, similar to "serf," "indentured servant," "peon," and the like. That was part of the "true meaning" of slavery. Can calling slaves "enslaved persons" remind students of the "essential humanity" of the slaves? Possibly so, but consider: if we lacked a conception of the humanity and individuality of soldiers, say, calling them "ensoldiered persons" is not likely to make good our deficiency.

35. See Bennett, *Comprehensive Multicultural Education*, pp. 11, 15, 23–9, 86; Gollnick and Chinn, *Multicultural Education in a Pluralistic Society*, pp. 21–3; and Banks, *Multiethnic Education: Theory and Practice*, pp. 58ff., 116ff.

36. Lynch, *Multicultural Education: Principles and Practice*, p. 5.

37. Gollnick and Chinn, *Multicultural Education in a Pluralistic Society*, p. 20.

38. Bennett, *Comprehensive Multicultural Education*, p. 91.

39. Carl Grant, "Education That Is Multicultural and P/CBTE: Discussion and Recommendations for Teacher Preparation," in Klassen and Gollnick, *Pluralism and the American Teacher: Issues and Case Studies*, p. 66.

40. Lynch, *Multicultural Education: Principles and Practice*, p. 11; Bennett, *Comprehensive Multicultural Education*, p. 91.

41. See Bennett, *Comprehensive Multicultural Education*, p. 30.

42. See Gollnick and Chinn, *Multicultural Education in a Pluralistic Society*, p. 28; Bennett, *Comprehensive Multicultural Education*, pp. 203–5.

43. See Manuel Ramirez and Alfredo Castaneda, *Cultural Democracy, Bicognitive Development, and Education* (New York: Academic Press, 1974), p. 10.

44. For example, the following list religion but never give it more than a paragraph or two: James Lynch, *The Multicultural Curriculum* (London: Batsford Academic and Educational, 1983); Cohen and Manion, *Multicultural Classrooms*; Arora and Duncan, *Multicultural Education: Towards Good Practice*; Ricardo L. Garcia, *Teaching in a Pluralistic Society: Concepts, Models, Strategies* (New York: Harper & Row, 1982); Kendall, *Diversity in the Classroom: A Multicultural Approach to the Education of Young Children*; Ramsey, *Teaching and Learning in a Diverse World: Multicultural Education for*

Young Children; Trevor Corner, ed., *Education in Multicultural Societies* (New York: St. Martin's Press, 1984); Banks, *An Introduction to Multicultural Education*; Gold, Grant, and Rivlin, *In Praise of Diversity*; Tiedt and Tiedt, *Multicultural Teaching*; Sleeter and Grant, *Making Choices for Multicultural Education*; Grant and Sleeter, *Turning on Learning*; and Bennett, *Comprehensive Multicultural Education*. Some discussion of religious beliefs and conflicts can be found in Nicholas Appleton, *Cultural Pluralism in Education: Theoretical Foundations* (New York: Longman, 1983), pp. 99–106; and a complete chapter on religion can be found in Gollnick and Chinn, *Multicultural Education in a Pluralistic Society.*
45. California Framework, pp. 13, 14–5, 58–61, 63, 66–7, 80–1.
46. In Klassen and Gollnick, *Pluralism and the American Teacher*, p. 3.
47. Banks wrote in a publication of the American Association of Colleges for Teacher Education. Ironically, in a 1979 set of essays published to accompany the AACTE's 1972 statement on multicultural education, "No One Model American," both religion and region counted equally with race, gender, and ethnicity. Subsequently, they largely disappeared from the multicultural screen.
48. Sandra Stotsky, ed., *Connecting Civic Education & Language Education* (New York: Teachers College Press, 1991).

Chapter 2

Antiracist civic education in the California History-Social Science Framework

LAWRENCE A. BLUM

The California History-Social Science Framework[1] is an impressive document in several respects. My interest here is in its articulate and detailed championing of ethically informed and civically responsible education. In its commitment to providing such an education to children from all ethnic and cultural backgrounds, the Framework distances itself (though not explicitly) from those who wish education to be morally neutral. It also avoids the anxious hand-wringing of those who want the schools to teach values but are worried about the basis for teaching some values rather than others. The Framework cuts through this philosophically interesting but pedagogically constraining concern about relativism largely by grounding, or attempting to ground, its conception of ethical education in a framework of "civic education."

In keeping with the American tradition of "social studies" as, in part, a training in the values and virtues needed for participation in a democratic polity, the Framework offers a plausible general description of those core values and virtues. This description comprises the first quarter of the document; the final three quarters consist of curricular suggestions evidently meant to exemplify the value guidelines set out in the first part.

The Framework, adopted in 1987, was responsive to multiculturalist currents in society and in the world of education of the past two decades. I want to examine the Framework primarily from the vantage point of one component of multicultural education – what I will call "antiracist education." Antiracist education is a dimension of moral education concerning right and wrong in the area of race and race relations. It takes as a core value racial equality – understood both as equal rights and opportunities for persons independent of their racial identity, and as an attitude of respect for members of other races as moral equals. Above all, antiracist education seeks means and methods by which this value can be taught in schools.

Antiracist education is an important component of the broader category of "multicultural education," and may even appear to describe its central motive and agenda. Multicultural education is, after all, a response to the historical legacy of racial discrimination, including the unequal educational opportunities and attainments of black, Latino, and Native American children. It seeks to address the persistence of racial prejudice, with its unequal valuing of different racial groups; the possible effect of this unequal valuing on the self-worth of children from those groups, and the consequent (at least alleged) negative impact on those children's functioning in school. Some multicultural initiatives, such as emphasizing the contributions of a particular racial or ethnic group to national life or to humanity as a whole, are explicitly intended to promote racial justice by contributing to equal educational opportunity, by correcting the racist prejudices of students who are not members of the group, or by fostering achievement in members of the group in question by removing or mitigating educational factors causing alienation.

Nevertheless, antiracist concerns do not cover the whole of what is of legitimate interest in the multicultural movement. There is an independent concern with what might be called "cultural acknowledgment and respect" – respect for another culture *in its difference from one's own*. It is true that when teachers emphasize the contributions of specific groups, their efforts may encourage both racial equality and cultural respect. Other multicultural initiatives may have this dual effect as well. Nonetheless, we can say that in promoting equal opportunity for, say, Hispanic-Americans, multicultural education serves a value distinct from that which it serves in promoting respect for the particular culture of Mexican-Americans.[2] Cultural respect is a value founded on recognition of difference. Antiracism, in contrast, is founded on sameness – on treating others as equals, according them equal rights and opportunities.[3]

By and large the California Framework treats racial equality as a defining value of the American polity, though acknowledging that this value has not been fully achieved. Citing equality, liberty, democratic participation, and dignity of the individual as core American values, the authors explicitly and implicitly present these values as implying a commitment to racial equality. I will premise my own argument on the validity of this claimed link between American civic values and racial equality, and will treat a commitment to racial equality as a core civic value for American schools. But I want at the outset to note a problem in grounding racial equality in the American civic tradition. For while the racial version of equality is directly entailed by the professed values of equality and dignity animating the Constitution and the Declaration of Independence, as well as by the popular understanding of the underpinnings of core American institutions in liberty and equality, this is not sufficient for declaring racial equality itself a core American value. For one thing, the Constitution itself in fact upholds some form of racial *inequality*. Second, the notion of "Americanness" has often been used to exclude some immigrant and racial groups and relegate them to second-class citizenship, rather than to accord them full equality.[4] Third, it is not clear that the *operative* values and ideals of the American populace do include a substantial commitment to racial equality. One lesson I want to draw from these ambivalences and ambiguities in the American civic heritage is that our own commitment to racial equality should not remain content with a purely "civic" grounding but must draw on other sources as well. (I return to this point at the end of the chapter.) With this caveat, I will proceed on the assumption that there are some important civic arguments for racial equality.

CITIZENSHIP, RACIAL INJUSTICE, AND RESPONSIBILITY

I've noted at the outset the strengths of the California Framework because in what follows I want to focus on some of its limitations. A first limitation concerns the Framework's notion of the content of "citizenship" in the context of a democratic polity. While there is no single place at which the Framework's conception of citizenship is fully and definitively spelled out, one can locate its core elements under two general rubrics. One is "citizenship" itself; the other is "ethical literacy." The relation between the latter and the former is not made very clear, though the authors certainly consider the values and skills mentioned under the "ethical" rubric to bear some connection to the values and skills of citizenship.

There are, roughly, two different levels of abstraction in the Framework's statements regarding citizenship. On the most general, foundational level, the document invokes the "American creed" of equality, drawn from the Declaration of Independence (20), and the "ethical" value of "the sanctity of life and the dignity of the individual" (14). The second level involves more specific rights, procedures, and values of a democratic society, such as fair play, due process, and freedom of religion.

From the perspective of racial equality and justice, the values stated on the specific level generally fail to capture a notion of citizenship adequate to the promotion and securing of racial equality. Consider two major statements of such specific values. The first is one of the guiding principles of the Framework:

> **This framework encourages the development of civic and democratic values as an integral element of good citizenship.** From the earliest grades students should learn the kind of behavior that is necessary for the functioning of a democratic society. They should learn sportsmanship, fair play, sharing, and taking turns. They should be given opportunities to lead and to follow. They should learn how to select leaders and how to resolve disputes rationally. They should learn about the value of due process in dealing with infractions, and they should learn to respect the rights of the minority, even if this minority is only a single dissenting voice. (6) (bold in original)

The second statement comes under the heading "Civic Values, Rights, and Responsibilities" (one of the components of the general "Goal of Democratic Understanding and Civic Values"):

> Students must understand what is required of a citizen in a democracy. They need to understand, for example, that a democratic society depends on citizens who will take individual responsibility for their own ethical behavior, control inclinations to aggression, and attain a certain level of civility by choosing to live by certain higher rules of ethical conduct. (22)

Certainly these features are all central to sustaining a democracy. But they are less pertinent to that aspect of democracy that involves instantiating the value of equality in a context of a history of racial injustice. While taking turns, sharing, and fair play constitute training in forms of democratic equality, these values come into play only in the context of an already-defined group. They do not help to define the group in the first place. If, for example, a child in a class feels excluded, she may not get to be part of the groups who are engaging in fair play and taking turns. There are many reasons that children may feel, or be, excluded from activities important to a class or school – because they are perceived as outsiders ("the new kid" syndrome), because of their gender, because of what they wear, because they do not understand common cultural reference points, because of some particular personal dynamic in the group in question, or for any number of other reasons. Race or ethnic prejudice is among such reasons. Exclusion based on race or ethnicity can take several forms: (i) active exclusion by members of the dominant group in the class; (ii) passive exclusion, in which the members of the dominant group, while not actively prejudiced, do nothing to make the children of minority cultures and races comfortable in joining in; and (iii) blocked inclusion, in which minority children, having internalized the message –

from the wider society, or from the culture of the school as a whole – that they are not entirely welcome, are therefore unable to respond to the dominant children's overtures when the latter *do* make positive efforts at inclusion. In all these instances, values of fair play, sharing, and taking turns do not go very far in correcting for those attitudes that contribute to racial and cultural exclusion, nor do they particularly involve the promotion of sensitivities to such issues of exclusion.

The civic values mentioned in the Framework also fail to respond to a broader form of exclusion: they do not raise questions about which children are present in a given school in the first place. If schools were truly racially and ethnically integrated, and if attitudes contributing to exclusion were not present, then taking turns and fair play would constitute a genuine training in citizenship for a nonracist democracy. But in fact most schools in the country are essentially racially segregated. In such settings none of the children – whether they belong to racial "minorities" or racial "majorities" – get to learn the civic abilities necessary to function in, and to strive to promote, a democracy embodying racial justice.

Perhaps it can be replied that the Framework does not set out to address systemic problems in national education such as racial segregation, and thus cannot be faulted for failing to do so. However, the Framework might at least have recognized – in a way that it very clearly does not – that the inculcation in civic virtues that it so strongly advocates will be severely limited by constraints placed on it by these systemic injustices.

The second passage I have quoted asserts a commitment to "a certain level of civility" and "controlling inclinations to aggression." But while the passage thus describes necessary behavioral and psychological attributes of a democratic citizen, it does not take us very far toward the positive notions of respect for dignity and regard for another person as an equal, especially across racial barriers. The notion of "civility," which is not clearly defined in this context, can readily be interpreted in a somewhat limited way, to refer to behavior that allows persons to get along with one another. It does nothing either directly to address injustices between persons or groups, or to promote attitudes of democratic respect and equality that would characterize a social order that conformed to the more abstractly stated ideals of equality and respect for dignity. Surely these attitudes of respect (especially across racial divides) and their behavioral manifestations should be counted among the "higher rules of ethical conduct" of a democracy. In short, the Framework's elaboration of specific democratic values should go much further to include values more centrally expressive of racial equality and justice.

The too-minimal conception of the responsibilities of citizenship in the Framework is connected to a more general lacuna – a failure to address citizenship responsibilities in the face of injustice, or, more generally, in the face of departures from democratic values. James Baldwin powerfully describes an incident in the early 1960s in which he and two black friends (all well past 30) were refused service in an airport bar on the grounds that they "looked too young." When they objected to this treatment, the manager emerged to defend the bartender. Baldwin continues, "The bar was very crowded, and our altercation had been very noisy; not one customer in the bar had done anything to help us."

Baldwin here describes a failure of citizenship on the part of the patrons of the bar. An adequate conception of democratic citizenship must surely involve some sort of responsibility by the patrons to intervene or protest against this violation of fundamental democratic treatment.[5] This responsibility is particularly applicable if the bartender and manager were doing something illegal, but it is not limited to illegal actions. Citizens should respond to behavior that violates norms of equal treatment, or relationships of mutual respect, or principles of racial justice generally. Such situations constitute occasions for civic intervention.

In *The Faces of Injustice*, Judith Shklar has this to say about "passive injustice" – standing by while an injustice is committed:

> [It] . . . is more than failing to be just, it is to fall below personal standards of citizenship. . . . Passive injustice defines the failure of these republican citizens to perform their chief tasks: to see to it that the rules of justice are maintained and to support actively those informal relations upon which a republican order depends and which its ethos prescribes. (40–1)[6]

This point about passive injustice applies to many domains of social and political life, but it is particularly pertinent to race and race relations in the United States. Both the group injustices and individual acts expressive of objectionable racial attitudes are corrosive of democracy, and a conception of democratic citizenship should help us articulate what the citizen's responsibility must be in facing them.[7]

The failure to articulate the full range of values encompassed by democratic citizenship is linked with another insufficiency in the Framework's conception. This concerns the abilities and dispositions, or virtues, students must develop in order to realize those core values. Here I have in mind what we might more broadly refer to as the "psychology" of democratic citizenship.

In the Framework, the civic virtues are integrated with general virtues such as taking turns, sportsmanship, and fair play. In order to develop these virtues, students must participate in activities requiring certain kinds of dispositions and abilities. Taking turns is not only something a child learns to *value*; it is also something she must learn to *do*. But the Framework shows inadequate recognition of the range of abilities and dispositions needed to realize the full complement of civic virtues, and the need for pedagogy to address the teaching of those virtues.

Baldwin's example suggests one kind of virtue required for the achievement of racial democracy – intervening appropriately in instances of racial discrimination. If our interventions are to be effective, it is not enough for us simply to choose to act; we must also be capable of acting in the right way.

In this regard it is noteworthy that the Framework speaks of respecting the rights of the single dissenting voice. What it does not highlight is the need, sometimes, to *be* the single dissenting voice, or even to be part of a collective dissenting voice.[8] That, too, is a necessary democratic virtue. Part of its value lies in the power it gives a potential agent to define the character of a situation for *other* potential agents. If no one speaks up in the face of injustice, then the silence sets a demoralizing process in motion: it gives potential agents a strong incentive to persuade themselves that the situation does not involve an injustice, or involves a very minor injustice, or involves an injustice that is none of their concern – one that does not call for any action on their part.[9] The Framework says that the curriculum "should help students grasp the enormous barriers black Americans had to overcome in their struggle for their rights as citizens" (99). The kinds of psychological qualities required to engage in that struggle are important civic virtues that the Framework does not mention.

It may seem in the Baldwin case that the virtues required for intervention can be displayed straightaway and do not actually need to be *developed*. Surely a patron in the bar could say to the bartender or manager something like "Hey, that's not right (or fair)" or "You should serve those guys." Simply challenging the assumption that refusing service to the black customers is appropriate, and a matter of concern only to the parties involved, might well do the trick.

Nevertheless, there is a "psychology of citizenship" issue here. Many people in a democratic society never contemplate challenging the behavior of someone else in a dispute that does not involve them personally (unless, perhaps, there is a possibility of averting violence). Such persons must go through certain developmental steps before they are able to instantiate the democratic virtues of appropriate intervention to challenge injustice.[10]

The precursors of such virtues of intervention can be taught to young people. Children can be taught, for example, when seeing one child bully another, that it is their responsibility to act, even if so doing involves only informing someone in authority. What about being in the presence of people telling racist jokes? First, the child needs to learn how to recognize that a joke is racist. But once she knows this, what does she say at the moment? Does she say, "I don't like that kind of joke"? "That joke is racist"? "That joke might really hurt somebody"? The best choice depends on several situational factors (what she knows about the people telling the jokes, how close she is to them, whether she has reason to fear their reaction, among others); but even the attempt to evaluate these factors will involve the development of skills in, or a psychology of, "intervening." This aspect of antiracist education will also involve recognizing when it is best not to intervene, learning the difference between appropriate interventions and "tattling," reading the signals that an intervention is not working, and knowing when to back off or try something new. Children may learn that often the best way to intervene in racist incidents is *not* by labeling the incident as racist, or, more important, not by labeling one of the principals as racist or as having done something racist.

Without attempting here to give an actual account of pedagogical methods for conveying antiracist civic abilities, we can distinguish at least two general sorts of pedagogical approaches. One directly teaches *about* racism itself and encourages students to combat, mitigate, and more generally do something about it. A discussion about interventions in racist incidents would be one example of this approach.

A second form of antiracist education does not focus directly on racism itself but nonetheless has the effect of steering students in an antiracist direction. For example, a teacher might help students become sensitive to forms of inclusion and exclusion (both in the classroom and outside it) which are pervasive in children's lives, and which provide significant opportunity for proto-civic education. Children can be led to see how hurtful it is to be excluded from a game or a group, and they can learn how to include children whom they might not otherwise have included. They can learn how to revise or slightly alter a game so that a new child can be made part of it. In the larger society, race is one of the most salient grounds for exclusions, whether explicit or implicit. But a teacher need not always emphasize the racial import of civic lessons in "inclusion/exclusion" in order to impart a lesson that students can apply later in racial contexts. Here, then, is an example of "indirect" antiracist civic education.

THE CONNECTION BETWEEN VIRTUE
AND CURRICULUM

The absence of serious attention to the nature and range of abilities and dispositions necessary for democratic citizenship is related to a further striking omission in the Framework. That is the absence of an attempt to draw explicit connections between the curricular suggestions that constitute the bulk of the Framework's recommendations, and the inculcation of the specific civic values and virtues urged in the document. The authors seem to imply, but do not state, that the civic, ethical, and other values described in the Framework's first part are realized in the curricular suggestions that occupy the remainder of the document.

Perhaps the authors are less concerned than they profess to be with how, through curriculum and classroom instruction, actually to *develop* the skills of citizenship. In several places in the document the curriculum is understood simply as giving students an *intellectual grasp* of the importance of American civic values. A noteworthy instance occurs in the final few pages of the Framework, where "Criteria for Evaluating Instructional Materials" are given as guides to prospective publishers. One of the fourteen criteria is that "Materials should reflect the significance of civic values and democratic institutions" (116).[11] The injunction is cashed out in the following way: "the writers of these materials should pay close attention to the evolution of basic democratic principles, such as universal suffrage, freedom of the press, freedom of religion. . . ." But describing the evolution of basic democratic principles hardly constitutes giving some thought to what might lead students to adopt and be able to live by such principles.

The authors may also be making the assumption that teaching the suggested subject matter will by itself have the effect of inculcating the appropriate civic values in the students. This assumption is quite implausible. Do the authors assume that if they teach historical events that concern the struggle against various forms of unfairness and discrimination, then the students will thereby have learned how to "play fair"? Certainly teaching such historical events can be *part* of such inculcation, but equally certainly it is far from sufficient. There must be some other kind of learning involving engaging in the activities in which fair play is appropriate. For whatever reason, the authors of the California Framework have failed adequately to address the issue of a form of pedagogy adequate to teaching the range of democratic virtues – either the wider range required for genuinely antiracist education, or even the narrower range mentioned in the Framework.

CULTURAL RESPECT

I want now to look at the way the Framework addresses the specific issue of multiculturalism, or cultural respect, as distinct from racism. And here I want to contrast the California Framework with the 1991 New York curriculum report, *One Nation, Many Peoples: A Declaration of Cultural Interdependence*.[12] The California Framework sees multiculturalism as a distinguishing feature of its approach, and states as one of its seventeen fundamental principles:

> This framework incorporates a multicultural perspective throughout the history-social science curriculum. It calls on teachers to recognize that the history of community, state, region, nation, and world must reflect the experiences of men and women and of different racial, religious, and ethnic groups. California has always been a state of many different cultural groups, just as the United States has always been a nation of many different cultural groups. The experiences of all these groups are to be integrated at every grade level in the history-social science curriculum. (5)

A specific conception of how multiculturalism figures in the teaching of U.S. history guides the Framework in its presentation of curricular materials. That conception is stated well in the sentence following the previous passage:

> The framework embodies the understanding that the national identity, the national heritage, and the national creed are pluralistic and that our national history is the complex story of many peoples and one nation, of *e pluribus unum*. . . . (5)

In other words, multiculturalism is seen as the expression of a (mostly) already-achieved conception of American nationhood. That conception is presumably meant to contrast with that of some conservative thinkers who would more explicitly frame national identity in terms of Anglo-Americans or Euro-Americans and their experiences and traditions. Rightly understood, the Framework implicitly argues, there is no tension between the cultural plurality of the American polity, and the unity necessary for nationhood and civic loyalty; for cultural plurality is one of the central features *of* that unifying conception of nationhood.

> We are strong because we are united in a pluralistic society of many races, cultures, and ethnic groups; we have built a great nation because we have learned to live in peace with each other, respecting each other's right to be different, and supporting each other as members of a common community. (56)

32

This multicultural conception is exemplified in the particular grade-level curricula suggested in the Framework. For example, the fourth-grade curriculum, focusing on the history of California, emphasizes the role of the Spanish, Spanish-Mexicans, Asians, and Europeans in the region's early history, as well as that of immigrants from Latin America and Asia in the twentieth century. Particular note is taken of "the presence of black explorers and soldiers in the earliest Spanish expeditions by sea . . . " (47). The Framework emphasizes the contributions and accomplishments of members of different groups. For example, it proposes that students "learn about the significant contributions that black men and women made to the economic, political, and cultural development of the nation, including its music, literature, art, science, medicine, technology, and scholarship" (55).

It is instructive to compare the New York report's approach to multiculturalism, or cultural respect, with that of the California Framework. The New York report implicitly contrasts an earlier period, when ethnic groups were largely content (or anyway compelled) to assimilate to the dominant culture, to our current situation in which these groups, "while anxiously embracing many of the advantages, opportunities and mores of this society, seem determined also to maintain and publicly to celebrate much that is peculiar to the cultures with which they identify" (vii). The contrast with earlier periods may be overstated; U.S. history has been rife with endeavors by immigrant ethnic groups to gain some recognition, validation, or assistance in preserving their traditions.[13] However, the recognition of both the current political context of demands for cultural validation and the historical dimension of the issue of assimilation is a useful complement, and even corrective, to the California Framework's attempt to affirm the multicultural dimension of American democracy as a timeless feature of our history, needing only to be recognized.

A second difference between the New York and the California approaches lies in the former's stronger emphasis on the distinct experiences of different groups, and the very different ways in which particular historical events may have been experienced by each.

> [T]he story of the early colonization in the eastern U.S. has too often been told from the perspective of the colonists, not the Native Americans already settled on the land. Or the story of the western United States is told as one of westward expansion, assuming the perspective of the migrating Easterners and disregarding the native men and women already there. (*One Nation, Many Peoples,* 18)

Often the California Framework glides over events and historical phenomena that call out for such a recognition of the conflicting meanings that these events had and have for different groups. The fifth-grade curriculum includes a unit on Westward Expansion that suggests, in the midst of a long description of the culture and economics of the pioneers, only that "students should discuss the reactions of the American Indians to the increasing migration and the reasons for their growing concern" (55). This brief statement is hardly adequate to the displacement, confinement and undermining of the Native Americans' traditional economy and social life brought in the wake of those pioneers. The fourth-grade curriculum states, "One reason for settling California was to bring Christianity to the native peoples" (47), but contains no indication of these native peoples' experience as the objects of this missionary activity, or what it meant for their native religious practices and cultures.[14]

While the California Framework's emphasis on *contributions* and *accomplishments* is important to developing cultural acknowledgment and respect, it is insufficient to that end. Also required is attention to the distinct *experiences* of different groups, and especially to the different meanings that a particular historical event may have for these different groups. Perhaps the California authors' guiding conception of a harmoniously multicultural and pluralistic America leaves insufficient room for this possibility of difference and conflict between groups.

To what extent, then, should teachers keep in mind the racial and ethnic identities of their students as they present lessons in history? On the one hand, it seems clear that teachers must be sensitive to those identities when they are discussing racially charged matters. The Framework's fifth-grade curriculum, for example, contains a unit on the Civil War, including a study of slavery and its abolition. A teacher needs to be aware of potential race-linked responses to this material. Some white students may feel defensive or guilty; they may want to distance themselves from the material, and may complain of it. White students whose ancestry in the United States postdates the end of slavery may adopt a different stance from those whose ancestry predates it. Some black students may feel angry, others shamed, by this material. Then again, some black students will be able to take pride, in a way that white and other students cannot, in figures like Frederick Douglass, Sojourner Truth, and Harriet Tubman.[15]

Some critics believe that multicultural education is itself responsible for these divergent responses – that by encouraging students to define themselves primarily in racial or ethnic terms, it necessarily pits students against one another, dividing them into separate, non-communicating groups, and fostering in minority children a debilitating sense of permanent victimization. But in the slavery lesson, for example, teachers who are sensitive to the different possible reactions of their students can make the history much less divisive than it might otherwise be. They can carefully avoid the implication that white Americans were or are a monolithic and oppressive group. They can point to the very different roles that different groups of whites played in the perpetuation, and abolition, of slavery – distinguishing between slaveowning and non-slaveowning whites, and highlighting the accomplishment of white abolitionists. In this way, teachers can mute a perhaps natural but misleading and quite civically damaging polarization, in which the history of slavery is perceived as a struggle of all black people against all white people.

At the same time, the stance and achievements of white abolitionists should not be allowed to mask – as they have so often done in school curricula – the role of slaves and free blacks in struggling for an end to slavery, and for an extension of democratic freedoms in the period after the Civil War. The California Framework does an admirable job of recognizing this achievement, emphasizing at several points the role of African-Americans in extending the reach of constitutional principles and ideals to groups not originally included.[16]

On the other hand, it would clearly be a mistake for a teacher to imagine that the students' reactions to material will systematically correlate with race. There is no reason to assume, for example, that a current student of Polish extraction will be in any better position to understand the psychology of slaveowners than are current Chinese-American, or even African-American, students, even though the former, like the slaveowners, are "white." One cannot even assume that the descendants of slaveowners are in a better position to understand slavery than are these other groups. Similarly, there is no reason to assume that an African-American student will come to class with a full understanding of the phenomenon of slavery just because she is African-American, though she might well be *more likely* than students of other backgrounds (all else being equal) to have learned something about slavery at home. The exercises in historical imagination and empathy required to understand the experiences of different historical groups will be required of students from *all* backgrounds.

THE NEW YORK CURRICULUM REPORT AND
ITS REJECTION OF A SHARED HISTORY

Unfortunately, while New York's *One Nation, Many Peoples* does a better job than the California Framework in recognizing divergent group experiences of common events, the New York report inflates this insight into a full-fledged epistemological pluralism and then takes this epistemological version of multiculturalism to be the true goal of social studies teaching.

> Especially in the humanities and social sciences, we are beginning to
> realize that understanding and the ability to appreciate things from
> more than one perspective may be as important as is factual knowl-
> edge, among the goals of education. . . . [T]he social studies should be
> concerned not so much with "whose culture" and "whose history" are
> to be taught and learned, as with the development of intellectual com-
> petence in learners, with intellectual competence viewed as having as
> one of its major components the capacity to view the world and under-
> stand it from multiple perspectives. (vii) (see also pp. 2, 18 and else-
> where)

While taking different perspectives on the same material is an important intellectual skill, this articulation of the point of multicultural
education is unsatisfactory. First, it masks or marginalizes the civic
and ethical purposes of multicultural education, by collapsing these
dimensions into a purely intellectual skills-development goal. Second, by attempting to bypass questions of "whose culture" and
"whose history," this conception essentially devalues the distinctive
disciplinary value of history itself, wherein questions of significance
and focus can hardly be avoided.

Third and most important, the report does not make it clear what
the student is meant to *do* with the multiple perspectives once she has
achieved them. While it is important in its own right to understand
that group A sees events in a certain way and group B in another, it is
also important to be able to assess whether either way of seeing
events is accurate, just, reasonable, plausible, and the like. Learning
the tools for this sort of historical assessment is as crucial an educational goal as the ability to grasp the perspectives in the first place.
Moreover, without them students are left with a potentially debilitating relativism in their understanding of history.[17]

Thus, it is true that Native Americans of the Eastern United States
experienced the influx of Europeans as something like an invasion,
and it is important to see events from their point of view so that this
perspective can be made intelligible. For their part, the Europeans
saw their movement to the New World as a source of opportunity,
and as a "discovery" of a land hitherto unknown. But we surely want
to say more than that these two groups had two different "perspectives" on this same event. It is important that both were in a certain
sense *right*. That is, the effect on the Native American tribes was
devastating in many respects, and the European influx was a genuine
threat to their way of life. On the other hand, for the European
colonists, the expansion was an opportunity for economic revitaliza-
tion for the Crown. There is no inconsistency between recognizing
both of these perspectives as valid ones. Yet the New York report

gives no indication as to how any of this is to be conveyed pedagogically.[18]

Moreover, the notion of different perspectives as a foundational
idea masks the fact that *interactions* between different groups had an
impact on each of them that shaped their subsequent identities and
ways of life.[19] No group's history can be understood without continually relating it to that of others. Moreover, by speaking so unequivocally of "differing perspectives" (attached primarily to different socially salient groups, such as ethnic and racial groups), the report fails to
acknowledge that these perspectives are perspectives on a *common
history*, and, indeed, that they are unintelligible outside this context.
For example, looking at historical events from an "African-American
perspective" requires taking seriously the "American" in "African-
American." What it means to be an African-American has been powerfully shaped by the experience of being American. The ways that
African-Americans have, for example, organized to extend civic recognition and rights to themselves make sense only as a part of American history.

One passage in the New York report suggests that its authors reject
this notion of a common history:

> There was a new recognition that the teaching of social studies as a
> single officially sanctioned story was inaccurate as to the facts of conflict
> in American history, and further, that it was limiting for white students
> and students of color alike. (4)

The authors are right to reject many of the "officially sanctioned"
versions of history, in particular those that deny group conflict or
effectively deny the deep strands of racism in our history; the California Framework, as we have seen, partakes too much of this sanitized
version of history. But it is a long step from that insight to a rejection
of the entire attempt to craft a coherent overall perspective – one that
builds in features of conflict and differing group-based experiences.
The New York report encourages an intellectual laziness that pre-
scinds from attempting to think through the perspectives of different
groups to a common framework without which they are in any case
meaningless.

Nathan Huggins suggests something of what that common framework might look like, at least in relation to whites and blacks in
America:

> The invaluable work done in recent years to unearth and reveal previ-
> ously disregarded aspects of African-American life, history, and culture
> has served to bring to life a people who were socially and historically
> dead. Left as "black history," however, it merely moves the story of the

black experience from the margins to the center, marginalizing in turn the "mainstream" history. The challenge of the paradox is that there can be no white history or black history, nor can there be an integrated history which does not begin to comprehend that slavery and freedom, white and black, are joined at the hip.[20]

INTEGRATING RACE INTO THE AMERICAN NARRATIVE

While the California Framework at least maintains the idea of an overall narrative within which the experiences of different groups are given meaning, the actual narrative provided by the California document is, as has been suggested, unsatisfactory. First, it presents the values of cultural pluralism too much as something already achieved, and needing only to be appreciated. It fails to mention how assimilationist pressures of earlier eras were a source of cultural and psychic damage and loss. It does not recognize that such pressures still exist, and that the continuing need to resist them helps explain the current trend toward ethnic preservation and pride.

A second systematic problem with the California Framework's "master narrative" is its failure to integrate American racial history into that narrative. Because of this failure, the multicultural framework that remains as one of the document's defining features becomes itself seriously misleading. Let us consider two of the California Framework's recommendations concerning the multicultural nature of the U.S.'s national identity:

> **Understand the special role of the United States in world history as a nation of immigrants**. The multicultural, multiracial, multiethnic, multireligious character of the United States makes it unusual among the nations of the world. Few, if any, nations . . . have opened their doors so wide to immigration and provided such relatively easy access to full citizenship. At the same time students should analyze periodic waves of hostility to newcomers and recognize that the nation has in different eras restricted immigration on the basis of racial, ethnic, or cultural grounds. (21)

> **Realize that true patriotism celebrates the moral force of the American idea as a nation that unites as one people the descendants of many cultures, races, religions, and ethnic groups.** (21) (bold in original)

The image of a "nation of immigrants," as an already-achieved multiculturalism, pervades the California document. This image is one of a fairly egalitarian state of affairs – all groups were immigrants; all cultures contribute; all groups are respected; all groups have and had an impact on American culture. While containing an important partial truth, this egalitarian image of the "nation of immigrants"

38

seriously distorts the place of African-Americans, of Native Americans, and (to a somewhat lesser extent) of Mexican-Americans and Asian-Americans. The roles that these groups played in American history were initiated not through immigration but through slavery or conquest. The multicultural-without-antiracist perspective of the California document assimilates the experience of these groups to that of immigrant groups – and thus assimilates their form of "ethnicity" to that of Polish-Americans, Italian-Americans, and the like. But white ethnicity is not a satisfactory model for non-white ethnicity within the American context.

The Framework's recognition that some immigrant groups did face *racial* restrictions on immigration, while an acknowledgment of the distinct racial dimension to cultural pluralism, still fails to capture the *non*-immigrant character of the aforementioned groups. Thus, it retains and even thereby reinforces "(white) immigrant ethnicity" as a model for groups understood in the American context (both by themselves and by others) primarily in *racial*, and not only *ethnic*, terms. Taking racism seriously would yield a different overall model of the actual history, one according a structuring role to the fact that non-white (immigrant and non-immigrant) groups are in general treated worse than white (immigrant and non-immigrant) groups, and that even now the former (and especially black, Native American, and some Latino groups) are generally not accepted fully into the mainstream.

The Framework's implied notion that all the different ethnic groups making up the American polity have something like equivalent experiences and roles in the national narrative is exemplified in its injunction to study the different "contributions" of different groups, and in the following passage from the ninth-grade curriculum (under the rubric "ethnic studies"):

> Students should study the social, economic, and political forces that caused people to come to America. They should gain insights into the barriers that various ethnic groups have had to overcome in the past and present. They should learn about the opportunities these groups encountered and the contributions made by each toward American society. (83)

The "every group contributing" perspective omits, first, that the recognition of contributions to the dominant European-American culture has long been biased to reflect the norms of that culture; for example, forms of spirituality of various Native American tribes or nations were and generally are not seen as "contributions," nor are distinct forms of communal and family life in African-American communities. Second, what *are* recognized as contributions are often filtered through the dominant culture's stereotypes of the group in question and may serve to reinforce those stereotypes. For example, the recognition that many blacks have achieved excellence in basketball plays into the stereotype that blacks are good at sports and other physical activities, but are not really good at activities requiring mental ability. Moreover, often the activities in which racial groups excel and to which they are known to "contribute" are themselves perceived through the lens of racial stereotypes. Thus, when blacks are proficient at basketball, their excellence is often seen by whites as a "natural physical talent" rather than as the embodiment of a distinctive cultural style that requires intellectual skill and an aesthetic sense as well.[21] Finally, the "every group contributing" model tends to overlook the fact that some groups have been prevented from making anything like equal or appropriate contributions (of any of the kinds mentioned above) because discrimination against their members deprived them of access to the educational, political, and cultural resources essential to developing their capacity for making contributions.

The failure to take seriously the racial dimension of American history shows itself not only in attempts to assimilate the experience of non-white groups to that of white ethnic groups, but also in the failure to recognize the ways in which white ethnicity itself was shaped by the racist character of our history. White ethnic groups from Southern and Eastern Europe or Ireland were offered an option to construe themselves as "white," a status that they were given to understand made them superior to blacks.[22] Despite significant cultural differences among these ethnic groups, and between them and the politically and culturally dominant Anglo-Americans,[23] they could define themselves in terms of a "white" racial identity that carried cultural as well as economic benefits.[24]

To take this racial history more seriously could have profound implications for our understanding of history in general. Orlando Patterson, for example, argues that the entire Western notion of "freedom" has its source in slavery; it is defined by contrast with slavery, and presupposes an understanding of slavery that those who wish to be "free" take as a paradigm for the condition that is freedom's opposite.[25] Similarly, Judith Shklar argues that American understanding of the status of "citizen" was constantly defined by contrast with the status of "slave."[26]

The California authors do of course recognize racism in its various forms as a blight on our shared history; and they not infrequently recognize that racial equality is something yet to be achieved. What they do not do is find a way to incorporate this recognition into the framing narrative of American history. Slavery, Jim Crow, segregation, and other forms of racial injustice remain, in Nathan Huggins's words, "aberrant and marginal to the main story of American history."[27]

DEMOCRACY ACHIEVED/ACHIEVING DEMOCRACY

A dominant image in the Framework that may contribute to blocking a more robust conception of citizenship – one that would face up to civic responsibilities in the face of racial injustice – is that democracy as a form of polity has *already been achieved*, and needs only to be appreciated and protected.

> We want [students] to understand the value, the importance, and the fragility of democratic institutions. We want them to realize that only a small fraction of the world's population (now or in the past) has been fortunate enough to live under a democratic form of government, and we want them to understand the conditions that encourage democracy to prosper. (2)

> Students need to understand the inherent strengths of the democratic system. But they also need to ponder its fragile nature and the processes through which democracies perish: through erosion of democratic protections, through lack of effective leadership or governance, through indifference of citizens to their rights and responsibilities under the Constitution and the Bill of Rights. . . . (23)

All this is unexceptionable, and importantly true. But is not the metaphor of "unfinished project" as apt as "fragile system" for the nature of our democracy? Is it not evident, especially in the area of race, that not everything we mean by "democracy" has yet been achieved? If so, then our conception of citizenship must involve more than appreciating and protecting, but must also include helping to realize, to bring fully into being, this democracy.

Interestingly, the Framework does say, "[O]ur national history is . . . the complex story of an unfinished struggle to realize the ideals of the Declaration of Independence and the Constitution" (5). "The American story is unfinished, for it is a story of ideals and aspirations that have not yet been realized. It is a story that is in the making" (21). But the Framework does not follow through on the implications of the "unfinished" metaphor for civic education. Discussions of specific virtues tend to remain within the ambit of the "appreciate and protect" metaphor. Despite the occasional recognition of the underside of American history, the authors have a tendency to elide the real and the ideal in their portrayal of the actual character of the American polity in its historical and contemporary dimensions. Ignoble events and trends are generally seen as exceptions to the "true meaning" of American life, rather than part of that meaning.

Perhaps the California authors' refusal to face up to systemic and pervasive deficiencies in our history and institutions stems partly from the idea that unless the "true" meaning of that history is entirely positive, teaching the history will not serve the civic function of providing inspiring ideals. Such an interpretation is suggested in an article by Diane Ravitch, one of the two principal authors of the California Framework. In this article, Ravitch criticizes what she calls a "particularist" approach to history for highlighting differences rather than stressing commonalities. "Particularistic education teaches children to see history as a story of victims and oppressors. . . . "[28] In another article she says that such education encourages "a sense of rage and victimization in those who are the presumed descendants of victims and a sense of resentment in those who are the presumed descendants of oppressors."[29]

While the full range of targets of Ravitch's negative characterization of "particularist" education is not clear,[30] she does appear to be countenancing a failure to face up to the facts of history in order to preserve a particular political/educational goal – namely, forging common identifications with American institutions across ethnic groups. For she appears to be saying that one should not emphasize that some groups were victims while others were oppressors and beneficiaries of that victimization, even if this is precisely what the facts reveal. It is both historically more truthful as well as educationally sound to face up to the dishonorable facts of our racial history, while finding ways of teaching these facts that do *not* produce the psychic ill effects Ravitch mentions. A flexible and sensitive antiracist pedagogy should be able to accomplish this, but Ravitch does not provide space for even the search for such a pedagogy.

It is ironic that Ravitch maintains such a view, since she elsewhere criticizes other curricula for subordinating scholarly and educational standards to political goals,[31] and here she appears to be doing that very thing. Her motivation appears to be the worry that unless the value orientation that she favors is presented as the sole or dominant strand in history teaching, then history will not be able to serve as a source of civic guidance and inspiration.

Such a view seems simplistic and unduly pessimistic. Knowing the "bad" strands in our history makes the search for how to realize the "good" ones much more realistic. Even if racism is more deeply woven into the fabric of American life than the California authors acknowledge, this does not make the antiracist ideal of racial equality, nor the multiculturalist ideal of respect for diverse cultures, any less worthy of our civic and ethical commitments. Nor does it deny that those ideals *are* genuine strands in American life (though perhaps not as prominent as the authors imply). The California authors are right to recognize, for example, that some of the driving forces of the antislavery and the civil rights movements were noble American ideals – a search for freedom on the part of blacks, belief in racial equality on the part of supportive whites. If we know how racism has operated and what its effects have been, we are much better positioned to craft a pedagogy to teach the appropriate form of American ideals of equality and freedom – to, as the Framework puts it, "inspire understanding of and commitment to the best principles in the American heritage" (117).

Speaking of "the best" principles is a way of acknowledging that the ethical and historical meaning of a country's history is not fully *determinate*. While we can identify some principles as "the best" ones, and some historical trends as "bad," what we cannot do is to declare definitively that the "best" ones represent what our historical traditions *really are*. The purpose of civic education is to work toward a realization of the best, in the hope that we will one day be in a better position to claim devotion to equality as a central meaning of American history.

This point is worth making because it offers an alternative view of what it means to face up to the deeply pervasive racism in American life. The more common view, at least at this historical moment, is that to see racism in this way requires a denial that American culture holds anything of value for people of color and especially for African-Americans. This is one of the sources of the Afrocentric movement in education, which searches for cultural and moral resources in the African origins of African-Americans and in developments entirely internal to the African-American community, unaffected by the allegedly corrupting Eurocentrism of the dominant American culture. It is not possible here to attempt an overall assessment of the complex and many-stranded Afrocentric movement. But we can say this: from the fact that American society has been and continues to be in many ways deeply racist, it does not follow that American culture and its European roots are devoid of essential moral and cultural resources for mitigating and remedying that racism.[32]

By the same token, while not embracing the doctrines of Afrocentrism, one need not reject those forms of cultural strength and significance derived from non-Western traditions and heritages. Chinese, African, Native American, and Latin American cultures can provide important sources of cultural sustenance, of intellectual tradition, of political imagination for people of color not yet treated as full equals in American society. Moreover, these non-European sources can further enrich mainstream American life as well, as they have already done. In this regard some trends in Afrocentrism have made important contributions to African-American cultural understanding, and to American self-understanding more generally. Though I have examined antiracist education in the context of the American civic tradition, it would, as I suggested earlier, be a mistake to confine our moral resources for a commitment to racial equality and justice to civic ones. Euro-Americans and Americans of color can find resources not only within the American civic tradition strictly construed, but also in specific cultural traditions outside it, as well as in intellectual arguments rooted in traditions of rational and critical thought less clearly culturally locatable.

I have criticized the California History–Social Science Framework for failing to provide a secure foundation for antiracist education – education for racial justice – within its framework of civic education; for failing to articulate a pedagogy adequate to its own civic goals; and for tailoring its view of American history to a conception of the requirements of civic education that constricts both historical and moral resources for education for racial equality. At the same time, the California Framework remains a document of unparalleled importance to the cause of civic education. It articulates in an intellectually substantial and ethically sound fashion a set of goals necessary for any responsible program of civic education within the context of the teaching of history and social studies. It will remain an important touchstone for debates about pre-college education for years to come.[33]

NOTES

1. *History–Social Science Framework for California Public Schools* (Sacramento: California State Department of Education, 1988). Page references given in parentheses in the text.
2. Mexican-Americans are one component group of "Hispanics," categorized so as to bring out its distinct cultural identity, which is masked by the term "Hispanic." The latter is a linguistic identification, but in common parlance and policy contexts is often treated as something more like a racial designation (as in "blacks, Hispanics, Asians, Native Americans"). Many Hispanics prefer the term "Latino," to emphasize Latin American rather than Iberian roots, and I will use this term. "Latino" is also closer to being a cultural designation than "Hispanic," yet neither is as fully or precisely a cultural or ethnic category as "Mexican-American" or "Puerto Rican."
3. For a more detailed exploration of the differences between "antiracism" and "cultural respect," see L. Blum, "Antiracism, Multiculturalism, and Interracial Community: Three Educational Values for a Multicultural Society" (Boston: Office of Graduate Studies and Research, University of Massachusetts, 1992) and "Multiculturalism, Racial Justice, and Community: Reflections on Charles Taylor's *The Politics of Recognition*," in *Pluralism and Multiculturalism: Conflicts and Controversies*, ed. L. Foster and P.

Herzog (Boston: University of Massachusetts Press, 1994). There the value I here call "cultural respect and acknowledgment" is referred to as "multiculturalism." In the current context I prefer to retain the latter term for the general educational movement containing several distinct strands, of which antiracism and cultural respect are two important ones. Robert Fullinwider's essay "Multiculturalism: Theme and Variations," *Perspective* 5 (Spring 1993): 1–19, contains an excellent, fuller discussion of the cultural respect strand of multicultural education. (See also his "Multicultural Education," *University of Chicago Legal Forum* ([1991]: 75–99.) In a sense, the term "multicultural" can be misleading, as it may suggest that concerns with discrimination and inequality may not be as central to the educational endeavor as matters concerned specifically with culture and cultural respect. Fullinwider appears to read the term "multicultural" in this way, on p. 10. There is undoubtedly a good deal of confusion surrounding the term. But I see no justification for conferring any lesser importance in the educational enterprise on issues of racial discrimination and equality than on those of cultural respect.

4. This point is made well by Henry Louis Gates, Jr., in "Am I Other?", a reply to Diane Ravitch (who will be discussed below) in *The Responsive Community* 1 (Summer 1991): 86.

5. James Baldwin, *The Fire Next Time* (New York: Dial Press, 1963), pp. 77f. (cf. passage following). I do not mean to imply that every case of racial injustice is as straightforward as this one, nor does the analysis provided here imply a particular viewpoint on controversial policy matters such as affirmative action programs.

6. Judith Shklar, *The Faces of Injustice* (New Haven, Conn.: Yale University Press, 1990). The example around which Shklar builds her own argument is that of being in a supermarket checkout line and witnessing the cashier shortchange a customer.

7. The Framework is not entirely without resources pointing in the direction of a robust conception of citizenship in the face of racial injustice. It says, for example, that children need to learn "how to work for change in a democratic society" (3), and, as mentioned, it articulates the ideals of equality and freedom in terms of which our current racial situation is seen to involve substantial injustices. Note, however, that the dimensions of citizenship I have been discussing are not all comfortably encompassed under the rubric of "working for change," as vague and general as that phrase is. Some of them simply concern what we do in the face of individual instances of injustice. It is a further step to aim those responses in the direction of changing unjust structures through political action. As important as the latter is, my focus in this paper is the more minimal one of what one does in the face of specific instances of injustice. I am not here advocating a conception of citizenship that *requires* citizens to work actively for structural change.

8. In the eighth-grade curriculum, the authors do make one of the strongest statements in the direction I am encouraging here: "Teachers should encourage discussion of the citizen's ethical obligation to oppose discrimi-

nation against individuals and groups and the converse obligation to work toward a society in which all people enjoy equal rights and a good life" (75).

9. On the role of observers or "bystanders" in constructing the moral character of situations, see "Studying the Pivotal Role of Bystanders," *New York Times*, June 22, 1993, p. C1, discussing the work of the psychologist Ervin Staub and others.

10. The process of this development is portrayed in the influential 1947 film *Gentleman's Agreement* (directed by Elia Kazan), concerning anti-Semitism. One major character is a well-meaning person who is not anti-Semitic and who disapproves of and is occasionally upset by manifestations of anti-Semitism in others. However, she never does anything in the face of such incidents, though she contemplates the possibility of doing so. The film portrays her development toward a painfully experienced recognition that she must take an active stand against bigotry, not merely disapprove of it passively.

11. This is the only principle in this section of the Framework that relates to civic education. Since this section spells out the criteria for selecting the material that teachers will actually use in the classroom, this seems an unfortunate lapse in the Framework's commitment to civic education.

12. New York State Social Studies Review and Development Committee, *One Nation, Many Peoples: A Declaration of Cultural Interdependence* (Albany: New York State Education Department, June 1991).

13. See Paula Fass, *Outside In: Minorities and the Transformation of American Education* (New York: Oxford University Press, 1990).

14. The difference between the New York and the California documents on this score is largely one of degree, however. For example, when discussing the slave trade in the fifth-grade curriculum, the California Framework suggests that students use their "growing sense of historical empathy to imagine how these young men and women felt, having been stolen from their families, carried across the ocean in a brutal voyage in a strange land, and then sold into bondage" (51). And the New York document does more in the way of *calling for* attention to different groups' experiences than it does in noting when and how this is to be done.

15. I am not saying here that students who are *not* African-American *cannot* take pride in Frederick Douglass, etc. Such students can take pride in these figures as, for example, great Americans. African-Americans have a *further* reason, connected with racial/ethnic identity. For more on the issue of multiculturalism and pride, see L. Blum, "Antiracism," esp. pp. 1of.

16. Cf. in the fifth-grade curriculum:

Attention should be given to what blacks did themselves in working for their own freedom: their organizations, which mobilized legal action; their petitions to Congress for redress of the fugitive slave laws and for emancipation of the slaves; the activities of leading black abolitionists such as Frederick Douglass, Charles Remond, and Sojourner Truth; and the direct actions of free blacks such as Harriet

Tubman and Robert Purvis in the underground movement to assist slaves to escape. (72)

17. The New York report actually goes this relativism one worse by occasionally infusing it with "social constructionism": "Principle 6. The subject matter content should be treated as socially constructed and therefore tentative – as is all knowledge. Knowledge is the product of human beings located in specific times and places; consequently, much of our subject matter must be understood as tentative" (13). This marks an even greater departure from the multicultural civic and ethical focus that the authors elsewhere profess. For there is a deep tension between this "tentative" view of knowledge and the moral authority which the authors mean to attach to their multiculturalist and antiracist conception of American history, and to the study of it. If their own view is no more than tentative, why should teachers feel compelled to teach it? How can their vision inspire loyalty to those values? How can they take themselves to be drawing on a tradition that carries some moral authority?

I should note that while I have chosen to focus on certain deficiencies in the New York report, *One Nation, Many Peoples,* to help bring out the character of the California Framework, I should say that in general the former does a better job than the latter in articulating the values both of cultural respect and of racial justice.

18. In general, the New York report, like the California Framework, gives inadequate pedagogical guidance as to how actually to accomplish even its stated aims. (Since the New York report, unlike the Framework, is primarily a critique of existing textbooks and curricula, this criticism has less force against it.) Note also that my brief discussion in this chapter does not consider the appropriate pedagogy for inculcating values of "cultural respect" (as distinguished from antiracist values) *specifically as civic values.* In my view, neither document is satisfactory in this regard.

19. The impact of Native Americans on the course of American history and American life is described well by James Axtell in "Colonial America without the Indians: Counterfactual Reflections," *Journal of American History* (March 1987): 981–96.

20. Huggins, "The Deforming Mirror of Truth: Slavery and the Master Narrative of American History," *Radical History Review* 49 (Winter 1991): 38. This essay is a shorter version of a new introduction that Huggins wrote for a reissue of his *Black Odyssey* (first published in 1977). For a widely respected attempt to provide an integrated history of the relation between European white colonists, black slaves, and Native Americans in the early years of the republic, see Gary Nash, *Red, White, and Black: The Peoples of Early North America,* 3d ed. (Englewood, N.J.: Prentice-Hall, 1992).

21. See Nelson George, *Elevating the Game: Black Men and Basketball* (New York: HarperCollins, 1992), on this point.

22. On this point, see Alexander Saxton, *The Rise and Fall of the White Republic* (New York: Verso, 1990), and David Roediger, *The Wages of Whiteness* (New York: Verso, 1991).

23. Some of these ambiguities and complexities of "white" identity are interestingly explored in the male Italian-American characters in Spike Lee's film *Jungle Fever* (1991).

24. In an interesting twist on this argument, Mary Waters argues in *Ethnic Options: Choosing Identities in America* (Berkeley: University of California, 1990) that the ethnic revival among white groups (Irish, Polish, Italian) in the 1970s and 1980s, while characteristically eschewing explicit mention of race, nevertheless constituted an attempt to draw on and reassert the cultural superiority of "whiteness."

25. Orlando Patterson, *Freedom: Freedom in the Making of Western Culture*, vol. 1 (New York: Basic Books, 1991).

26. Judith Shklar, *American Citizenship: The Quest for Inclusion* (Cambridge, Mass.: Harvard University Press, 1992).

27. Nathan Huggins, "The Deforming Mirror," p. 30.

28. Ravitch, "Pluralism vs. Particularism in American Education," p. 38.

29. Diane Ravitch, "Diversity and Democracy: Multicultural Education in America," *American Educator* (Spring 1990): 16.

30. One prime target in the "Pluralism vs. Particularism" article is an early report from the New York Commissioner of Education, called "A Curriculum of Inclusion," which is a good deal more extreme in its condemnation of American institutions than the *One Nation, Many Peoples* report discussed in this essay.

31. See Ravitch, "The Plight of History in American Schools," in *Historical Literacy: The Case for History in American Education*, ed. Paul Gagnon (New York: Macmillan, 1989), cited in Robert Fullinwider, "Patriotic history," Chapter 9, this volume.

32. One may roughly distinguish "moderate" Afrocentrism that involves a special and distinct concern with the problems of African-American students, and a desire to ensure a recognition of the character, historical importance, and contributions of both African-Americans and African civilizations; and "extreme" forms that claim that European civilizations hold nothing of cultural or ethical worth but only oppression to members of the African diaspora (often combined with highly debatable claims about the African origins of all civilizations, including European). An influential Afrocentric work that contains both moderate and extreme strands is Molefi Kete Asante, *The Afrocentric Idea* (Philadelphia: Temple University Press, 1987).

33. I wish to thank Robert Fullinwider and especially Judith Smith for acute critical comments on this chapter.

Chapter 3

A conflict of visions: multiculturalism and the social studies

GILBERT T. SEWALL

In the extraordinary debate over multicultural education, Americans are struggling to define how they want their children to see themselves, their nation, and the world. Important matters are at stake. In a country that celebrates diversity, agreement on an irreducible, universal core of basic knowledge remains elusive, especially as the franchise of "diversity" expands beyond race and religion to encompass gender, sexuality, and disability. Multicultural education has become a pressing issue not only for elected officials and prominent combatants in the "culture wars," but also for councils trying to set national curriculum standards, test designers, educational publishers, and professors of education and the humanities.

The pressure for multiculturalism and multicultural education is not hard to understand. American elementary and secondary schools, especially in metropolitan areas, have increasingly large proportions of black, Hispanic, and Asian students. The multiethnic nature of the United States, and more intimate cultural and commercial relations between nations and continents, make any "monocultural" curriculum or "canon" seem provincial and obsolete.

On the face of it, multicultural education may seem an unlikely catalyst of division and controversy. Most scholars, educators, and policymakers agree on some central points: that social studies ought to recognize and respect cultural diversity; that children should not be given sanitized or ethnocentric versions of history; that race, gender, and class should have a place in historical explanations; that schools should teach students to respect one another, to appreciate the customs, religions, and languages that differentiate them, and to see the commonalities that lie behind their differences.

The problem may lie not in these propositions but in the different constructions that some multiculturalists give them. Construed in certain ways, multicultural precepts endorse a pedagogy that weak-

49

ens rather than strengthens the impulse for civic integration. In many schools, social studies classes are increasingly filled with reductive lessons that take a dim view of Western civilization in general and the white Anglo–Saxon patriarchy of the United States in particular.

Some multiculturalists want to rewrite the American story in such a way as to repudiate "the idea of a national identity, and the emotion of national pride," Richard Rorty recently asserted in the *New York Times*. "We live in a time when great efforts are being made to falsify the record of the past and to make history a tool of propaganda; when governments, religious movements, political parties, and sectional groups of every kind are busy rewriting history as they would wish it to have been," Bernard Lewis has warned. "All this is very dangerous indeed, to ourselves and to others, however we may define otherness – dangerous to our common humanity."[1]

In 1981, examining the recent phenomenon of historical revisionism, C. Vann Woodward pointed out that many historians now tend to invert old myths of American innocence, replacing them with a new, astringent, and occasionally demonic view of Anglo-American culture. These "inverted myths," Woodward argued, present Americans – at least, European-Americans – with a new image of themselves and their cultural heritage:

> The first English settlers . . . never should have come in the first place. Invasion was their initial offense. The pattern of collective rapacity and inhuman cruelty to darker peoples that characterized their westward conquests of the Pacific shores and on across the ocean ever westward through Asia is seen as existing from the very outset. From this point of view the line of precedents stretched from the slaughter of braves in the Pequot War of 1637 on for three centuries and more to Lieutenant Calley at My Lai, with little more than changes in the technology of annihilation. Thus interpreted, American history becomes primarily a history of oppression, and the focus is upon the oppressed. The primary objective in all this would not seem to be so much the exposure of evil or the identification of transgressors as it is an oblique exercise in the analysis of national character.[2]

Much of the multiculturalism fashionable in schools today is hardly an "oblique exercise." During the 1980s a skeptical and shaming view of national history and character prevailed in many social studies manuals, frameworks, and guidelines. Multicultural educators active and influential in promoting change in social studies content rejected any hint of national "triumphalism" or "commonwealth." Their discomfort with, or animus toward, the "rise of the West" was undisguised. The roots of their mind-set are to be found in the educational activism that surfaced three decades ago.

CLEANSING THE TEXTBOOKS

The curriculum disputes of our times originate partly with the Council on Interracial Books for Children. Founded in 1966, CIBC described itself as a group of "writers, editors, illustrators, teachers and parents committed to effecting basic change in books and other media." The "basic change" had to do with attitudes toward race and gender. Viewing the public school curriculum as one of the sources of racism, the CIBC demanded that textbooks and lesson plans free themselves from racial stereotypes and broaden their accounts of American history to include fully the role that blacks, women, and other groups have played in it. The CIBC criticized textbooks as "anti-human" vehicles of "racism, sexism, ageism, classism, materialism, elitism, and other negative values." It promised to provide "critical analyses of racist and sexist stereotypes prevalent in children's books and learning materials." The CIBC saw its mission in clear political terms. Words were political weapons, and books – children's books and schoolbooks – were not politically innocent items of instruction. "In our racist and sexist society, our decisions about word usage are political decisions," the CIBC asserted.[3] In its 1976 "guidelines for parents, educators and libraries," the CIBC declared:

> In any given society, children's books generally reflect the needs of those who dominate society. A major need is to maintain and fortify the structure of relations between dominators and dominated. The prevailing values are supportive of the existing structure; they are the dominator's values.[4]

Writers of children's books do not consciously set out to fortify the system of domination: "[M]ore often than not, they are unconscious tools of that system." To promote "human liberation," children's books had to be scouted not just for language and content but for more subtle features as well.

According to the CIBC, individualism and competitiveness are twin buttresses of the system of domination. Unlike individuality – defined as "the possession of individual characteristics" and as a value to be encouraged – individualism "is the cult of human separateness, the doctrine that each person is, indeed, an 'island.'" Competitiveness is understood to be individualism in an extreme form. The CIBC observed that individualism "has not always existed in every human society," and supported this claim with specious assertions about the character of non-European cultures. Native American societies, it claimed, "were more accepting of diversity, offered greater individual freedom and were more 'community' oriented and less competitive than European societies."[5]

The CIBC was not inclined to relax its vigilance in favor of esthetic considerations – or the imperatives of historicism. A poorly written book, it conceded, could not be redeemed by the presence of "good values," since "beautiful writing and art . . . are values, too." But if bad writing counted against a book with otherwise "good values," could beautiful writing count for a book containing "bad values"? In short, no. About books that were "stylistically admirable but that had anti-human values," CIBC was particularly stern:

> With such books, one can hardly talk about their "beauty": the inner ugliness of their racism or sexism, ageism or elitism, corrupts the very word itself. This type of book is especially venal because, by the very skill of its writing or pictures, it is likely to impress a child more. The more exciting, the more compelling, the more realistic it seems, the more damage it can do; its smooth surface masks its true nature all the more effectively.[6]

History texts were faulted for using incorrect language and for adopting "white" perspectives. They were criticized for various "distortions," that is, interpretations at odds with the CIBC's own revisionist views of American history. Texts were chided for saying that there had been "marked progress" or "impressive advances" in honoring the civil rights of blacks; for comparing "the immigrant experience to the Black experience"; for failing to emphasize the Constitution as a "pro-slavery" document; for describing the Iroquois as "a fierce and warlike people"; and for implicitly assuming that the United States is a "true democracy."[7] The CIBC was highly influential in lobbying textbook publishers and in shaping the presentation of race and gender in books. It influenced the people who play leadership roles in curriculum and textbook development today.

Publishing houses formulated standards for internal use and for textbook screening committees seeking to eliminate textbook "bias" against minority groups and women. The content of textbooks, their language, and the choice of subjects for illustration were all affected. Mass-market textbooks began to incorporate into their accounts of American history the experiences of blacks, immigrant groups, women, and native Americans, sometimes with finesse, more often awkwardly, to satisfy demands for "inclusion." Houghton Mifflin published *Eliminating Stereotypes* (1981), which examined such themes as gender, minority groups, disparities in students' economic and environmental backgrounds, and language. The handbook was quite prescriptive: "Show boys as well as girls: interested in small furry animals and birds, planning meals, shopping for clothes." In 1988, the New York City Board of Education published a guide entitled *Promoting Bias-Free Materials*, which noted a variety of problem areas in the social studies curriculum, including "contextual invisibility," historical distortion and omission, language bias, and inaccurate or stereotypic visual images. ("Do illustrations and images portray women and men of all races, ages, physical abilities, and social classes interacting with each other; or are they predominantly white, nondisabled males?")[8] California and other states enacted compliance criteria that required review of all educational materials for "inclusion" and "diversity."

While the CIBC is now defunct, its influence remains unmistakable in recent schoolbooks, multicultural education materials, and textbook analyses. Indeed, a leading anti-bias education handbook, distributed nationally by the National Association for the Education of Young Children, explicitly names the CIBC as the foundation of its initiatives and curricular agenda. The 1989 guide's rhetoric is virtually identical to that of old CIBC publications, and it ignores the vast changes in content that have occurred in the last three decades.[9]

CURRICULUM ISSUES TODAY

The CIBC view of curriculum reform remains significant, since its prevailing viewpoint dominated efforts to reshape history curricula and textbooks for more than twenty years. In 1989, the New York State task force report entitled "A Curriculum of Inclusion" made headlines by insisting that current education in the state harmed African-American, Asian-American, Native American, and Puerto Rican/Latino youth "because of its hidden assumptions of 'white supremacy' and 'white nationalism.'" The New York public school system was "contributing to the miseducation of all young people through a systematic bias toward European culture and its derivatives," the report charged. "Stringent measures" should be taken to revise the curriculum so that African-American, Asian-American, Native American, and Puerto Rican–Latino children "will have higher self-esteem and self-respect, while children from European cultures will have a less arrogant perspective."[10] The revisionism the task force had in mind as a way of raising the self-esteem of some children while refuting the arrogant perspectives of others prompted public denunciations from some of the nation's most prominent journals and historians.

One of the four academic consultants to the "Curriculum of Inclusion" task force, and a contributor to the main text of the report, was Leonard Jeffries of the City College of New York, which in 1992 tried to relieve Jeffries from his post as chair of its black studies program for making anti-Semitic remarks. In an appendix to "A Curriculum of Inclusion," Jeffries claimed that New York's existing treatment of European history "fail[ed] to reflect the conflict, chaos, and war which characterized Europe after the Crusades and corruption of the Catholic Church." Jeffries went on to explain, "This situation in Europe contributed directly to the development of negative values and policies that produced aggressive individuals and nations that were ready to 'discover, invade, and conquer' foreign land because of greed, racism and national egoism." New York had also failed to do justice to the American experience. On the creation of the Constitution and the American political process, Jeffries wrote, "[T]here is something vulgar and revolting in glorifying a process that heaped undeserved rewards on a segment of the population while oppressing the majority." Jeffries saw nothing redeeming in the American experience except the "constant struggle" of the oppressed, who alone had managed to wrest any "potential" or "promise" from the Constitution.[11]

"A Curriculum of Inclusion" generated such public controversy that New York Commissioner of Education Thomas Sobol empaneled a second committee to review the state's social studies curriculum. In the summer of 1991, the new group released its report, *One Nation, Many Peoples: A Declaration of Cultural Interdependence*, to more headlines and media attention, when two historians on the committee, Kenneth Jackson and Arthur Schlesinger, Jr., dissented from its findings.

The two reports were not identical. While extolling "global perspectives" and making ritual bows to the "social construction of knowledge,"[12] the second report stated that the purpose of the social studies is to teach students "the significance of our democratic rights and principles, and the importance of playing an active role in preserving and extending them to everyone." The new committee was not "revolted" at the idea of making the ideals embodied in the Constitution a central part of student learning. *One Nation, Many Peoples* recommended that the social studies curriculum address the "shortcomings" as well as the "successes" of U.S. domestic and foreign policy. It advised teaching history from "multiple perspectives," exploring "all the applicable viewpoints of the historical and social protagonists" involved, "paying special attention to the ways in which race, ethnicity, gender and class generate different ways of understanding, experiencing, and evaluating the events of the world." However, the new report endorsed these approaches in the context of an education that aimed to inspire a "common loyalty" to "our national traditions and values," an education that, while recognizing our differences, nevertheless gives "special attention . . . to those values, characteristics, and traditions which we share in common."[13]

The principles and recommendations expressed in *One Nation, Many Peoples* clearly masked larger tensions within the committee itself. Co-chairs Edmund Gordon and Francis Roberts appended a personal statement to the report, observing, "Some of us were shocked at the depth of feelings about diverse renditions of history" among members of the committee. They noted that members had difficulty stating their differences "dispassionately." It is not hard to imagine the range of some of these differences. Some committee members issued individual statements indicating that they would have liked the document to take a more explicitly anti-Western perspective. Diane Glover, a New York City teacher, said: "The educational community needs to know . . . the role of European scholarship in promoting psychological and historical inferiority. They need to know or to try to understand how racism has impacted on children of African descent and its relationship to self concept, economic, and sociological variables." Wrote Ali A. Mazrui, a professor of humanities at the State University of New York at Binghamton, "American children need to know that genocide was part of the birth of *this* nation. The holocaust began at home."[14]

DEFENSES OF AFROCENTRISM

"A Curriculum of Inclusion" faulted the New York state curriculum for failing "to outline clearly the significance of Africa in the world." The nature and extent of this significance, however, have themselves become controversial with the introduction of "Afrocentric" curricula in public schools. Leonard Jeffries is a prominent Afrocentrist, and Afrocentrism's influence on the report and later state deliberations was evident.

In Afrocentric education, the ordinary tests of historical proof are suspended. According to its proponents, Egypt was a black civilization, a fact purposefully obscured by racist European scholarship of the eighteenth and nineteenth centuries. Similarly obscured was the influence of Egypt on Greece, which European civilization honors as its fountainhead. Science, literature, mathematics, advanced technology and engineering – all flourished in Egypt while Greece was still a rude backwater. And they continued to flourish in successor civilizations in Africa into the Middle Ages. These and similar lessons constitute the heart of Afrocentric education, the main elements of which were embodied in the curriculum materials first devised by the Portland Public Schools in 1983 and disseminated among urban, black-dominated school systems in the ensuing decade.

Of the three kinds of Afrocentrism, two fully reject the West. The first wants curricula to reflect "the true role of Africa, especially Egypt, in the development of Western Civilization." A Eurocentric curriculum alienates black students, and diminishes their self-esteem.

They don't feel a part of what they are learning. By contrast, a curriculum infused with "African-centered history" will increase the self-esteem of black children, it is said, and support academic and career achievement.

A second kind of Afrocentrism operates on a particular theory of cultural inheritance and continuity. All people of African descent, wherever they are and however many generations they are removed from Africa, are still connected to their original African culture. They are heirs to an "unbroken African cultural continuity"; they participate in a "collective consciousness." People of African descent become a weakened people when they adopt European or other alien cultural attitudes and values. To succeed in life, African-American children must be imbued with cultural values and perspectives properly their own – African values and perspectives. Thus, Afrocentric curricula are said to be of crucial importance for black students. This rejection of the West – and of Western behavior and values – rests on a cultural essentialism: African-Americans have a "nature" that can flourish only with cultural values appropriate to that nature. African-Americans must learn their own values just as European Americans learn theirs.

A third variety of Afrocentrism rejects Western values and modes as deeply flawed, even evil. It isn't that they aren't fit for Africans; they aren't fit for humanity. Western civilization is characterized by "possessive materialism" and by "anti-humanistic individualism." It separates people from nature and alienates them from their intuitive selves by reliance on a dominating alphabetic linearity. It is, in the characterization by Leonard Jeffries and his like-minded colleagues, essentially rapacious and violent. By contrast, African values harmonize man and nature, prize community and collectivity, remain open to intuition and spirituality, and forswear hatred, greed, or violence. Clearly, then, African-American children ought to be protected from Western values – but so ought everyone else.[15]

NCSS GUIDELINES

Thus the treatment of race in history classes was already problematic when, in September 1992, the National Council for the Social Studies staked a position on multicultural education. The NCSS is the professional organization for social studies teachers in the United States, and its statements and guidelines consequently carry considerable authority, at least among educators active in curriculum development. Its "Curriculum Guidelines for Multicultural Education," a revision of a 1976 NCSS statement on multiethnic education, were written by James A. Banks, one of the nation's most influential promoters of multicultural education. His *Teaching Strategies for Ethnic Studies* (1975; fourth edition, 1987) and *Multiethnic Education: Theory and Practice* (1981; second edition, 1988) are staples of curriculum and instruction courses in schools of education.

The defining ideal of multiculturalism that Banks set forth in the 1992 NCSS Guidelines was unexceptional:

> Multicultural education helps students understand and affirm their community cultures and helps free them from cultural boundaries, allowing them to create and maintain a civic community that works for the common good. Multicultural education seeks to actualize the idea of *e pluribus unum* within our nation and to create a society that recognizes and respects the cultures of diverse people, people united within a framework of overarching democratic values.[16]

In the NCSS Guidelines, Banks placed his own views about multicultural education as a mediating voice of reason between white ethnocentrism and Afrocentrism, as though the two rested on a continuum. In his other writings, however, Banks often appears to reject the possibility of transcending "cultural boundaries" or articulating an inclusive American ethos. For example, in *Multicultural Education: Issues and Perspectives*, he pictures social studies education more as a contest across cultural boundaries. "Mainstream-centric curriculum," as he calls it,

> presents events, concepts, issues, and problems primarily or exclusively from the point of view and perspectives of the mainstream society and the dominant ethnic and cultural group in the United States, White Anglo-Saxon Protestants. The mainstream-centric curriculum is also usually presented from the perspective of Anglo males.[17]

And in this passage from *Teaching Strategies for Ethnic Studies*, Banks suggests that the oppression of minorities on the basis of their ascriptive characteristics will outlive any effort at cultural assimilation:

> [A]lthough non-White ethnic minorities may become totally assimilated culturally (i.e., in cultural characteristics they may become indistinguishable from Anglo-Saxon Protestants), they will still be victims of discrimination and racism because of their different physical characteristics.[18]

Assimilation, racial comity, and a "color-blind" society are impossible, Banks suggests. Ethnic separation is foundational to culture and society. The United States is a culture and nation divided into particular racial blocs, forever polarized, where a white majority forever excludes minorities from full participation. Banks does not fully subscribe to Woodward's "inverted myth" and does warn against an American history that only emphasizes "how ethnic groups of color have been oppressed by Anglo-Americans."[19] Yet Banks also leans reflexively toward CIBC-style curriculum criticism, recommending to teachers CIBC's *Guidelines for Selecting Bias-Free Textbooks and Storybooks* as a "helpful guide" for scouting out "Anglocentric and Eurocentric points of view."[20] Untrained as an historian, Banks warns against "oppression history," but his warning is compromised by his own credulousness toward historical work of dubious quality and arguable bias.

THE END OF TRIUMPHALISM

When Banks and others object to whitewashed history of the past, they have in mind the shadow of Euro-American triumphalism, a legacy of the nineteenth century. A hundred years ago, most Europeans and Americans had a different view of themselves than they have today. Not only was democratic capitalism freed from a "feudal" past. Technological progress produced secular miracles. Europeans possessed ocean liners, railroads and streetcars, and after about 1880, telephones and electric lights. They had hospitals and orphanages. All this seemed evidence of human achievement and excellence. The nineteenth-century European ideal of civilization, however, was not exclusively materialistic. It was also "liberal" and "reformist." Correct or truthful knowledge was held to be a civilized attainment – scientific knowledge of nature, in place of superstition or demonology; geographical knowledge, by which civilized people were aware of the earth as a whole and its diverse inhabitants. Literary, musical, and philosophical refinements were taken to be a basic provision of education and higher forms of culture.[21]

Before 1914, Europeans and their transatlantic counterparts assumed that people throughout the world should respect the same social ideals. If the "primitive" inhabitants of distant lands were unwilling or unable to adopt them, they were perceived as "backward." Insofar as they did adopt them, they became "civilized." Thus the world was to be made over according to Euro-American standards. An Englishman, Isaac Taylor, in his *Ultimate Civilization* (1860), listed the "relics of barbarism" soon to disappear with the advance of European civilization: polygamy, infanticide, legalized prostitution, capricious divorce, sanguinary and immoral games, infliction of torture, caste and slavery.[22]

By now European hubris has fairly exhausted itself. Claims of European cultural supremacy have long been open to question or repudiated. Many Western intellectuals today admire non-Western native cultures, not only out of scholarly interest but also on aesthetic grounds. Western democracies today may exhibit justifiable pride over the constitutional liberties and technical achievements that make life more fair, safe, clean, and comfortable in such places than in many non-Western societies. But this pride is mixed with regret, self-doubt, and even guilt over past colonial adventures and the mixed legacies of development.

Any responsible history of the United States and the world now takes into account the impact of Western expansionism on non-European societies, religions, and cultures. Ethnocentric and triumphalist accounts that sweep out of sight a sometimes violent, brutal, and sorry record will no longer do. During the last twenty years the curriculum – in mandates and published texts – has reflected increased appreciation of ethnic groups, including people of color, and non-Western cultures formerly misrepresented or marginalized in the curriculum. Textbooks have become more "honest." Yet history is not a plastic subject where interpretation can free itself from evidence. In the historical study of U.S. institutions, in particular, the influence of European – especially English – manners, ideas, and laws cannot be discarded or swept aside without great cost to the subject's integrity.

The United States inherits a complex political philosophy rooted in the rule of law and the ideas of justice, rights, and property, most of it borrowed from the English tradition. It is organized under a limited government of citizen-based consent, in a tradition of representative democracy, and in explicit recognition of ideas such as human rights, liberty, equality, reform, and progress. English is not only the public language of the nation. It is the *lingua franca* of educated people on all continents. Euro-American systems of finance, communication, and information exchange are global standards, as are its achievements in medicine, sanitation, and energy production.

American history is not merely a story of unfulfilled idealism and oppression but also one of great opportunity and creativity. American and European society are not characterized just by the "cult of human separateness" but also by political ideals and institutions that secure stability, justice, and liberty on an unprecedented scale. The trouble with the "inverted myth" is that it takes away any satisfaction or inspiration from this, except for the "heroic" resistance of the oppressed against the nation's and Western civilization's institutions, political and economic systems, and "philosophies of life."

Most American parents believe that the United States is a symbol of opportunity and freedom to people throughout the world, many of whom face excruciating want, disease, malnutrition, civil wars, and peonage. They see public schools as tax-supported instruments that give their children keys to knowledge and success. They are not likely to abide social studies curricula that present their nation's past and present as manifestations of an inherently oppressive, racist, and evil system that children should learn to distrust or even dislike. Where educators seek a revised curriculum informed by various degrees of Woodward's "inverted myth," multicultural education will not likely enhance the quality of school curricula, help build public support for public schools, or contribute to a vigorous and multiethnic American republic.

NOTES

1. Richard Rorty, "The Unpatriotic Academy," *New York Times*, February 13, 1994, p. A15; Bernard Lewis, *Islam and the West* (Oxford: Oxford University Press, 1993), p. 130.
2. The passage first appeared in the November 1981 *Bulletin* of the American Academy of Arts and Sciences and was reprinted in C. Vann Woodward, *The Future of the Past* (Oxford: Oxford University Press, 1989), pp. 119–27.
3. Racism and Sexism Resource Center for Educators, *Human and Anti-Human Values in Children's Books: A Content Rating Instrument for Educators and Concerned Parents* (New York: Council on Interracial Books for Children, 1976), pp. vii, viii, 4, 5.
4. Ibid., p. 1.
5. Ibid., pp. 3, 4, 18; Racism and Sexism Resource Center for Educators, *Stereotypes, Distortions, and Omissions in U.S. History Textbooks* (New York: Council on Interracial Books for Children, 1977), p. 129. The concept of individualism, as Robert Fullinwider observes, is a moving target in *Stereotypes, Distortions, and Omissions*. Chicanos, we are told, reject the "individualism and competitiveness" of European society in favor of "their traditional values of mutual help and collectivity" (p. 56). Have Chicanos derived these putative "traditional values" from their Native American rather than their Spanish heritage? If Chicanos obtained their "traditional values" from Spain, then the simple contrast between community-oriented Native American societies and competitive European societies utterly fails.
6. *Human and Anti-Human Values in Children's Books*, pp. 21–2.
7. *Stereotypes, Distortions, and Omissions in U.S. History Textbooks*, pp. 20–3, 28, 29, 72, 128.
8. Houghton Mifflin, *Eliminating Stereotypes: School Division Guidelines* (1981), p. 6; New York City Board of Education, *Promoting Bias-Free Curriculum Materials* (1988), pp. 5, 16.
9. Louise Derman-Sparks, *Anti-Bias Curriculum: Tools for Empowering Young Children* (Washington, D.C.: National Association for the Education of Young Children, 1989), n.p.
10. Task Force on Minorities: Equity and Excellence, "A Curriculum of Inclusion" (Albany: New York State Department of Education, July 1989), pp. iii-iv, 3, 7, 34.
11. *New York Times*, September 12, 1990; "A Curriculum of Inclusion," p. 22; Appendix 4, pp. 21, 26, 28, 29.
12. "The subject matter content [in history and social studies] should be

treated as socially constructed and therefore tentative – as is all knowledge," said the preamble to *One Nation, Many Peoples*. Jean Bethke Elshtain recently dismissed the view of history and theories of knowledge that this idea underwrites:

> To go beyond the reality of perspectives to the claim that there are only perspectives, that facts themselves are arbitrary inventions and that there is only "my reality" and "your reality," is to embrace nonsense. And to go still further and argue that the conditions of knowledge change with a change in gender, that men and women [or blacks and whites] inhabit separate epistemological universes, is to embrace not only nonsense but dangerous nonsense. (*The New Republic*, Sept. 6, 1993, pp. 32–3)

The attitude that Elshtain criticizes – allergic to distinctions of achievement, intelligence, and aesthetics – smiles upon elusive and futile quests for truth. For the left flank of multiculturalism, the unstated use of the "social construction of knowledge" is to press forward the idea that all cultures are of equal value and quality.

13. New York State Social Studies Review and Development Committee, *One Nation, Many Peoples: A Declaration of Cultural Interdependence* (Albany: New York State Education Department, June 1991), pp. 1, 5, 7, 8, 13.
14. Ibid., p. 31, 39, 41.
15. I am indebted to Robert Fullinwider for the design of this paradigm, which draws inter alia on *African-American Baseline Essays* (Portland, Oreg.: Portland Public Schools, revised edition, 1990); Molefi Kete Asante, *Afrocentricity: The Theory of Social Change* (Buffalo, N.Y.: Amulefi, 1980), pp. 4–5, 9–10; William M. King, "Challenges Across the Curriculum," *American Behavioral Scientist* 34 (November/December 1990): 176.
16. "Curriculum Guidelines for Multicultural Education," *Social Education* 55 (September 1992): 282.
17. James A. Banks and Cherry A. McGee Banks, eds., *Multicultural Education: Issues and Perspectives* (Boston: Allyn & Bacon, 1992), p. 328.
18. James A. Banks, *Teaching Strategies for Ethnic Studies*, 4th ed. (Boston: Allyn & Bacon, 1987), p. 69.
19. Banks, "Curriculum Guidelines," p. 282.
20. James A. Banks, "Integrating the Curriculum with Ethnic Content: Approaches and Guidelines," in *Multicultural Education: Issues and Perspectives*, ed. Banks and Banks, p. 205.
21. Theodore H. Von Laue, *The World Revolution of Westernization: The Twentieth Century in Global Perspective* (Oxford: Oxford University Press, 1987), pp. 13–34; R. R. Palmer, *A History of the Modern World*, 2d ed. (New York: McGraw-Hill, 1964), p. 556.
22. Quoted in Palmer, p. 556.

PART II
Culture and identity

Chapter 4

Culture, subculture, multiculturalism: educational options

K. ANTHONY APPIAH

It is a truism that in the United States of America "we live in a multicultural society." But the obviousness and apparent clarity of this truism, like the apparent clarity and obviousness of most such truisms, dissolves upon inspection. To begin with what is, perhaps, the least patent difficulty, what people normally have in mind when they pronounce this slogan, is that the United States is a multicultural *nation*. This is by no means obviously the same thought, since that we in America constitute a nation is, so to speak, a juridical and constitutional fact, while our being a society requires, I should have thought, both more and less than this.

The people of Martinique, after all, are French nationals: but there is surely such a thing as Martinican society as distinct from French society – the society of the "hexagon" – and it is not obvious that Martinicans generally are participants in the latter. Similarly, many Native Americans, who live on reservations, while clearly American nationals, might be thought to live in a separate society from the rest of us; and we might also argue, less uncontroversially, that soldiers on bases, the inhabitants of Bel Air, or of South Central L.A., or of San Francisco's Chinatown, live in societies separate from those of the people whose lives go on around them.

The point is that our word "society," used in this context, means something like a group of people with probably a shared geography,[1] and certainly shared institutions and a common culture: and, granted the geographical unity of the (continental) United States and the existence, under the Constitution, of American institutions, the question whether we are a society in this sense is the same as the question whether there is such a thing, at some level, as a shared American culture.[2] To speak of American society as multicultural in this sense, as composed of groups of people with distinct cultures, might seem to be, at best, confusing; at worst, actually contradictory. And the fact

65

is that the problems of the many cultures within the boundaries of the American state are usually thought of as flowing from the yoking together of societies, groups of people with a common culture and common institutions, within a single set of political institutions and in a shared social space.

Still, to speak of America as a collection of societies, a gathering of cultures, is, in one way, rather misleading. For while some of the cultural variety of the current United States arises from the presence of people who grew up and were acculturated in other places,[3] most of America's cultures have been largely shaped by experience in the United States: if there is an overarching set of beliefs, ideas, and practices that make up an American culture, most of America's cultures were shaped by that common culture. And even if that common culture is pretty thin gruel, America's cultures have mostly been shaped by interaction with each other. America's many cultures, its various societies, have grown up together, belong in a single system of cultures; they are not the mere logical sum of a series of unrelated historically independent elements.

QUESTION 1: ARE WE REALLY A SOCIETY?

If, as I have suggested, a society is a group of people with probably a shared geography, and certainly shared institutions and a common culture, then understanding whether we are a society will depend on both a) whether there are American institutions and b) whether there is an American common culture.

The first of these questions is easily enough answered: for the political institutions of the American nation are shared by all who live in the United States. (Some of us live here without being citizens, and thus without being entitled to participate in those institutions as voters, jurors, and so on; but we all have the right to participate in other politically created institutions – heterosexual marriage, for example, or property ownership – and the obligation to live under American laws.)

It is equally plain, however, that these constitutional institutions – the political structure of the American republic – take up only a small part of the lives of many who live in the United States; they have the interest and affection of a significant number of the people who live in the United States but by no means of all.

Many citizens, for example, do not vote, and their disengagement from the constitutional political process means more than that their participation in the institutions of the American nation may be minimal; more importantly, it means that they may have little investment in those institutions. (That they have no subjective investment does not, of course, mean that they have nothing at stake: the homeless may not be well enough treated in our society but they do – and they should – take advantage of their legal rights.) And this lack of investment means not sharing certain values, values that might be thought of as American.

Which brings us, then, to the second question: the question of an American culture. Suppose it is correct to speak, as many do, of American culture as centrally constituted, in part, by, for example, democratic and republican values. Then, so it seems, something central to American culture may not be held in common by all who live within the American nation. And if that is so, then, in the relevant sense, there may be no American society, nothing bound together both by American institutions and by a unitary American culture.

QUESTION 2: WHAT IT WOULD MEAN TO HAVE A COMMON CULTURE?

But we will not get much further with these issues until we explore the concept of culture, an idea that immediately reveals itself to be extremely elastic. In my dictionary I find as one definition for culture "The totality of socially transmitted behavior patterns, arts, beliefs, institutions, and all other products of human work and thought."[4] This is not, I think, quite right. There is, to begin with, no obvious incoherence in the idea of a non-human culture: we can reasonably speak of the culture of some primates or imagine, in science fiction, the culture of non-terrestrial creatures.

But the definition surely picks out a familiar constellation of ideas. "Culture," in one sense, does indeed name all the "products of human work and thought." That is, in fact, the sense in which anthropologists largely use the term nowadays. The culture of the Ashanti or the Zuni, for the anthropologist, includes every object they make (clothing, pottery, houses – which, taken together, we call their "material culture") and everything they think and everything they do; or, more precisely, everything that they do that is the product of thought (which is to say, invoking a familiar philosophical distinction, not every bodily movement, but every action).

You will notice, however, that the dictionary definition could have stopped there, leaving out the talk of "socially transmitted behavior patterns, arts, beliefs, institutions," because these are all products of human work and thought. They are mentioned, of course, because they are the residue of an older idea of culture than the anthropological one. Here what the dictionary draws attention to is something more like the idea of a civilization: the "socially transmitted behavior patterns" of ritual, etiquette, religion, games, arts; the values that they engender and reflect; and the institutions – family, school, church, state – that shape and are shaped by them.

There are two tensions between the anthropologist's idea of a culture and the idea of a civilization. First, there is nothing in the anthropologist's idea that requires that the culture of a group should be a totality in any stronger sense than being what I called the mere logical sum of all the things they make and the actions they undertake.

American civilization, on the other hand, would not be just a simple logical sum of the doings and thoughts of Americans. It would have to have a certain coherence. Some of what is done in America and by Americans would not belong to American civilization because it was too individual (the particular bedtime rituals of a particular American family); some would not belong because it was not properly American, because (like a Hindi sentence, made in America) it does not properly cohere with the rest.

The second, connected, difference between what I am calling the anthropological idea of culture and the idea of a civilization, is that the latter takes values to be more central to the enterprise, in two ways. First, the civilization of a group is centrally defined by its moral and aesthetic values, and the coherence of a civilization is, primarily, the coherence of those values with each other and, then, of the group's behavior and institutions with its values. Second, civilizations are essentially to be evaluated: they can be better and worse, richer and poorer, more and less interesting. Anthropologists, on the whole, tend now to avoid the relative evaluation of cultures, adopting a sort of cultural relativism, whose coherence philosophers have tended to doubt. And they do not take values as more central to culture than, for example, beliefs, ideas, and practices.

Because there are these differences I want to reserve the word "culture" for the anthropologist's notion: henceforward I shall use the word "civilization" for the older notion I have been sketching. The habit of shaking hands at meetings belongs to culture in the anthropologist's sense; the works of Sandro Botticelli and Martin Buber and Count Basie belong to culture also, but they belong to civilization as well.

DISTINGUISHING BETWEEN CULTURE
AND CIVILIZATION

The move from "civilization" to "culture" was the result of arguments, not a simple drift of usage. The move away from evaluation came first, once people recognized that much evaluation of other cultures by the Europeans and Americans who invented anthropology had been both ignorant and biased. Earlier criticisms of "lower" peoples turned out to involve crucial misunderstandings of their ideas (Levy-Bruhl's talk of a "pre-logical" mentality, for example); and it eventually seemed clear enough, too, that nothing more than differences of upbringing underlay the distaste of some Westerners for unfamiliar habits. It is a poor move from recognizing certain evaluations as mistaken to giving up evaluation altogether, and anthropologists who adopt cultural relativism often preach more than practice it. Still, this cultural relativism was a response to real errors. That it is the wrong response doesn't make the errors any less erroneous.

The arguments against "civilization" were in place well before the mid-century. More recently, anthropologists began to see that the idea of the coherence of a civilization got in the way of understanding important facts about other societies (and, in the end, about our own). For even in some of the "simplest" societies, there are different values and practices and beliefs and interests associated with different social groups (women as opposed to men; elders as opposed to young men; chiefs as opposed to commoners; one clan as opposed to another). To think of a civilization as coherent was to miss the fact that these different values and beliefs were not merely different but actually opposed.[5] Worse, what had been presented as the coherent unified worldview of a tribal people often turned out, on later inspection, to be merely the ideology of a dominant group or interest.

I believe there is much of value in these anthropological criticisms of the idea of a civilization.[6] I shall refer back to the idea of civilization from time to time, however, where it helps us understand some of our contemporary debates. In the meanwhile, we need another distinction within the idea of culture.

A MULTICULTURAL SOCIETY

We customarily refer to the small-scale, technologically uncomplicated, face-to-face societies, where most interactions are with people whom you know, as traditional. In many such societies every adult who is not mentally disabled speaks the same language. All share a vocabulary and a grammar and an accent. While there will be some words in the language that are not known by everybody – the names of medicinal herbs, the language of some religious rituals, the vocabulary of secret societies – most are known to all normal adults. (I shall speak loosely, from now on, of what is known to – or believed by – all who are not mentally disabled – or hugely miseducated – as universally known or believed.) To share a language is to participate in a complex set of shared expectations and understandings, but in such societies it is not only linguistic behavior that is coordinated through universally known expectations and understandings. People will share an understanding of many practices – marriages, funerals, other rites of passage – and will largely share their views about the general workings not only of the social but also of the natural world. While ethnographers in the past may sometimes have overstated the extent to which basic theories of nature are universally believed in a society, even those who are skeptical about particular elements of belief will nevertheless know what everyone is supposed to believe, and they will know it in enough detail to behave very often as if they believed it, too.

A similar point applies to many of the values of such societies. It may well be that some people, even some groups, do not share the values that are enunciated in public and taught to children. But, once more, the standard values are universally known, and even those who do not share them know what it would be to act in conformity with them and probably do so much of the time.

In such a traditional society we may speak of these shared beliefs, values, signs, and symbols, as the common culture;[7] not, to insist on a crucial point, in the sense that everyone in the group actually holds the beliefs and values, but in the sense that everybody knows what they are and everybody knows that they are widely held in the society.[8] There will be beliefs and values – those of the skeptics – in the society that are not part of its common culture, because they are the results of individual defections from a norm. There will be beliefs and values that are not socially shared, but are the property of families or other associations of social life. And there will be material culture, which is shaped by social transmission, but not the common property of all.

But even in a traditional society there will be other elements of culture that are not held in common. Skills, for example, are not beliefs or values, nor are they material culture, but hunting or singing, for example, or ritual practices are socially transmitted. These will fail to belong to the common culture not because they are the products of individual or family deviations but because they are the result of the special training associated with particular groups. I am going to call the shared beliefs, values, and practices of a socially recognized subgroup a subculture.[9] And I shall say that a nation that contains subcultures wider than the family is multicultural.

Since this definition is going to do some work later, let me point out at once some things that it does not entail. On this way of thinking of subcultures, there doesn't have to be one common culture shared by the members of all the national subcultures taken together. A subculture is "sub" because it belongs to a recognized subgroup of the nation, not because its members share the national culture plus some other more specific culture. My definition doesn't assume there is some culture in common to all the national subcultures; but it isn't meant to rule that out, either.[10]

It is also important that the overarching group is the nation, not the society. For, in the way I have been using the word "society," it is an open question whether fellow nationals share a society, because it is an open question whether there is a national common culture.

MULTICULTURAL SOCIETIES ARE NOT INTRINSICALLY PROBLEMATIC

No one is likely to make much fuss about the fact that a nation is multicultural in this sense. For, in this sense, many simple and all large-scale societies have been multicultural. Once you have division of labor and social stratification, there will be people who do and people who don't know about music and literature and pottery and painting; if we call all these specialized spheres together the arts, then everyone will participate in the arts to varying degrees, and there are likely to be subgroups (opera lovers, say, or dedicated moviegoers, or lovers of poetry) who share significant practices and ideas with each other that are not shared with everyone else.

If being multicultural is a problem, it is not because we have different artistic subcultures: pace those who seem preoccupied with stopping multiculturalism at the NEH or the NEA, the problems created by our many subcultures largely lie elsewhere. Since the arts were central to the idea of civilization, those who worry about the existence of artistic subcultures may be conflating the question whether there is a shared civilization in the United States with the question whether there is a common culture. If a shared culture means shared arts – a single civilization – the United States has never had a shared culture: the social meaning of the fine arts includes their not been shared; high and low are mutually constitutive categories. But, as we have seen, there is more to culture, in the sense of the term that I have chosen to focus on, than the arts.

QUESTION 1 ANSWERED: THE UNITED STATES IS NOT A SOCIETY BECAUSE THERE IS NO COMMON CULTURE

What I have called the common culture is what a social group has socially in common: it is what people teach their children in order to make them members of their social group. By definition, a common culture is shared; it is the social bottom line. It includes language and table manners, religious ideas, moral values, theories of the workings of the natural and social worlds.[11] To have a common culture, to repeat the crucial point, is to have a common language and a common vocabulary of values and theories, even if some individuals or sub-groups are skeptical of the theories and reject the values. (It does not, thus, require shared commitment to the central values and theories of the natural and social world.)[12]

I associate cultures with social groups, not with nations, because I want to insist again that a group of persons living together in a common state, under common authorities, need not have a common culture. There is no single shared body of ideas and practices in India, or, to take another example, in most contemporary African states.

Thus, many, but by no means all, Ghanaians know (some) English. There is no language known to all (or even most) of us. There are Moslems and Christians and practitioners of the traditional religions of many ethnic groups. There are matrilineal and patrilineal concep-tions of family; there are traditions of divine kingship and less hier-archical notions of politics. The modern constitutional order – the Presidency, the parliament, the courts – is not well understood by many and unknown to quite a few.[13]

Now I think it is fair to say that there is not now and there has never been a common culture in the United States, either. The reason is simple: the United States has always been multilingual, and has always had minorities who did not speak or understand English. It has always had a plurality of religious traditions; beginning with Native American religions and Puritans and Catholics and including now many varieties of Judaism, Islam, Buddhism, Jainism, Taoism, Bahai . . . and so on. And many of these religious traditions have been quite unknown to each other. More than this, Americans have also always differed significantly even among those who do speak English, from North to South and East to West, and from country to city, in customs of greeting, notions of civility, and a whole host of other ways.

To say this is not to deny that for significant parts of American history there has been a good deal of mutual knowledge across re-gional, religious, ethnic, and even linguistic barriers. My point is that the notion that what has held the United States together historically over its great geographical range is a common culture, like the com-mon culture of a traditional society, is not sociologically plausible.

NATIONAL CULTURE VERSUS NATIONAL COMMON CULTURE

The notion that there is no American national culture will come as a surprise to many: observations about "American culture," taken as a whole, are common. It is, for example, held to be individualist, litigious, racially obsessed. I think each of these claims is actually true, because what I mean when I say there is no common culture of the United States is not what is denied by someone who says that there is an American culture.

Such a person is describing large-scale tendencies within American life that are not necessarily participated in by all Americans. I do not mean to deny that these exist. But for such a tendency to be part of what I am calling the common culture, they would have to derive from beliefs and values and practices (almost) universally shared and known to be so. And that they are not.

RECOGNIZING A DOMINANT CULTURE

At the same time, it has also always been true that there was a *dominant* culture in these United States. It was Christian, it spoke English, and it identified with the high cultural traditions of Europe and, more particularly, of England. And, until recently, when people spoke of American culture, this is what they meant.

This dominant culture included the common culture of the dominant classes – the government and business and cultural elites – but it was familiar to many others who were subordinate to them. And it was not merely an effect but also an instrument of their domination. Because the dominant norms of language and behavior were those of a dominant class, their children, for example, were likely to have preferred access to the best educations – educations which themselves led to dominant positions in business, in government, and in the arts.

As public education has expanded in the United States, America's citizens, and especially those citizens educated in public elementary schools in this country, have come to share a body of historical knowledge, and an understanding – however tenuous – of the American political system. And it is increasingly true that whatever other languages children in this country speak, they speak and understand English, and they watch many of the same television programs and listen to much of the same music. Not only do they share these experiences, they know that they do; and so they can imagine themselves as a collectivity, the audience for mass culture. In that sense, most young Americans have a common culture based in a whole variety of kinds of English, but it is no longer that older, Christian, Anglo-Saxon tradition that used to be called American culture.

The outlines of this almost universal common culture, to which only very few Americans are external, are somewhat blurry. But it includes, for example, in its practices, baseball; in its ideas, democracy; in its religion, Christianity;[14] in its arts, rap music and music videos and many movies. This culture is to a large extent, as I have implied, the product of schools and of the media. But even those who share this common culture live in subcultures of language, religion, family organization, and political assumptions. And, more than this, most who are black and Hispanic have, irrespective of their incomes, radically different experiences and expectations of the state.

MULTICULTURALISM AS AN ALTERNATIVE TO IMPOSING THE DOMINANT CULTURE

Now I take it that multiculturalism is meant to be the name of a response to these familiar facts: that it is meant to be an approach to education and to public culture that acknowledges the diversity of cultures and subcultures in the United States and that proposes to deal with that diversity in some other way than by imposing the values and ideas of the hitherto dominant Anglo-Saxon cultural tradition. That, I think, is the common core of all the things that have been called multiculturalism.

I think this common idea is a good one. It is a good idea for a number of reasons. It is a good idea, first, because the old practice of imposing Christian, Anglo–Saxon tradition was rooted in racism and anti-Semitism (and sexism and heterosexism . . . but that is another story). But it is a good idea, second, because making the culture of one subculture the official culture of a state privileges the members of that subculture – gives them advantages in public life – in ways that are profoundly anti-egalitarian and, thus, anti-democratic.

Yet agreeing to this idea does not tell you much about what you should do in schools and in public culture. It tells you that you mustn't impose certain practices and ideas, but it doesn't tell you what you should do affirmatively. I want to suggest that one affirmative strategy in this area is a bad idea for public education and that there are other strategies that are better. And then, in closing, I want to say something about why living together in a multicultural society is bound to turn out to be difficult.

THE DISTINCTION BETWEEN CULTURES AND IDENTITIES

There is one final piece of apparatus I need, however. I have been talking of "subcultures" and defining what I mean by this. And it would be natural to assume that the primary subgroups to which these subcultures are attached will be ethnic and racial groups (with religious denominations conceived of as a species of ethnic group). It would be natural, too, to think that the characteristic difficulties of a multicultural society arise largely from the cultural differences between ethnic groups. I think this easy assimilation of ethnic and racial subgroups to subcultures is to be resisted.

First of all, it needs to be argued, and not simply assumed, that black Americans, taken as a group, have a common culture: values and beliefs and practices that they share and that they do not share with others. This is equally true for, say, Chinese-Americans; and it is *a fortiori* true of white Americans. What seems clear enough is that being African-American or Asian-American or White is an important social identity in the United States. Whether these are important social identities because these groups have shared common cultures is, on the other hand, quite doubtful; not least because it is doubtful whether they have common cultures at all.

With differing cultures, we might expect misunderstandings arising out of ignorance of each other's values, practices, and beliefs; we might even expect conflicts because of differing values or beliefs. The paradigms of difficulty in a society of many cultures are misunderstandings of a word or a gesture; conflicts over who should take custody of the children after a divorce; whether to go to the doctor or the priest for healing.

Once we move from talking of cultures to identities, whole new kinds of problems come into view. Racial and ethnic conflicts, for example, have to do with the ways in which some people think members of other races and ethnic groups should be treated, irrespective of their cultural accomplishments. It isn't because a black man won't understand his daughter, or because he will value her differently from a white man, or because he does not know some important facts, that Archie Bunker wouldn't want his daughter to marry one. Mr. Bunker's bigotry does not require him to differ culturally in any significant respect from black people. He would be as opposed to the marriage if the potential son-in-law had exactly the same beliefs and values (on non-race-related matters) as he had himself. Similarly, in Bosnia it is not so much that what Croats do makes them hateful to Serb bigots; or vice versa. It is rather that those things are hateful because Croats (or Serbs) do them.

These cases bring out the ways in which ethnic and racial identities are contrastive: it is central to being African-American that you are not Euro-American or Asian-American; *mutatis mutandis*, the same goes for being Euro-American or Asian-American. And these distinctions matter because (some) people think it appropriate to treat people differently depending on which of these categories they fall into; and these ways of treating people differently lead to patterns of domination and exploitation. Racial and ethnic identities are, in this way, like genders and sexualities. To be female is not to be male; to be gay is not to be straight; and these oppositions lead some to treat people differently according to their gender or sexuality, in asymmetrical ways that usually privilege men or straight people.

Now it is crucial to understanding gender and sexuality that women and men and gay and straight people grow up together in families, communities, denominations. Insofar as a common culture means common beliefs, values, and practices, gay people and straight people in most places have a common culture; and while there are societies in which the socialization of children is so structured by gender that women and men have seriously distinct cultures, this is not a feature of most "modern" societies.[15]

I take the fact that questions about feminism (gender) and gay and lesbian identity (sexuality) come up often in thinking about multiculturalism (especially in the university) as an indication that what many people are thinking about is not the multiple subcultures of the nation but its multiple identities. All I want to insist on for now is that these are not the same thing.

A MULTICULTURAL NATION'S PROBLEMS WITH PUBLIC EDUCATION

I have been trying to explore the ways in which we are a multicultural nation, because, as I say, I want to say something about the consequences of this situation for public education.[16] But we should notice that it is not obvious what special problems the multicultural character of the American nation creates for the curriculum.

Once you have conceded what I claim is the key multiculturalist contention – that you should not use the public schools to impose the subculture of a dominant group – you might think you could proceed simply by asking what is worth teaching to American children and teaching that. This was, after all, the basis of the older curriculum; and if that curriculum confused what was worth teaching with what was valued in the subculture of the dominant class – the particular masquerading in a familiar way as the universal – the obvious correction would be to try to answer the question of what is worth teaching in a less (sub)culturally biased way.

The fact is that the older notion that we should instruct all children in "American culture" was, itself, a potentially democratic and egalitarian one. The advantages that the children of the dominant class gained by the fact that it was their home culture – their dialect of English, their table manners, the literature their parents read and admired – that was taught in schools and presupposed in public life, could be eradicated, if all children were given access to that culture

76

through schooling. The multicultural critique might lead you to feel that it was unfair to give the dominant class a head start in this way (a fact we could deal with, for example, by refraining from preferring their dialect in official speech). But I do not see that it would require you to do anything else to reflect the multicultural character of the nation in the curriculum.

Yet if we read the National Council for the Social Studies statement on multicultural education, it is clear that this influential group of educators take it for granted that much more is required. To begin with, they move freely (as I have urged we should not) from talk of multiculturalism to talk of ethnic identities. Though they agree that not every student cares much about an ethnic identity and that children should be free not to identify themselves ethnically,[17] they also insist that ethnicity should be an important factor in shaping educational policy:

(1) Personal ethnic identity and knowledge of others' ethnic identity is essential to the sense of understanding and the feeling of personal well-being that promotes intergroup understanding. . . . (278)

(2) Students cannot fully understand who they are . . . until they have a solid knowledge of the groups to which they belong. (282)[18]

In the background here are widespread assumptions about what is going wrong in our "multicultural" schools: that violence between children (which is plainly a barrier to learning) often grows out of intergroup misunderstandings; that minority students (especially African-Americans and Hispanics) underachieve because they and their cultures are not respected in the school. But if the conflict in the schools is a matter of contests between identities, there is no reason to think that teaching about various cultures will eradicate it. Understanding may not help with problems that do not arise from misunderstanding. What is required, very often, is not understanding of cultures but respect for identities; and a curriculum that takes the cultural works of African-Americans seriously may be helpful here, even if it does not communicate a deepened understanding of African-American culture.

And if the "solid knowledge" of my group is to be taught as a distinct body of beliefs and ideas, then it may actually lead me to be more culturally different from my peers of other races and ethnicities (who are taught different, though, no doubt, equally solid things about "their" tradition) and thus generate more possibilities for misunderstanding. Passage (2) thus proposes a policy that increases the likelihood of the danger passage (1) seeks to avoid.

TWO RATIONALES FOR SEPARATISM

Implicit in passage (2) is the thought that the way to deal with our many cultures in public education is to teach each child the culture of "its" group. This is the strategy of some (but by no means all) Afro-centrists and of some (but by no means all) of those who have favored bilingual education for Hispanics.

This is the strategy I oppose.

To explain my first basis for objection, I need to elicit a paradox in this approach, which we can do by considering the answer that this approach – I shall call it, tendentiously, Separatism – proposes to the question, Why should we teach African-American children something different from what we teach other children? The answer will come in two parts: the first part says that we should do so because they already come from a different culture; the second part says that we should do so because we should teach all people about the traditions from which they come.

It's the first answer that is paradoxical, at least if you think that the plurality of cultures is a problem. It is paradoxical because it proposes to solve the problems created by the fact that children have different cultures by emphasizing and entrenching those differences, not by trying to reduce them.

I should make it plain that I have no problem with the argument that children's home cultures need to be taken into account in deciding how to teach them: there's no point in giving kids information in languages or dialects they don't understand, or simply punishing them – rather than dealing with their parents or guardians – for behavior that they are being taught at home. But to admit that is to admit only that culture may sometimes make a difference as to how you should teach, not that it should make a difference as to what you should teach. And defending teaching children different histories (Afrocentric history) or different forms of speech or writing (Black English) on the grounds that this is already their culture simply begs the question; if we teach African-American children different histories from other children, then, indeed, it will become true that knowing that history and not knowing any other history will be part of the culture of African-Americans.

But the fact is that if we don't enforce cultural differences of this kind in the schools, surely they will largely disappear. And what that means is that the only serious argument for Separatism that survives is the second answer I considered earlier: the claim that we must teach each child the culture of "its" group because that is the right thing to do, because we should.

EXPLORING THE SECOND RATIONALE

That idea is much more powerful. It is presumably at the basis of the thought that many non-observant Jews share with observant Jews (who have other reasons for believing this), namely, that it is good to teach their children Jewish history and customs, because they are Jewish children. It is the argument – "we have Plato to our father" – that led to the sense of exclusion that many African-Americans felt when the history and culture of the United States were taught to them as the continuation of a white Western tradition; the argument against which so much Afrocentrism is a reaction.[19]

I myself am skeptical of all arguments of this form: my instinct is to believe that traditions are worth teaching in our public schools and colleges because they are beautiful and good and true – or, at least, interesting and important and useful – never because they are ours or yours, mine or thine. I was brought up a Protestant; but after my first seder, it struck me that this was a tradition worth knowing about for everybody, Jew or Gentile; and I have always valued the experience of family community among my Moslem cousins at Ramadan.[20]

It may be worth spending a little time reflecting on the unfashionableness of my instinctive view and insisting on some of its virtues, which may have been forgotten. I mentioned just now the "older view" that public education should teach an American culture. What was done in the name of that older view too often obscured the variety of the sources of America's cultures, as well as giving too rosy and unconflicted a view of the relations between America's various ethnic, racial, and religious subgroups. None of these mistakes needs resurrecting.

But this older view surely also held that what we should teach in public schools should be knowledge worth knowing, values worth respecting, practices useful in children's lives outside the school. Contemporary feminist, anti-racist and anti-ethnocentrist skepticisms lead us to ask, Worth knowing for whom? By whose standards? And these are fair questions. But in answering them we should take them seriously as questions about the curriculum as a practical business.

And this requires remembering some simple facts: the school curriculum contains, of necessity, an extremely small proportion of what is known; we read only the minutest sample of what has been written; and we have time to study only a fraction of the known history of the world, only the most basic scientific knowledge.

How, given these facts, can we pick from all these riches? To say we should favor truth over falsehood is to utter a truism worth holding on to; but it leaves vast decisions to be made. (It also neglects the fact that the whole truth is complicated, too complicated often to learn all at once, so that we teach children simplified versions of it, first of all – Newtonian half-truths before Einstein.) To say that in selecting what literature and art we should teach we should seek to transmit an appreciation of literary and aesthetic values is also fine enough; but to do this we need to read the mediocre and the near-great as well as the magnificent. More than this, while literary judgment can be reasoned about, it is also essentially contestable, so that part of what we need to teach is the idea that there are reasonable differences in matters of literary and artistic taste, differences that we cannot rely on argument or evidence to settle. Each of these complications makes the principle that we should teach the beautiful a poor instrument for discriminating among all the range of the arts those we should teach; and it offers little guidance as to how we should teach them.

Finally, of course, schools should teach the young what is good and evil: and also what is courageous and what foolhardy; what is compassion and what is sentimentality; where loyalty to family and friends ends and our responsibility to our fellow citizens, our fellow creatures, begins; and how to make all these moral discriminations. But there is here no easy consensus; there are too many hard cases, and we cannot expect that teaching young people to make these discriminations – which means helping them learn to think ethically – will be uncontroversial in a society where certain moral views are associated with particular group identities. For the schools will regularly be asked to recognize, say, religious identities by teaching their views.

I concede all these difficulties: indeed, thinking about them strikes me as a useful place to begin reflecting on the curriculum. But I repeat that I do not think it will help us in public education to add to our baggage of reasons for offering an element of a school curriculum to a child the thought: I teach you, this particular child, this thing because it is your tradition.

This is because I think this an inadmissible ground for the curriculum of a public school, not because I think that we should never hear such arguments. Indeed, they are among the most compelling arguments that a family or a church or temple or mosque can offer to a child. "In our family," I might tell my nephew, "we have done this for many generations. Your great-grand-uncle did it, in Asante, in the late nineteenth century; your grandfather did it when he was a boy in Kumasi." There are things and practices I value because we – my ancestors and I – have done them for generations, because I take pleasure in the sense of continuity with them as my ancestors.

If I had been to a Catholic or a Jewish or a Muslim school, I would have learned such traditions, too, not as my traditions but as some-body else's. I would have learned them not because the teachers and the school believed in them as traditions, but because they believed in them *tout court*. And because one can value them not just as traditions but as truths, I could decide to make them mine.

In the modern world many have sought to hold on to the profound pleasures of tradition even after they have left their faith behind. But, to repeat, in most Catholic or Jewish or Muslim schools, before the modern period, what was taught was taught as the truth about life, the universe, and conduct; and though people might have taken plea-sure in thinking of it as a matter of the tradition of a family and a community, if they had not thought it true, they would have thought it worthless. For these schools one notion of the good and the true, a contested notion, attached to one identity, was a presupposition of the curriculum.

AN ALTERNATIVE VIEW

The public schools of a multicultural, multiethnic, religiously diverse society should not operate like these older religious schools: the pub-lic schools should not propagate one faith, support the traditions of one group, celebrate the heritage of one ethnicity. They should not teach particular traditions and religions; though, of course, they should teach *about* them.

The view I am articulating here is a view about the division be-tween public and private spheres in the education of children: on such a view, ethnicity and religion are not to be transmitted by the organs of the state. Both, rather, are created and preserved outside the state by families, and by wider communities, including religious ones. Because there are many such cultures – and identities – created outside the state, in civil society, and because for many of us they are central to our conceptions of ourselves and of our lives, the school must acknowledge them. Because they have a great deal of impact on our relations, in communities and in the political life of the state, we are all better prepared for life in this nation if we know something of the cultures and identities of others and if we learn to engage in respectful discourse with them. Outside the school, children can be preached a specific religion; within it, they can hear about their own traditions, along with others, but they should not be proselytized, even on behalf of their families.

If there is any doubt about the stability of such a view, consider the alternative: a policy in which the public schools set out to teach children according to their identities and subcultures; that not only taught about collective identities but set out to reinforce and transmit them. If carried to its ultimate, this policy would require segregation into cultural and religious groups either within or between public schools, in ways that would be plainly unconstitutional in the United States since the *Brown* decision. For if we did have unsegregated classes teaching Jewish history, and African-American history, and Anglo history and Hispanic history and Chinese history in our schools, by what right would we forbid children from going to the "wrong" classes?

Of course there are things that we surely all believe that we should teach all American children: in particular, we should teach them something of the history of the American political system. And here is a reason why we cannot hope to teach each child only "its" cultural tradition: for understanding the American constitutional system and its history requires us to know about slavery and immigration, about the Civil War and Reconstruction, the Underground Railroad and Ellis Island. If there is a sense in which each of these belongs more to the history of some social groups than others, there is also a clear sense in which they belong to us all.

And it is *that* idea that motivates the approach to dealing with our multicultural society that I favor, that undergirds my multiculturalism. For it seems to me that what is ideal in a multicultural society, whose multicultural character is created outside the state in the sphere of civil society, is that the state should seek in its educational systems to make these multiple subcultures known to each other. A multicultural education, in my view, should be one that leaves you not only knowing and loving what is good in the traditions of your subculture but also understanding and appreciating the traditions of others (and, yes, critically rejecting the worst of all traditions).[21] This approach has its practical problems also: a curriculum filled with the history of Korean-Americans and African-Americans and Anglo-Americans and Jewish Americans and so on risks being a curriculum with a shallow appreciation of all of them. But the principle of selection is clear: we should try to teach about those many traditions from around the world that have come to be important at different stages of American history. This means that we begin with Native American and Protestant Dutch and English and African and Iberian cultures, adding voices to the story as they were added to the nation. Because different elements are important to different degrees in different places today, we can assume that the balance will be and should be differently struck in different places. (All of which presupposes a general improvement, I should add, in the quality of American elementary and secondary education.)

A FINAL OBJECTION TO SEPARATISM

I have a final argument against Separatism. It is that it is dangerous, for reasons that have to do with the final point I want to make, which is about the difficulty of managing multicultural – plural – societies.

I said earlier that no one is likely to be troubled by the variety of subcultures in high culture. Why is this? Because however important our participation in high culture is, it is unlikely to be at the heart of our ethnicity. High culture crosses ethnic boundaries to an extraordinary degree. (The boundaries that it crosses with less ease are those of class.) The result is that subdivisions of high culture are not so likely to become central to the organization of political life. The United States is not threatened by the cultural autonomy of the American Philosophical Association or (even) the American Medical Association. In this respect the associations of high culture are like many elements of popular culture: the next New York mayoral election is not going to be between followers of the Mets and of the Yankees.

But differences in what I have called subcultures are rather different. We pass on our language to the next generation because we care to communicate with them; we pass on religion because we share its vision and endorse its values; we pass on our folkways because we value people with those folkways.

I have insisted that we should distinguish between cultures and identities, but ethnic identities are distinctive in having cultural distinctions as one of their primary marks. Ethnic identities are created in family and community life. These – along with mass-mediated culture, the school and the college – are, for most of us, the central sites of the social transmission of culture. Distinct practices, beliefs, norms go with each ethnicity in part because people want to be ethnically distinct: because many people want the sense of solidarity that comes from being unlike others. With ethnicity in modern society, it is often the distinct identity that comes first and the cultural distinction that is created and maintained because of it, not the other way around. The distinctive common cultures of ethnic and religious identities matter not simply because of their contents but also as markers of those identities.

Culture in this sense is the home of what we care about most. If other people organize their solidarity around cultures different from ours, this makes them, to that extent, different from us in ways that matter to us deeply. The result, of course, is not just that we have difficulty understanding across cultures – this is an inevitable result of cultural difference, for much of culture consists of language and other shared modes of understanding – but that we end up preferring our own kind; and if we prefer our own kind, it is easy enough to slip into preferring to vote for our own kind, to employ our own kind, and so on.

In sum: Cultural difference undergirds loyalties. As we have seen repeatedly in recent years, from South Africa to the Balkans, from Sri Lanka to Nigeria, from South Central Los Angeles to Crown Heights, once these loyalties matter they will be mobilized in politics and the public square, except to the extent that a civic culture can be created that explicitly seeks to exclude them. And that is why my multiculturalism is so necessary: it is the only way to reduce the misunderstandings across subcultures, the only way to build bridges of loyalty across the ethnicities that have so often divided us. Multiculturalism of this sort – pluralism, to use an older word – is a way of making sure we care enough about people across ethnic divides to keep those ethnic divides from destroying us. And it must, I believe, be a central part of the function of our educational system to equip all of us to share the public space with people of multiple identities and distinct subcultures. I insisted early on the distinction between cultures and identities. It is especially important here. Teaching young people to respect those with other identities is not the same thing as teaching them some of the central practices and beliefs of a different subculture. When we teach Toni Morrison to children with serious attention, we are demonstrating respect for the cultural work of a black person in a culture where there is still pressure not to respect black people. We are showing that respect to black children; we are modelling that respect for other children. Each of these is something that a decent education can seek to do; neither is simply a matter of introducing people to a culture.

It seems to me that it will be important, too, to teach children to reflect critically on their identities, including their ethnic identities, if they care about them.

IDENTITY AS AN IMPORTANT PART OF EDUCATION

Locke famously argued that the trans-temporal unity of the self was created through memory. Contemporary work on this question has argued that this answer to the problem of identity is at best question-begging. For if I think I did something in the past and "remember" it from the perspective of a participant, that only shows that I am remembering what happened to me if that belief is true; and its being true, if it is a belief with a first-person perspective, requires not just that some person had such experiences but that I did. The role of "memory" in constituting the trans-temporal identity of a person should more appropriately, I think, be taken another way. To be a person is to have a sense of yourself as a creature with a history.

Memory here is a route into the recalled experiences whose existence, if they are veridical, certifies the story I tell of myself. But the oft-suggested parallelism between memory and history should remind us that a history of a self is not just "one damn thing after another." Our personal histories are as narratively constructed as our collective stories. For most of us the history of myself is Whig history, with a telos, or more likely, a plurality of ends, with anticipations in childhood, intimations of what is to come. Part of the function of our collective identities, of the whole repertory of them that a culture makes available to its members, is to structure possible narratives of the self.

Across cultures, people care to give a certain narrative unity to their lives: each person wants to tell a story of his or her life that makes sense. The story – my story – should cohere in the way appropriate to a person of my culture. In telling that story, how it fits into the wider story of various collectivities is, for most of us, important. It is not just that, say, gender identities give shape (through rites of passage, for example) to one's life; it is also that ethnic and national identities fit that story into a larger narrative. And some of the most "individualist" of individuals value such things. Hobbes spoke of the desire for glory as one of the dominating impulses of human beings, one that was bound to make trouble for social life. But glory can consist in fitting and being seen to fit into a collective history; and so, in the name of glory, one can end up doing the most social things of all.

Once I consciously grasp (as opposed to merely presupposing) the significance and value of my identity for me, I can see what the significance and value of their collective identities would be for others. I will also learn, from history and from social studies, both that such identities are probably humanly inevitable and that the cost of conflicts between identities can be very high, as we see now in the Balkans and in Somalia. A reasonable response to this fact is to recognize the need to accommodate others within my state with different identities. Once ethnic identities cease to be unreflective, as such a line of thought is bound to make them, I will also come to see my identity as something that can be molded, if not individually then at least as part of a common political project, or indeed as something that can be put away altogether.

What is wrong with our collective identities is not that that is what they are; it is rather that we need to restrain the persistent urge for one identity to go on the rampage against others. To do this, we may have to reshape them. Because the same "facts" can fit into many different stories, this reshaping is something we are indeed capable of. The picture I suggested earlier, in which public education simply acknowledges the ethnic identities created outside the state, is too simple. In reflecting on these identities we cannot but alter them; at least some of the children we teach about other cultures will not maintain the unreflective sense of the superiority of their own. To conceive of multicultural education in this way – as the teaching of cross-subcultural understanding and of respect for other identities – is to seek to constrain identities so that they may share a single society.

WHY NOT SIMPLY INSIST ON A SINGLE CULTURE?

Having argued that the school in our society should not simply leave everything ethnically where it is, the question of a single common culture is likely to resurface. Why not argue out democratically a common culture, making sure to learn the lesson of multiculturalism that this must not simply be the cover for a sectional interest?

My answer is, Because we do not have to do so. The question presupposes that what we really need is shared values, a common culture. I think this is a mistake. What I think we really need is provided in a conjunct of our original definition of a society, something so obvious that we soon left it behind. "Common institutions and a common culture," I said, but dropped talk of the common institutions almost immediately.

But to live together in a nation what is required is that we all share a commitment to the organization of the state – the institutions that provide the overarching order of our common life. This does not require that we have the same commitment to those institutions, in the sense that the institutions must carry the same meaning for all of us.

The First Amendment separates church and state. Some of us are committed to this because we are religious: we see it as the institutionalization of a Protestant insistence on freedom of conscience. Some of us are committed to it because we are Catholics or Jews or Moslems, who do not want to be pressed into conformity by a Protestant majority. Some of us are atheists who want to be left alone. We can live together with this arrangement provided we all are committed to it, for our different reasons.

There is a useful analogy here with much mass culture and other mass-produced goods. People in London and in Lagos, in New York and New Delhi, listen to Michael Jackson and drink Coca-Cola. They exist, in part, as an audience for his work, as consumers of that drink. But nobody thinks that what either of these products means in one place must be identical with what it means in every site of its consumption. Similarly, the institutions of democracy – the election, the public debate, the protection of minority rights – have different meanings to different subcultures. Once more, there is no reason to require that we all value them in the same way, for the same reasons. All that is required is that everybody is willing to "play the game."

A shared political life in a great modern nation is not like the life of a traditional society. It can encompass a great diversity of meanings. When we teach children democratic habits, through practice in public schools, what we are creating is a shared commitment to certain forms of social behavior. We can call this a political culture, if we like. But the meanings citizens give to their lives, and to the political within their lives, in particular, will be shaped not only by the school, but by the family and church, by reading and by television, in their professional and recreational associations.

Maybe, in the end, there will be a richer American common culture; maybe it will lead to a consensus on the value of American institutions. Certainly cultural homogenization is proceeding apace. But it has not happened yet. And, so far as I can see, it doesn't have to happen in order for us to live together. Competing identities may be having a hard time living together in new democracies. But in this, the oldest democracy, so long as our institutions treat every significant identity with enough respect to gain its allegiance, we can muddle along in the meanwhile without a common culture. That, after all, is what we have been doing, lo, these many years.

NOTES

1. The shared space is probably what distinguishes this sense of the term from the sense of society in the expression "international high society." We wouldn't normally speak of the latter as "a society," despite the shared institutions (Ascot, the Kentucky Derby, the fall fashions in Paris, the London season) and common culture (conventions of address).

2. My dictionary gives as the relevant sense of the word "society," "A group of human beings broadly distinguished from other groups by mutual interests, participation in characteristic relationships, shared institutions, and a common culture." *American Heritage Dictionary III for DOS*, 3d ed. (Novato, Calif.: Wordstar International Incorporated, 1993).

3. It is increasingly true, of course, that the cultures of other places are shaped by American culture – notably through the movies – so that the distinction between a culture shaped *in* the United States and one shaped *by* the United States is less sharp than it used to be.

4. *American Heritage Dictionary III for DOS*.

5. There is nothing absurd in holding that the different practices and beliefs of, say, women and men in a society cohere – not in the sense of forming a single logically consistent system, but in the sense that the reason why women engage in one practice is connected with the reason why men engage in another different practice and that a society in which women

87

and men engage in these different practices is, in part, held together by that fact. But even that notion came under attack when the functionalist notion that every element of practice in a society was adaptive was subjected to criticism.

6. Though, as I say, I do not think you need to react by becoming a cultural relativist.

7. I here exclude material culture – clothing, houses, pottery, weapons, and the like – from the common culture, though not the signs and symbols which adorn it.

8. Some, of course, may believe that they are universally held. This definition of the common culture excludes material culture. I believe the study of material culture is extremely important; but its relevance for debates about multiculturalism has to do with its symbolic resonance, and thus to do with language, ideas, values.

9. This is not the only way the term could be used. Some want to reserve the term for the culture of subordinate groups. I want to avoid that implication in my usage.

10. This way of defining subcultures also means that the shared beliefs and values of a subgroup of the nation need not be exclusive to them: it may be, for example, that there are some American Jewish subcultures whose shared central values and beliefs are also shared with some Jewish groups in Britain or Italy or Israel.

11. Not every society will distinguish between the natural and the social in the sort of way we do. So this formula is not meant to imply that every society has separable theories of what we call the natural and the social.

12. What I have been calling a subculture, then, consists of people who share specific practices, beliefs, and values that constitute the common culture of a subgroup of the nation.

13. Given that the constitution is about a year old as I write (it was promulgated in 1992 and came into full effect in 1993), this is not too surprising, I suppose. But much of the structure has been in place since independence with few changes.

14. This is not, remember, to claim that most Americans are Christians by belief. It is to say only that some of the central ideas and practices of Christianity are known to and understood by most Americans.

15. Men and women may have characteristically distinct experiences; but that doesn't, by itself, guarantee distinct cultures.

16. The arguments of this section are based on suggestions from Bob Fullinwider. I have taken up many suggestions he made in his helpful criticisms of my first draft. I accept full responsibility for these ideas, as I have expressed them, but I don't claim to have come to all of them myself.

17. National Council for the Social Studies, "Curriculum Guidelines for Multicultural Education," *Social Education* 55 (September 1992): 278.

18. Ibid.: "Multicultural education should stress the process of self-identification. . . ."

19. There is another problem with this way of thinking: it suggests that Western culture belongs to some American children more than others in virtue of their descent. This is doubly troubling: first, because the culture

we teach in school belongs only to those who do the work to earn it; second, because it proposes to exclude certain children from certain educational experiences on what look like racial grounds.

20. Of course, I do not think – absurdly – that everyone should become both a Jew and a Moslem while holding on to Protestantism. The sort of participation in Jewish or Moslem celebrations that I am talking about is the participation of a guest, a visitor, a friend.

21. Postmodernism urges people to respond, "Worst by whose criteria?" My answer is, In the real world of intercultural moral conversation, nobody – except a postmodernist – defends his position by claiming that it follows simply from his criteria and leaves it at that. If we argue with those who practice clitoral excision and say it ought to be stopped, we need to tell those who practice it why. If we argue that it causes pain to girls and years of low-grade infections to women, and raises the risks of pregnancy; if we say that women who have not been circumcised are not, ipso facto, sexually insatiable; if we say that the practice deprives women of a source of pleasure; if we observe that the practice is not, in fact, recommended by the Koran: nobody, except in a rhetorical moment of weakness, is going to defend the practice by saying that these facts – if such they are – are relevant only by our criteria. And when they suggest to us that "we" mutilate women – through cosmetic surgery; or that "we" practice male circumcision, which also reduces men's capacity for pleasure; or that an uncircumcised girl cannot get a husband: these facts – if such they are – do not strike us as relevant only by our criteria. (And, in any case, there are people here who are not so sure about the badness of the practice, and people there not so convinced of its goodness.) And this is in a hard case of intercultural disagreement. Most American subgroups share so many substantial ethical assumptions that the "Says who?" response is usually offered only by those who are losing an argument.

Chapter 5

Multiculturalism and mélange

JEREMY WALDRON

In order to think clearly about multicultural education, we need to think what it is for a person to grow up and form an identity in a culturally plural society. Official prescriptions for the study of history and social studies give a lot of attention to the multiplicity of cultures in the United States; but they say much less about what that diversity implies for the identities of particular individuals. This is a pity because questions about community and identity are complex and illuminating, and the array of possible answers poses an interesting challenge to our preconceptions about the role of culture in individual lives. Does cultural plurality at the social level imply cultural plurality in the constitution and identity of each individual member of the society? Or does it rather presuppose cultural homogeneity at the individual level, so that even though the society emerges as a patchwork, each constituent person or group is cut from whole cloth? If "[t]he United States is a microcosm of humanity today,"[1] does that make each citizen also a microcosm, so that she reflects in her relationships, aspirations, and experiences a little of each of the country's constitutive cultures? Or is the United States a microcosm in which the integrity of each person's identity is secured by the culture and ethnicity of some group in particular?

The questions are not just about the existing characteristics of a multicultural society; they are also about what a society of this kind should aspire to. The aim, we are told, is to reconcile national unity with respect for difference: *e pluribus unum.*[2] Does the hope for this unity-in-diversity lie in the synthesis that each individual forges among the various cultural experiences and encounters that make up her life? Or is it to be purely a social and political synthesis, welded externally among culturally disparate individuals and groups? If the latter, how is the social synthesis to be sustained? How, for example, can it be rooted in the consciousness of the various persons that make

90

up the society in question without at the same time undermining and compromising the integrity of the particular cultures and ethnicities that secure each person's identity? How, as a matter of identity, can one belong to one culture in particular and still be a good citizen of a multicultural society?

TWO MODELS

In this essay, I want to explore two models of the relation between culture and identity in the context of ethnic plurality. The first is the "One Person: One Culture" model (I shall call it "the One Culture model," for short): it assumes that each individual constructs her identity within the framework of one culture, the culture of the particular group or community to which she belongs. The second is the "One Person: Many Fragments" model (I shall call it "the Many Fragments model," for short): it assumes that each individual constructs her identity in the wider society in which she lives and that, if the society is multicultural, her identity will comprise a multiplicity of cultural fragments, bits and pieces of various cultures from here and there.

The two models are of course "ideal types," in Max Weber's sense.[3] They are intended as polar guides to thinking these issues through, rather than as exhaustive categories for social taxonomy. For many of us, the truth lies somewhere in between: a person's identity may be *predominantly* of one culture, for all that it is "supplemented" or "contaminated" by fragments of, or influences from, other cultures existing adjacently in the same society. All the same, it makes a difference what ideal types we have in mind when we approach the complexity of real-world cases, and it is worth exploring that difference even when we accept that, of course, a sensitive approach to particular instances will have to be much more nuanced than either of these ideal types suggests.

My hunch is that many who favor replacing traditional modes of education with multicultural curricula tend to adopt the One Culture model quite uncritically as the basis of their thinking about the respect that is owed to different cultures.[4] By contrast, I believe the Many Fragments model is both more realistic and more attractive as an account of individual identity. By "more realistic," I mean that it offers the analytical basis for a more accurate account of how most people in fact form an identity for themselves in a society of this kind. By "more attractive," I mean that the processes it describes offer a better prospect for society and for the individuals who have to live in the world. The Many Fragments model is, I think, one that we would do well to recognize and promote, instead of disparaging it as a deviant case of impurity or eclecticism. To articulate principles of respect for persons in terms of that model is wiser than persisting in the assumption – implicit in the One Culture approach – that cultural purity and solicitude for particular ethnic frameworks should be the key to public policy in these areas.

Clearly the Many Fragments model has a provenance in liberal individualism. It does not follow, however, that the model justifies complacency about modern education, or a rejection of multiculturalism and a return to "Great Books" and courses on "Western Civilization." The Many Fragments model calls in question the purity and hegemony of the dominant culture as much as that of any of the minority ethnic traditions: the identity of most white Anglophone persons is to be regarded as no less of a mélange than that of anyone struggling to make a life in this cultural bazaar.[5] Instead, the Many Fragments model may provide a different way of thinking the issue through. If we are less concerned about cultural integrity as the key to human identity, we may be less hung up on the issue of what it is to acquaint students fully and faithfully with a variety of cultures in the classroom. By the same token, we may (if this ever worried us) be less alarmed at the thought that some "essential" ingredient of our culture (*Billy Budd*, perhaps, or Plato's *Republic*) is being neglected in favor of a reenactment of the Bantu migration.

Above all, I hope the Many Fragments model will help us to reconsider the essentialism that is associated with the individuation of cultures, and the artificiality that this tends to engender in the bright lines we draw between one culture and another, and between different ethnic groups. If we are less insistent that each person is to be located in just one culture, there may seem less point in individuating cultures from one another. I am sure that will be a tremendous improvement from a sociological point of view: it will lead quite simply to saner social science. But it will be morally valuable as well. At the moment, respect too often takes the form of reverence for the culture *imputed* as a basis of identity to the person we claim to be respecting. A shift to the Many Fragments model portrays each of us as making what she can, alone or with others, in a veritable sea of cultural materials that often have little more to bind them together than that they are the ones that in fact impinge upon us. To respect a person is to respect her effort in that regard, rather than to respect some particular aspect of her background with which we insist she must "identify."

ONE PERSON: ONE CULTURE

Let me begin the discussion, now, by outlining the constructive and normative features of the first of the two models we are considering.

The first step in the construction of the One Culture model is to posit a multicultural society as one in which a number of distinct cultures coexist. I shall say more about what "culture" means or is taken to mean at the beginning of the next section; for now, we may take the term to refer to a number of ways of living, acting, and relating, affecting many or most of what are taken to be the more important as well as the more mundane aspects of life, and integrated more or less tightly into a single shared set of meanings, that is, a single way of life.

Cultures, of course, do not exist in the abstract; they characterize communities of people. "Community" refers to the sociological infrastructure of culture: a community is an enduring human group in which membership is taken to have ramifications for one's life and actions across the board and in an open-ended sort of way, in virtue of the sharing of a set of practices that can be regarded as a single culture. So the second step in constructing this model relates persons to cultures through the notion of community. Each community comprises several generations of persons. The idea is that, as youngsters begin to make lives for themselves, they find that they belong to a community and that its culture is their culture in virtue of that belonging. This is the basis of the "One Person: One Culture" correlation I have referred to in the label attached to this model.

The third step is to insist that it is normally within the framework of one's own culture – that is, the culture of the community to which one belongs – that one thinks about making a life for oneself, and that it is within this framework that one leads the life one has embraced.[6] Those who use this model do acknowledge that people sometimes incorporate influences into their identity which are alien to the culture their community has furnished for them. But often they see this as a special case, and they regard it as a quite unsatisfactory starting point for thinking about what people and communities need in a multicultural society.

The normative implications of the One Culture model rest in various ways on this connection between identity and the sharing of a culture. In the first place, the model suggests that great harm can be done to persons if a culture or a traditional way of life is allowed to die out, or if the conditions that make possible the practice of that way of life are allowed to degenerate. Since each person belongs to just one culture, if her culture is dying out, her opportunities for the construction of an adequate identity will die out with it. The alienation or anomie of the members of some Native American groups is often cited as an example of the experience of people who have difficulty establishing an identity for themselves, because the cultural framework of their community is withering away.[7]

In the second place, if (as the first model suggests) my culture is implicated in who I am, then to cast aspersions on my culture (to make fun of its religion, for example, or denigrate its traditions) is to attack *me*, at the core of my being. Respect for a given person, on this model, entails respect for the particular culture that has made her who she is.

Moreover, the fact that the culture that makes me what I am is one that I share with others means that I am also vulnerable to attacks upon others. If I am an Irish-American and I become aware that another Irish-American has been discriminated against because of her Irish background, then I suffer at least indirectly because there is an affront, via the attack on her Irishness, to the group to which both of us belong, the group deeply implicated in our individual identities. Because parts of our identities are *shared* in this strong sense, the model implies certain limitations on a purely individualistic account of rights and wrongs. It indicates that we should talk perhaps of group rights, and of the possibility that groups may be harmed in various ways, and that this should be incorporated into our social morality and our jurisprudence.[8]

The third normative implication concerns *difference* so far as the treatment of individuals is concerned. It has long been an assumption of liberal philosophy that whatever rights we have are either universal in character (i.e., *human* rights) or (in the case of contractual, promissory or other "special" rights) generated on the basis of universal principles.[9] This means it is possible to tell pretty quickly what rights another person has: she has just the rights that I have. The duties and the respect that I owe to her are simply the counterparts of the duties and respect she owes to me. But that tidy assumption presupposes that all persons share enough, by way of a common "human nature," to ground such universal rights. If identity is instead an artifact of culture, and if people forge their identities in distinct cultural settings, it may be a mistake to insist that rights remain the same. The job of rights is to protect crucial interests, and if the structures of people's interests vary according to the community to which they belong, the rights it is proper to attribute to them may vary accordingly.

An example may help here. For someone who has been brought up in a traditional church, it may be important that she have a right to freedom of worship – the freedom to come together with others to engage in religious ceremonial – whereas a person brought up in a secular, materialist culture, never having had anything to do with a church, may have no use for such a right. If the latter is asked whether freedom of worship is an important liberty for *every* human individual, she may quite reasonably answer, "No," saying that it depends on how important practices like worship loom in one's culture, community, and conception of the good. No doubt, we could abstract from the term "worship" and find some very vague description (freedom of conscience, perhaps conjoined with freedom of assembly) which could be recognized as a right that everyone needed. But – and this I think is the crucial point about difference – such an abstraction might end up being distracting and unhelpful in the process of working out what respect for particular others really requires.

Other examples spring to mind under the heading of religious freedom. Some of us value the freedom to revise or rethink one's faith and we take this freedom to be opposed to the idea that "apostasy" should be a matter of concern or condemnation. But many fervent adherents of Roman Catholicism or Islam deny that such a freedom is to be valued at all, and certainly they would not claim it for themselves. To do so would amount, in their eyes, to a weakening of their religious commitment. Those same adherents may, however, claim other rights that secular atheists are happy to disown. They may claim, for example, the right to be protected from blasphemy or from demonstrations of disrespect for their cherished beliefs. If the line of argument I am exploring here is correct, it is no reply to this claim that secular atheists are willing to disown any such protection. The fact that I do not need to be protected from cultural ridicule, for example, in order to pursue my own good does not show that others don't need such protection in order to pursue theirs. Different aims may require different liberties and different protections.

The consequences of this concession are interesting. In a simple two-person case, we may have a situation in which the rights claimed by P, as necessary to protect her identity, are different from the rights claimed by Q, as necessary for the protection of his. Now of course the rights claimed by Q will be correlative to duties imposed on P, and vice versa. The picture I have in mind is this:

P	Q
RIGHTS	rights
duties	DUTIES

with the difference between upper-case and lower-case indicating the difference in content between the two sets of rights and duties. Though P's rights are correlative to Q's duties, and P's duties correlative to Q's rights, Q cannot simply take the set of rights that he has and the set of duties that he has and, replacing proper names with variables, regard them as correlative. He is therefore no longer able to work out what duties he has simply by considering what would be correlative to the rights that he claims. He must really pay attention to the rights and needs of the other person, P, because what counts as

95

respecting her may differ significantly from anything he can extrapolate from his own case.

In the extreme individual case, this means that respect for rights requires a high degree of sensitivity to the distinctive needs and interests of others.[10] In the context of the first model of multiculturalism, however, what it requires is sensitivity to other *cultures*. Hence the link with education. We need to learn about other cultures in order to learn what our fellow citizens are and how to respect them.

A PLURALITY OF DISTINCT CULTURES?

To say that a society is pluralistic is not the same as saying it is multicultural: pluralism may relate to individual lifestyles, vocations, religious faiths, ethics, politics, and experiences, with no assumption that these differences coalesce into the shared and abiding entities we call "cultures." Pluralism is the genus; cultural diversity is a species of it.[11] For the purposes of the first model, "culture" and "community," as we have seen, are defined in an interlocking way. "Culture" refers to a set of related practices and traditions associated currently and historically with a community – that is, with a human grouping larger than a family or a village, abiding longer than just a few generations, permeating the lives of its members in a constitutive way, and amounting in some sense to an *ethnos*, a people or a nation. Membership in a community, unlike membership in an organization, a club, a party, or a church, is usually taken to be ascriptive rather than voluntary, and to have implications across the whole range of one's actions and relations with others, not just some specialized activity or concern. The culture of a community is a way of doing things, particularly the things that are done *together*, throughout the whole course of human life: language, governance, religious rituals, rites of passage, family structures, material production and decoration, economy, science, warfare, and the sharing of a sense of history. It is a way that its members have, as they think their ancestors had and as they hope their descendants will have, of enjoying and enduring the joys and vicissitudes of human life together.

If culture and community are tied together in this way, what is it (on the first model) for *several* cultures to coexist in a single society? The notion of such coexistence makes sense only on the assumption that society is not necessarily coextensive with community (in the sense of "community" that refers to the human grouping whose traditions and practices are identified as one culture). "Society" may be characterized as a loose and abstract term, referring to *any* human grouping whose characteristics (as a grouping) are important to us for some reason: thus we may veer easily between talking of world society, or North American society, or United States society, or high society in Beverly Hills. A use of the term "society" *may* refer to a community in the sense we have been discussing, but it need not. Usually, when we talk about a multicultural society, "society" refers to a large-scale human grouping delineated purely in terms of its being under the authority of a single sovereign state. We say, for example, that the United Kingdom is a multicultural society, meaning roughly that the British state presides territorially over a human grouping in which a number of cultures (and thus a number of communities) coexist. Or to put it another way, those who live together in the British Isles in the sense of being subject to a common political authority find that they do not share a single culture, but that many cultures coexist among them.

Such plurality may come about in a number of ways. The four with which we are most familiar are the following: (1) A single culture may split into separate cultures as the community it characterizes grows and becomes differentiated. An example of this process is religious differentiation in European communities in and after the sixteenth century, but it may also include the development of what are known as "subcultures" in modern societies, of which the growth of gay culture and the self-conscious evolution of African-American culture in the United States are two prominent examples. (2) A community with one culture may conquer a community with another culture, either moving into the latter's territory or expanding its own domain to include that territory. The subjugation of the aboriginal communities of North America by European colonists is a clear example of this. (3) Two or more communities may voluntarily confederate for political or security reasons, coming sufficiently to terms with one another to constitute a common polity or state. The Act of Union between England and Scotland is one of the best-known examples of this. (4) Finally, members of a given community may migrate to another society, and when they arrive, they may join with other migrants to preserve what they can of the culture of their provenance. This is typical of many communities in the United States: Chinese, Italian, Jewish, Amish, Korean, Irish, and so on.

This last way of constituting a multicultural society may seem more problematic than the others, inasmuch as the migrants are attempting to sustain a sense of shared culture among themselves without the infrastructure of enduring community which originally bore that culture.[12] Their community may have evaporated with their diaspora or they may have a sense of having left their community behind in their homeland and of having brought with them at most just a homesickness, a longing, or an aspiration to re-create or reproduce it in their new environment. It would be a mistake, however, to draw too sharp a line between those cultures and ethnicities that remain rooted in a located and enduring community, and those that have been, so to speak, "cut adrift" from a sociological point of view. We are dealing with a spectrum of cases, ranging from North American aboriginal nations at the one extreme, which combine a shared culture and ethnicity with a highly concrete and comprehensive embodiment of community, to (say) Irish-Americans at the other extreme, clinging gamely to some relics of a shared heritage and shared grievances while being largely integrated into the polyglot mainstream of American society without much social structure of their own. In between there are cases like Chinese-Americans or Pakistani Muslims in the U.K. – peoples who have managed to re-create quite formidable and enduring structures of community in the lands to which they, their parents, or their grandparents migrated.

However it comes about, the characterization of a society as "multicultural" is in the first instance simply a matter of fact. The coexistence of separate communities implies only that these various cultures and their respective communal infrastructures are *here*. It does not necessarily imply that they are all flourishing, nor that they are in any sense equal or mutually tolerant. Equal respect and toleration are often the aims of those who deploy the One Culture model; but in their view the hegemony of one culture in particular is often the ugly reality.

It is a crucial feature of the "One Person: One Culture" model that the cultures coexisting in modern society be seen as distinct. Certainly users of the model will concede that the differentiation is not absolute: the mere fact of coexistence militates against that (and I shall argue later that this point needs to be taken much more seriously than it usually is). Nonetheless, it is expected that the sets of traditions and practices that constitute the various cultures will be qualitatively different from one another in many important respects. The languages will be different; there will be quite different approaches to religion and faith, and different ways of thinking about family, sexuality, gender, and the passage from one stage of life to another.

Everyone acknowledges, of course, that in reality there will be similarities. Quite apart from cultural interaction, there is the fact that the communities in question are *human* communities, and there are likely to be broad similarities in the way things are done in community which reflect the fact that all humans are organisms of a similar kind facing similar problems, opportunities and vicissitudes. For example: all communities have to come to terms with disease; all communities have to deal with the vicissitudes of the human life cycle, of reproduction and the special needs of infancy; most communities meet their economic needs with some sort of division of labor; and so on. Sometimes the similarities are much more concrete than this: metallurgy developed in many different regions as a similar and intelligible human response to a naturally provided opportunity and resource; all communities explore their natural habitat for what we call pharmaceutical materials; children pursue at the level of play safe versions of adult activity (such as hunting, housekeeping, and warfare) as part of their recreation and preparation for adult life; all societies seem to have a conception of the spiritual or the divine; all societies organize some structure of collective memory that has an authoritative impact on collective and individual decision-making.[13]

In addition, most of the individual communities in question have consciously shared a world with at least some other communities. Culture, we know, does not stay local; ideas and practices, ways of doing things, are propagated and transmitted. Persons and peoples are curious and gregarious: they find ways of talking and trading across cultural divides, as well as fighting, conquering, or attempting to insulate themselves from adjacent cultural influences. Thus we would expect neighboring communities to have many similarities in their respective cultures: Breton culture and Irish culture will not be exactly the same, but they may be very similar in a number of important respects (a common Christian heritage, for example).

One sometimes hears it said that what is important about each culture is its *distinctiveness*. "Diversity" is commonly used as a synonym for "pluralism."[14] That view, I think, is characteristic of the model we are considering. If diversity *per se* is important, then what is to be taught under the auspices of multicultural education is *respect for the qualitative distinctiveness of each culture.*

It is worth noting, however, that this view may be seriously mistaken, both as a description of the consciousness of the communities in question and as a prescription about what respect ought to involve. Consider the example I just mentioned: the Breton and Irish cultures. These cultures are markedly different in a number of respects, but there are also marked commonalities. In both, for example, the Catholic Church plays a crucial – and a remarkably similar – role in people's lives. That prompts the following question: to the extent that a Breton or an Irish person actually thinks self-consciously about her culture (a problematic notion to which I shall return in a moment), is it the *distinctiveness* of the culture that will be important to her – that is, the respects in which her culture differs from others (in the region) as opposed to the respects in which it is similar? I doubt that we can assume this. It seems not only possible but probable that an inhabitant of Brittany would regard the teachings and sacraments of the Church as the most important aspect of her culture. If so, it is likely to be both implicit in and essential to that thought that her Church be regarded as *catholic*,[15] in precisely the sense of being something shared by other communities. That feature of her life – that *as a Breton* she shares a faith and a church with Irish, Italians, Poles, Brazilians, and Filipinos – may be much more important to her identity than anything which (say) a Tourist Board would use to highlight her cultural distinctiveness.

More abstractly, one must not assume that thoughts about the distinctiveness of one's culture loom very large in one's own involvement in the cultural life of a community. What one does is simply speak, or marry, or worship. One does not in doing so assert anything or evince any particular attitude about, say, the distinctive features of the Breton tongue, or the peculiarities of the marriage dress. As I have argued elsewhere, one keeps faith with the mores of one's community by just following them, not by announcing self-consciously that it is the mores of one's community that one is following.[16]

What I am driving towards is the paradoxical suggestion that the "essence" of a culture – if there is one – need not consist in its distinctiveness. One culture does not need to be clearly and importantly *different* from another, either in its appearance to an outsider or in the consciousness of its practitioners, in order to be the culture that it is. A taxonomist may be interested in qualitative differentiation, and we may want there to be lots of colorful differences in costume, language and ritual so that we can, in a sense, *display* our commitment to multiculturalism to even the most superficial glance. But all this is beside the point so far as the culture itself is concerned. A culture just is what it is, and its practices and rituals are constitutive of it in virtue of their place in a shared way of life, not in virtue of their peculiarity.

Why, then, the emphasis on diversity? It has to do, I think, with the way cultures and communities overlap in a multicultural society. Suppose there are Breton and Irish immigrant communities in an American city and they have managed to preserve large parts of their cultures. The faith and worship that the two communities share in common may well mean that instead of having two distinct communities, each with its own Catholic church, we have a single Catholic church that serves the needs of both communities. The similarities between the communities' practices and traditions lead to actual social overlap between them. If this happens often enough or on a broad enough front, it may be hard to discern the separateness of the communities except in terms of their differences. For epistemic and taxonomic purposes, then, it will seem that the key to cultural identity *is* distinctiveness. But that is a kind of optical illusion. The fact that its members involve themselves in the lives of the local Catholic church remains a crucial part of, say, Irish culture, even if that church is one they share with Catholics from other communities.

Another way of putting this is to say that what I have called "overlap" is not the same as assimilation. The latter term means something like being compelled by force or circumstance to come to terms with practices and traditions that are not one's own. But for an Irish Catholic to worship in a Catholic congregation which comprises people of many cultures and which is even perhaps dominated by people of the dominant culture in the society is not assimilation. For even at home in Galway the Irish person's faith and attachment to her Church is understood to be an attachment to an institution which admits of – indeed, which treasures and is organized around – just such universality.

WILL KYMLICKA ON THE IMPORTANCE OF CULTURAL MEMBERSHIP

The "One Person: One Culture" model is characterized not only by the assumption that plurality is diversity, that our pluralistic society divides neatly into an array of different cultures, but also by the assumption that what every person needs is just one of these entities – a single, coherent, distinctive culture – to give shape and meaning to her life.

In this section, I want to criticize that second assumption, and I shall do so in the context of a critique of Will Kymlicka's recent book, *Liberalism, Community, and Culture*.[17] Kymlicka's aim is to rehabilitate liberal political philosophy, and make it more sensitive to communitarian concerns. He wants to show that liberal theorists, such as John Rawls and Ronald Dworkin, have radically underestimated the importance of culture as a primary good for the self-constitution of individual lives. He wants to fill that gap and enlist liberal theories in the cause of the preservation of minority cultures. Thus Kymlicka's starting point is not so much a communitarian commitment to the intrinsic value of community and culture, but a Rawlsian conviction about the importance to persons of the freedom to form, reform, and revise their individual beliefs about what makes life worth living.[18] He concedes that in order to sustain that freedom, one needs a certain amount of self-respect, as well as familiar protections, guarantees, opportunities, and access to the means of life – all the things that figure already on Rawls's list of the primary goods to be governed by a theory of justice.[19] To make the case that culture is also one of these primary goods, Kymlicka argues that people cannot choose a conception of the good for themselves in isolation, but that they need a clear sense of an established range of options to choose from:

> In deciding how to lead our lives, we do not start *de novo*, but rather we examine "definite ideals and forms of life that have been developed and tested by innumerable individuals, sometimes for generations." . . . The decision about how to lead our lives must ultimately be ours alone, but this decision is always a matter of selecting what we believe to be most valuable from the various options available, selecting from a context of choice which provides us with different ways of life.[20]

Kymlicka elaborates the point by insisting that what we choose among are not ways of life understood simply as different physical patterns of behavior:

> The physical movements only have meaning to us because they are identified as having significance by our *culture*, because they fit into some pattern of activities which is culturally recognized as a way of leading one's life. We learn about these patterns of activity through their presence in stories we've heard about the lives, real or imaginary, of others. . . . We decide how to lead our lives by situating ourselves in these cultural narratives, by adopting roles that have struck us as worthwhile ones, as ones worth living (which may, of course, include the roles we were brought up to occupy).[21]

It follows, he argues, that

> [l]iberals should be concerned with the fate of cultural structures, not because they have some moral status of their own, but because it's only through having a rich and secure cultural structure that people can become aware, in a vivid way, of the options available to them, and intelligently examine their value.[22]

On the face of it, the argument is a convincing one. Of course, choice takes place in a cultural context, among options that have culturally defined meanings. But in developing his case, Kymlicka is guilty of something like the fallacy of composition. From the fact that each genuine option must have a cultural meaning for the person who faces that option, it does not follow that there must be *one cultural framework* for that person in which each available option is assigned a meaning. Meaningful options may come to us as items or fragments from an incommensurable variety of cultural sources. Kymlicka is moving too quickly when he says that each culturally meaningful item is given its significance by some entity called "our culture." It may be a mistake to infer that there are big things called "cultural structures" whose integrity must be guaranteed in order for people to have meaningful choices. Kymlicka's argument shows that people need cultural materials; it does not show that what people need is "a rich and secure cultural structure." He shows the importance of access to a variety of stories and roles; but he has not shown, as he claims to have shown, the importance of something called *membership* in *a* culture.

Kymlicka's claim about the difference between physically and culturally defined options is an echo of an argument made earlier by Alasdair MacIntyre, and it may reinforce my point to discuss that argument as well. According to MacIntyre:

> We enter human society . . . with one or more imputed characters – roles into which we have been drafted – and we have to learn what they are in order to be able to understand how others respond to us and how our responses to them are apt to be construed. It is through hearing stories about wicked stepmothers, lost children, good but misguided kings, wolves that suckle twin boys, youngest sons who receive no inheritance but must make their own way in the world and eldest sons who waste their inheritance on riotous living and go into exile to live with the swine, that children learn or mislearn both what a child and what a parent is, what the cast of characters may be in the drama into which they have been born and what the ways of the world are. Deprive children of stories and you leave them unscripted, anxious stutterers in their actions as in their words.[23]

Again, it is important to see that MacIntyre's roles are performed by heterogeneous characters (and none the worse for that) drawn from a variety of disparate cultural sources: from first century Palestine, from the heritage of Germanic folklore, and from the mythology of the Roman Republic. They do not come from some *thing* called "the structure of our culture." They are familiar because of the immense variety of cultural materials, various in their provenance as well as their character, that are in fact available to us. In correspondence on this issue, Kymlicka has written to me that "the fact that these stories originated in different cultures does not show that they have not been integrated into our culture or that their availability to us does not depend on this integration."[24] He is right about that as a matter of inference. But we must beware of defining the term "culture" so that the bare fact that a person has access to or is familiar with a given set of materials constitutes those materials as part of a single cultural framework. Indeed, if we were to insist that they are all part of the same framework simply because there is an identifiable group of people (*us*) to whom they are in fact available, we would trivialize the individuation of cultures beyond any sociological interest. Any array of materials would count as part of a single culture whenever they were familiar to a given person or group of persons, whether those materials had internal relations of coherence and harmony among them or not. It would then be *logically* impossible for an individual to have access to more than one cultural framework. The idea of a cosmopolitan heritage would have been ruled out by verbal fiat.

Kymlicka has also suggested that what matters for the integrity and identity of a cultural framework is *language*: "[T]he center of a community's cultural structure is its shared language."[25] In regard to the MacIntyre examples that I have mentioned, he writes:

> I did not learn Grimm's tales by reading German, and if they had not been translated, they would not provide meaningful characters to me. . . . It's true that the practices which are rendered vivid by our language come from a variety of cultural sources, but what renders them vivid to us is that they are now part of the cultural structure centred on our language.[26]

I think, however, that it is a mistake to assume *a priori* that language is the key to culture in this sense. A global language like English – vast, voracious, and cosmopolitan – cannot plausibly be identified with a single cultural framework; in the modern world it operates more as a cultural clearinghouse, far outstripping the traditions and practices of any one community of users. The fact that something is translated into English means only that it is available to at least a quarter of the world's population; it does not mean that it has been integrated into a secure and harmonious framework of culture which is the peculiar property of Englishmen. It is true that for some smaller communities, a particular language may be a treasured part of a cultural heritage; it is true too that part of its being treasured may be that it is taken to provide an indispensable framework for the representation of the rest of the culture in question. But that is true of some languages, some cultures, some communities and not others; it may or may not be a distinctive feature of the way a given cultural heritage is conceived. Not everything that we might individuate as *one culture* has its own language; and not everything that is represented in a given language is constituted thereby as part of one culture.

If this is correct, then the ethical importance of cultural wholes or integrated cultural frameworks is thrown in question. With it goes the idea that it is important for each person to be related to a secure and integrated framework *via* her membership in some community in particular. None of this has the importance Kymlicka claims it has, at least not at a general level. A person needs cultural meanings; but she does not need a homogeneous cultural framework. She needs to understand her choices and the options facing her in contexts in which they make sense, but she does not need any single context to provide commensurable meanings for all the choices she has. To put it crudely, people need culture, but they don't need cultural integrity. And since no one needs a homogeneous cultural framework or the integrity of a particular set of meanings, no one needs to be immersed in one of the small-scale communities which, according to Kymlicka and others, are alone capable of securing this integrity and homogeneity. Some, of course, may still prefer such immersion, and welcome the social subsidization of their preference. But it is not, as Kymlicka has maintained, a necessary presupposition of rational and meaningful choice.

RUSHDIE AND MÉLANGE

So we come to the second of our models, the "One Person: Many Fragments" model (or "the Many Fragments model," for short). I want to begin my discussion of it, rather tendentiously, with an extended quotation from an essay entitled "In Good Faith," which Salman Rushdie wrote in 1990 in defense of his execrated book *The Satanic Verses*:

> If *The Satanic Verses* is anything, it is a migrant's-eye view of the world. It is written from the very experience of uprooting, disjuncture and metamorphosis (slow or rapid, painful or pleasurable) that is the migrant condition, and from which, I believe, can be derived a metaphor for all humanity.
>
> Standing at the centre of the novel is a group of characters most of whom are British Muslims, or not particularly religious persons of Muslim background, struggling with just the sort of great problems that have arisen to surround the book, problems of hybridization and ghettoization, of reconciling the old and the new. Those who oppose the novel most vociferously today are of the opinion that intermingling with a different culture will inevitably weaken and ruin their own. I am of the opposite opinion. *The Satanic Verses* celebrates hybridity, impurity, intermingling, the transformation that comes of new and unexpected combinations of human beings, cultures, ideas, politics, movies, songs. It rejoices in mongrelization and fears the absolutism of the Pure. *Mélange*, hotchpotch, a bit of this and a bit of that is *how newness enters the world*. It is the great possibility that mass migration gives the world, and I have tried to embrace it. *The Satanic Verses* is for change-by-fusion, change-by-conjoining. It is a love-song to our mongrel selves. . . .
>
> I was born an Indian, and not only an Indian, but a Bombayite – Bombay, most cosmopolitan, most hybrid, most hotchpotch of Indian cities. My writing and thought have therefore been as deeply influenced by Hindu myths and attitudes as Muslim ones. . . . Nor is the West absent from Bombay. I was already a mongrel self, history's bastard, before London aggravated the condition.[27]

These remarks intimate a picture of the relation between culture and identity that is quite different from that asserted in the One

Culture model. It suggests that in the modern world – in the wake of imperialism, global communication, world war, mass migration, and frequent flying – people are not in a position to absorb their cultures whole and pure. We wake to a deafening babel of cultural materials, in a bazaar in which no prices have been fixed and no commensurabilities established for the bewildering variety of goods on offer. In what seems like chaos or anarchy from the point of view of the One Culture model, each of us makes a discovery about herself. We are not so lost or timid that we cannot build an identity for ourselves without the guiding hand of a pre-established framework. Indeed, we find ourselves with an identity – usually a coat of many colors – long before we have the chance to reflect on our ontological relation with community. The Maori *haka* and the Book of Common Prayer were already present in their different languages in my consciousness before I had a chance to wonder whether they could really fit comfortably within a single cultural frame.

That is the way in which we find ourselves constituted, and managing an identity is making the best of it. Of course, we are not always passive in the matter. As each of us grows up, we take more control of the materials to which we will expose ourselves and the interests and avocations we will pursue.[28] From time to time, each of us finds that the identity we have, partly given and partly constructed, is a source of unhappiness or anomie. But we do not, as we reflect on the various sources of this discomfort, turn naturally to purge from our identity those elements that do not conform to a pre-given pattern prescribed by a community as "our culture." On the contrary, the pre-given pattern embraced by a person obsessed with the distinctiveness and integrity of "her" culture may be the least *comfortable* to live with in the world we face. The curious, anxious, and imaginative animals that we are may find it much easier to live with an identity that is appallingly compromised from the point of view of the first model, because the world around us elicits questions for our curiosity that radically disconcert any attempt to hold cultural or communal boundaries constant and impermeable.

When I discuss the Many Fragments model with my colleagues, I encounter two responses. The first is that the second model may be fine for an extraordinary individual like Salman Rushdie. But he is exceptional, say the critics; the idea that people will feel at home in a cosmopolitan mélange, they say, is bound to be confined to a tiny and privileged elite.[29] I am sure that is true, certainly in regard to the form in which Rushdie expresses this vision. Most ordinary people have neither the opportunity nor the inclination to engage in anything like the conscious cultivation or celebration of cosmopolitanism that my Many Fragments model has intimated. By the same token, however, few people – other than the members of a somewhat *different* tiny elite – have the opportunity to worry very explicitly about the integrity, the purity, and the survival of particular cultural frameworks. As I acknowledged at the beginning of this paper, the models under consideration are ideal types in relation to the complexity of ordinary life. Each of these models has its explicit elite version, and each organizes an array of mundane, messy versions for ordinary use. The question is which of the ideal-typic models provides the better starting-point for understanding the complexity of the everyday life of (say) your average non-intellectual French-Canadian worker. In her more political moments, the *Québécoise* may loudly proclaim the importance of the One Culture model and refuse to speak anything but French. But such proclamations cannot always be trusted; given the mélange of Coke bottles, Levi jeans made in Korea, North American ice hockey leagues, Chinese food, Montreal folk singers, American movies, Japanese computers, Canadian politics, and Catholic guilt that might be taken to characterize her ordinary life and experience, my money is on the Many Fragments model as the more honest basis for understanding the cultural character of her identity.

The second response to the Rushdie picture that I encounter goes as follows: "There could not *be* a bazaar of cultural materials available to cosmopolitan intellectuals like Rushdie or their non-elite counterparts unless there had once been a variety of cultures and communities, each relatively pure and homogeneous, to serve as the sources for this mélange. So we surely owe *something* to the integrity of particular cultures, if only to preserve the sources for cultural diversity in the future."[30]

That response is premised on a certain view of the history of cultural mélange. Once upon a time there were pure cultures, one to each community, existing in different parts of the world. Then, for the reasons we have previously considered, the members of various communities mingled, bringing their respective cultural heritages into relation with one another, and mixing them all up in the ways I described. The mixture is assumed to be rich now only because of the distinctive character of each pure ingredient. If the supply of pure ingredients ever dries up, the argument goes, the mixture will become impoverished.

But what if these historical assumptions are false? What if there has been nothing but mélange all the way down? What if cultures have always been implicated with one another, through trade, war, curiosity, and other forms of inter-communal relation? What if the mingling of cultures is as immemorial as cultural roots themselves? What if purity and cultural homogeneity have always been myths? I don't mean that all cultures have always been implicated with all others;

certainly there are some that have developed in relative isolation. But that may be an anomaly, with purely geographical explanations. Perhaps we should not make too much of it so far as our general ontology of culture and community is concerned; perhaps we should not make it our point of reference in thinking about how to live in a society of which it is evidently false. Maybe cultural homogeneity is not, in any interesting sense, the *normal* state of a human community at all, but simply something that happens when, for whatever reason, the members of a given community do not have the opportunity to interact with others on a basis that enables them to indulge what appears to be a hard-wired human curiosity and to learn from each other and appropriate or copy various practices and traditions.

In any case, it should be clear that the key to the richness of Rushdie's mélange is not necessarily original purity. The key is sheer plurality. What matters is the experience of human curiosity, creativity, and ingenuity: new and startling ways of dealing with the world. We know enough about new beginnings to understand that they do not necessarily have to be nurtured in a cradle of cultural purity. As Rushdie suggests, the newness that enters the world enters as often in the clash of old materials as in the immaculate conception of the raw materials for such a clash.[31]

It is true that in the world Rushdie describes, the category of *the exotic* may eventually fade away;[32] we may less and less have the experience, so dear to nineteenth-century anthropology, of being confronted with cultural materials *wholly different* from those with which we are familiar. But, again, novelty is not the same as newness. The constitution and dissemination of human creativity – the emergence of new ways of thinking and new ways of doing things – can go on from within a given society. It does not appear to need a constant input of exogenous materials. As John Stuart Mill noted, whether a society continues as creative or lapses into a stationary condition depends on how it organizes itself in regard to the choices, the courage, and the creativity of its members, rather than on the continual accumulation of essentially "foreign" experience.[33]

In general, then, we should not be beguiled by images such as "the melting pot" into thinking that the upshot of the mingling of cultures is eventual homogenization. Homogenization under the influence of fashion, consumerism, and conformism is always a possibility. But, again, avoiding it seems to be a matter of how we organize ourselves and not a matter of the relative purity of the cultural materials we are dealing with. It remains the case that the most strikingly new ideas are hybrids of the old. There is simply no correlation between the creative value of the hybrid and the proximity (in time or purity) of its raw materials to any allegedly pristine cultural roots. The American image of the melting pot does suggest that under certain conditions the blend may become bland. Under other conditions, however, the heat of the pot might cause the diversity of materials to proliferate. Neither possibility is guaranteed. Which one is realized depends in part on the respect we accord to each other's imaginative ability to develop new and disconcerting combinations. It depends, in other words, on our respect for precisely those human capacities that challenge the bonds of cultural purity.[34]

THE MONGREL SELF

The second model, like the first, is supposed to depict the relation between culture and the constitution of individual identity. But what in fact *becomes* of identity, on the second model? If we draw our communal allegiances from here, there and everywhere, if bits of cultures come haphazardly into our lives from different sources, where is the guarantee that they will all fit together? At least if a person draws her identity, as Kymlicka suggests, from a single culture, she will obtain for herself a certain degree of coherence or integrity. The coherence which makes her particular community a single cultural entity will confer a corresponding degree of integrity on the individual self that is constituted under its auspices.[35] By contrast, identity constituted under the auspices of a multiplicity of cultures may strike us as chaotic, confused, incoherent. Such a self is surely going to require *management*, just to keep its house in order.

The trouble is that if we talk too much in this way about management, we will fall into the trap of postulating the existence of the self as a managerial entity, an agent existing in distinction from each of the disparate elements that constitute the person in question. We have to postulate the "I," the true self who somehow contrives to keep the whole house in order. Listen, for example, to the following passage from George Kateb:

> One must take responsibility for oneself – one's self must become a project, one must become the architect of one's soul. One's *dignity* resides in being, to some important degree, a person of one's own creating, making, choosing rather than in being merely a creature or a socially manufactured, conditioned, created thing.[36]

But who is this entity that takes responsibility for its self-creation? How does it make its decisions? How does it know what sort of being to create?

Certainly, the self imagined in the second model does not answer to the more earnest or high-minded characterizations of the liberal individual in modern political philosophy. Modern liberal theorists place great stress on the importance of an autonomous individual's formulation and execution of a life-plan. Liberals stress the importance of each individual's selection of a particular conception of the good, a view about what makes life worth living; and they define a person's rights as the liberties and protections she needs in order to be able to choose and follow such values on equal terms with others who are engaged in a similar enterprise. The approach to life sketched out by Rushdie in the passage we quoted earlier has little in common with this, apart from the elements of freedom and decision. It has none of the ethical *unity* that the autonomous Kantian individual is supposed to confer on her life: it is a life of kaleidoscopic tension and variety. It is not the pursuit of a chosen conception of goodness along lines indicated by Ronald Dworkin,[37] nor does its individuality consist, in Rawls's words, in "a human life lived according to a plan."[38] Instead, it rightly challenges the rather compulsive rigidity of the traditional liberal picture.[39] If there is liberal autonomy in the model of mélange, it is choice running rampant, and pluralism internalized from the relations *between* individuals to the chaotic coexistence of projects, pursuits, ideas, images, and snatches of culture *within* an individual.[40]

Given the ontology of the Many Fragments model, the liberal self would be suspect in any case. One dominant theme in recent communitarian writing has been a critique of the idea of the independent self – the homunculus manager, standing back a little from each of the items on the smorgasbord of its personality. In order to manage the disparate commitments and see that they fit with one another, in order to evaluate each item and compare it with others on the cultural menu, the self would have to be an ethereal sort of entity, without any content or commitments of its own. Michael Sandel has quite properly raised the question of whether this is the way we should view our personality and our character:

> [W]e cannot regard ourselves as independent in this way without great cost to those loyalties and convictions whose moral force consists partly in the fact that living by them is inseparable from understanding ourselves as the particular persons we are – as members of this family or community or nation or people, as bearers of this history, as sons and daughters of that revolution, as citizens of this republic. Allegiances such as these are more than values I happen to have or aims I "espouse at any given time." . . .
>
> To imagine a person incapable of constitutive attachments such as these is not to conceive an ideally free and rational agent, but to imagine a person wholly without character, without moral depth. For to have character is to know that I move in a history I neither summon nor command, which carries consequences none the less for my choices and conduct.[41]

Sandel's critique seems to present the defender of the Many Fragments model with an unhappy dilemma. Either she must embrace the ethereal self of liberal deontology – the self that chooses but is not identified with any of its choices; or she must admit that the self can have a substantial character of its own, a character essential to its identity. If she adopts the former, she gives a wholly unrealistic account of choice, for on what basis can this ghost choose if it has no values or commitments or projects of its own? If, however, she tries to avoid the imputed shallowness of this approach by adopting a conception of the self with a substantial essence of its own, then the model itself begins to look unsatisfactory. For now the self must have, not just cultural characteristics in all their plurality and variety, but *a character*, and it has not been proved that this is something one can have except in the framework of a particular given culture.[42]

To avoid the dilemma, we should go back and question the image of *management* and the assumptions about *identity* that are presupposed in this critique. So long as we think that the management of the self is like the personal governance of a corporation, we will be driven to ask embarrassing questions about the specific character of the "I" in its capacity as CEO. Suppose we think instead about personal identity in terms of the democratic self-government of a pluralistic population. Maybe the person is nothing but a set of commitments and involvements, and maybe the governance of the self is just the more or less comfortable (or at times more or less chaotic) coexistence of these elements. The threat, of course, is what we vulgarly term schizophrenia; but that may be better understood as radical conflict or dissonance rather than mere unregulated plurality.

An image that may help to dispel the various threats that are operating here is that of the self-governance of a group of friends living and working together. Each friend has a character of her own, and strengths and weaknesses of her own; they are quite different, but their variety and their frictions may be the key to their association and to their ability to undertake different projects and enterprises. No one, I hope, thinks that a friendship can be sustained only if one or the other friend is recognized as being *in charge*, or only to the extent that all parties are agreed on some specific common purpose or charter. Friendship doesn't work like that, nor, I think, do the internal politics of the self. There may, on occasions, be antagonisms within the self (as indeed there are among friends). All of us, even the most culturally and psychologically secure, have the experience of inner conflict. But far from detracting from the self's integrity, the possibility of such conflict, and the variety and open texture of character that make it possible, seem indispensable to healthy personality. It may be this limitless diversity of character – Rushdie's mélange or hotchpotch – that makes it possible for each of us to respond to a multifaceted world in new and creative ways.

These are speculations, and they need to be matched more closely to recent work in the psychology of personality. Still, I hope that thinking in these terms may help to indicate how misleading it is to indict a picture of human life or action, such as the Many Fragments model, on the basis of simplistic assumptions about what the self *must* be like. Human character is not a simple thing. The openness and diversity of the second model may well hold more of a key to understanding the role of character in a changing world than the simple assumption of Sandel's critique that character is to be identified compulsively with pre-established cultural role.

MANY FRAGMENTS AND MULTICULTURALISM

In a previous section entitled "One Person: One Culture," I outlined what I took to be the main normative implications of the first model of culture and identity. I want to conclude by doing something similar for the "One Person: Many Fragments" model. Some of the normative implications of the second model simply contradict those of the first. If individual identity is not constituted by the framework of a single culture, it is neither sufficient nor perhaps even necessary to understand a whole culture in order to respect an individual.

That it is not sufficient is obvious. Even if a person, P, is identified as a *member of* or as *coming from* a given community, still, respecting her involves understanding not only the aspects of that community's culture that are important for her identity, but also the way she has come to terms with the cultures of the other communities that surround her. Someone may object that this is unnecessary in the case where P has lived her life wholly within the confines of the given community; there would be no need for any other member of that sheltered community to take into account the cultures of the surrounding communities in her dealings with P. But even in that case, the other person's familiarity with the culture of their common community would not be *sufficient* for respecting P;[43] she would also have to know P's position in that culture, and increasingly, for almost all cultures under the pressure of (post-)modernity, she would have to know something about the cultural choices that P has made, choices which cannot easily be predicted simply by studying P's characteristics in relation to the given cultural frame.

Anyway, the question of respect usually only arises in a *multi*cultural setting when the person who is according the respect does not hail from the community of the person to whom the respect is to be accorded. Suppose, then, the issue arises for a person whose background is in a quite different culture from that of P's community: what is it for *this* individual to respect a person like P? In order for that question to arise, it must be the case that the two cultural worlds *already* impinge on one another. It therefore follows from its being a question for the second person that she must consider what role elements of *her* background culture have played in the constitution of P's identity.

It might seem harder to establish that understanding a whole culture is not a necessary condition for respect in a case like P's. But if we agree that the natural condition of cultures and communities is interaction and overlap, continuous growth and development, the point is easier to accept. To think – as one does with the "One Culture" model – that in order to respect P one has to respect some *cultural framework* as the basis of her identity, means that one has to pin down a favored version of the cultural framework to be understood in this regard. But cultures and communities are developing things – their boundaries blur and their identities shift. If we try to solve the problem by specifying a favored version of the culture first, and then imposing that as a condition of respect for P, we run the risk of oppressing P's own identity in favor of some version of it *we* have constructed. This is what happens, for example, in those invidious cases where a member of some ethnic group is not permitted to benefit from affirmative action programs because she has not "self-identified" with some favored version of her ethnicity.[44] But if we come at it from the other direction, taking our cues from P herself, it will be an entirely contingent matter – dependent on what she says and thinks – whether it is necessary to understand the whole culture in order to understand and respect P.

This is not to say that the second model rejects the idea of *difference* (as discussed in the section "One Person: One Culture"). But difference is relegated now to the individual level, rather than to the level of group membership. It is genuine difference – sensitivity to the uniqueness of each person's self-constitution – rather than the bogus difference which takes refuge in the artificially constructed homogeneity of each of a variety of cultures.

With that in mind, we may also have to revise what the One Culture model indicated about group rights and wrongs. Each person's identity is given not only by the culture of the community to which she belongs (if there is such a community), but also by the effect on her of the other cultures that surround or impinge on her. That is partly a matter of her choices, and partly independent of her choices, but it is at any rate not something that can be predicted from a study of the culture that we call (in virtue of the person's background) "hers." Thus an attack on P in virtue of her ethnicity or cultural background cannot automatically be assumed to be an implicit attack on another person with the same background, for we cannot assume that a common cultural heritage has played the same role in the constitution of their respective identities. What the attack on P does to the other person's dignity and self-respect will depend (at least in part) on what the latter has made for herself of the relations between the culture they share and the communities and cultures that surround them.

There is (as I suggested at the beginning of the paper) one respect in which the Many Fragments model and the One Culture model do overlap in their normative implications. Both reject the hegemony of the dominant culture as the key to understanding and respect in a multicultural setting. But they do so for different reasons. The Many Fragments model rejects it utterly, because it denies that any culture has a necessarily privileged place in the constitution of any individual, or in the determination of what it is to respect her. The One Culture model rejects it, but only contingently. Its logic is to suggest that something like "Great Books" and "Western Civ." *would* be appropriate for understanding and respecting "Anglos" if they were not in fact surrounded by members of other ethnic communities. Worse still, it suggests that something like a "Great Books" approach *is* the appropriate vehicle for understanding and respecting other cultures; the only difference is that it should be proliferated so that we can study a privileged version of *each* culture, rather than just a privileged version of the dominant one.

The advantage of the Many Fragments model is that it rejects all such nonsense. Under modern conditions, boundaries between cultures are permeable, and materials of quite disparate provenance make themselves available for the constitution of individual lives. We need a notion of respect for persons that is sensitive to those conditions, and to the fact that for every man and woman the construction of an identity under these conditions is a painfully *individual* task. We need, accordingly, a conception of multicultural education that is sensitive to the fact that *each individual's identity is multicultural* and that individuals can no longer be regarded in the modern world (if indeed they ever could) as mere artifacts of the culture of the one community to which we think they ought to belong.

NOTES

1. New York State Social Studies Review and Development Committee, *One Nation, Many Peoples: A Declaration of Cultural Interdependence* (Albany: New York State Education Department, June 1991), p. 1.
2. For example, the National Council for the Social Studies (NCSS) "Curric-

ulum Guidelines for Multicultural Education," *Social Education* 55 (September 1992), p. 274: "Multicultural education seeks to actualize the idea of *e pluribus unum* within our nation and to create a society that recognizes and respects the cultures of its diverse people, people united within a framework of overarching democratic values. . . ."

3. See Max Weber, *Economy and Society,* ed. Guenther Roth and Claus Wittich (Berkeley: University of California Press, 1978), pp. 19–22.

4. This seems to be the implication of the NCSS Guidelines, p. 277: "For individuals, group identity can provide a foundation for self-definition. Ethnic and cultural group membership can provide a sense of belonging, of shared traditions, of interdependence of fate. . . . When society views ethnic and cultural differences with respect, individuals can define themselves ethnically without conflict or shame."

5. There is an excellent discussion in David Bromwich, *Politics by Other Means: Higher Education and Group Thinking* (New Haven, Conn.: Yale University Press, 1992), pp. 55–97.

6. Lest this point sound too individualistic for the first model, we may add (i) that people make lives for themselves individually or together within the culture to which they belong, and (ii) that the process of thinking about a life for oneself (or themselves) need not be a matter of autonomous or existential choice, but may be a matter of, as it were, finding one's place in the life of the community, discovering who one is.

7. See, for example, Will Kymlicka, *Liberalism, Community, and Culture* (Oxford: Clarendon Press, 1989), p. 169, and Philip Selznick, *The Moral Commonwealth: Social Theory and the Promise of Community* (Berkeley: University of California Press, 1992), pp. 7ff.

8. See the discussion in Iris Marion Young, *Justice and the Politics of Difference* (Princeton, N.J.: Princeton University Press, 1990), particularly chap. 2.

9. For the distinction between "general" and "special" rights, see H.L.A. Hart, "Are There Any Natural Rights?" in *Theories of Rights,* ed. Jeremy Waldron (Oxford: Oxford University Press, 1984), esp. pp. 83–8, and Jeremy Waldron, *The Right to Private Property* (Oxford: Clarendon Press, 1988), pp. 106–24.

10. See Seyla Benhabib, "The Generalized Other and the Concrete Other," in her collection *Situating the Self: Gender, Community and Postmodernism in Contemporary Ethics* (New York: Routledge, 1992).

11. That pluralism is not necessarily ethnic diversity is recognized in the NCSS Guidelines, p. 4: "For many persons, then, ethnic criteria may be irrelevant for the purposes of self-identification. Their identities stem primarily from, for example, gender, social class, occupation, political affiliation or religion." What is interesting, however, is that our conception of ethnic affiliation has the "totalizing" or "comprehensive" character associated with "community," whereas the other categories mentioned in the quotation I have just given do not have this character or have it to a much lesser extent. It may seem possible for a person to think of herself as a Navajo, for example, and have that be the key to a large part of her identity; whereas a person could not possibly think of her being a Democrat or a realtor as a key to her identity in this way. For a

discussion of the totalizing tendency of community, see Selznick, *The Moral Commonwealth*, p. 358.

12. I am grateful to Will Kymlicka for making me think harder about this issue.

13. See H.L.A. Hart, *The Concept of Law* (Oxford: Clarendon Press, 1961), pp. 185–95 for reflections, along these lines, concerning "the minimum content of natural law."

14. See, for example, the discussion of the first and second "Principles of Ethnic and Cultural Diversity" in the NCSS Guidelines, pp. 2–3.

15. In the sense of the second meaning of "catholic" given in Merriam-Webster's Collegiate Dictionary: "**1 a** . . . : of, relating to, or forming the church universal **b** . . . : of, relating to, or forming the ancient undivided Christian church or a church claiming historical continuity from it." *Merriam-Webster's Collegiate Dictionary, Tenth Edition* (Springfield, Mass.: Merriam-Webster, 1993), p. 181.

16. See Jeremy Waldron, "Particular Values and Critical Morality," *California Law Review* 77 (1989), pp. 578–81 and 589, reprinted in Jeremy Waldron, *Liberal Rights: Collected Papers 1981–91* (Cambridge: Cambridge University Press, 1993).

17. Will Kymlicka, *Liberalism, Community, and Culture* (Oxford: Clarendon Press, 1989). The argument that follows is adapted from Jeremy Waldron, "Minority Cultures and the Cosmopolitan Alternative," *University of Michigan Journal of Law Reform* 25 (1992), especially pp. 781–6.

18. John Rawls, *A Theory of Justice* (Cambridge, Mass.: Harvard University Press, 1971), p. 178. See also John Rawls, "Reply to Alexander and Musgrave," *Quarterly Journal of Economics* 88 (1974): 641: "[F]ree persons conceive of themselves as beings who can revise and alter their final ends and who give first priority to preserving their liberty in these matters."

19. Rawls, *A Theory of Justice*, pp. 90–5.

20. Kymlicka, *Liberalism, Community, and Culture*, p. 164, quoting also from Rawls, *A Theory of Justice*, pp. 563–4.

21. Kymlicka, *Liberalism, Community, and Culture*, p. 165.

22. Ibid.

23. Alasdair Macintyre, *After Virtue* (London: Duckworth, 1981), p. 201.

24. Letter from Will Kymlicka to the author, June 16, 1992.

25. Kymlicka, *Liberalism, Community, and Culture*, p. 177.

26. Kymlicka, letter to author, June 16, 1992.

27. Salman Rushdie, *Imaginary Homelands: Essays and Criticism 1981–1991* (London: Granta Books, 1991), pp. 394 and 404.

28. See the discussion by Joseph Raz in *The Morality of Freedom* (Oxford: Clarendon Press, 1986), pp. 387–90. See also Jeremy Waldron, "Autonomy and Perfectionism in Raz's Morality of Freedom," *Southern California Law Review* 62 (1989), pp. 1109 and 1113.

29. Once again I am indebted to Will Kymlicka's letter of June 16, 1992, for this criticism.

30. I am grateful to Radhika Rao for pressing this point.

31. On the topic of "new beginnings," see also Hannah Arendt, *The Human*

Condition (Chicago: University of Chicago Press, 1958), pp. 8–9 and 176–8.

32. For the dangers of confusing the importance of the new with a depraved intoxication with the exotic, see Hannah Arendt, *The Origins of Totalitarianism* (New York: Meridian Books, 1958), chap. 3.

33. See John Stuart Mill, *On Liberty* (Indianapolis: Bobbs Merrill, 1955), chap. 3.

34. See also Waldron, "Particular Values and Critical Morality," p. 586. See also Bromwich, *Politics by Other Means*, p. 182.

35. This may be exaggerated. However we define and individuate cultures, can we simply assume that each culture is coherent in this sense? Aren't some cultures, even some traditional ones, riven by contradictions? And isn't the artifice of "cultural preservation" likely to heighten any contradictions that already exist as well as introducing new ones? Moreover, are we really in a position to assume that coherence means the same in the context of a social entity, like a cultural framework, and an individual entity, like a person constituting a life?

36. George Kateb, "Democratic Individuality and the Claims of Politics," *Political Theory* 12 (1984): 343. This passage was drawn to my attention by an excerpt in William Galston, *Liberal Purposes: Goods, Virtues and Diversity in the Liberal State* (Cambridge: Cambridge University Press, 1991), p. 230.

37. See Ronald Dworkin, *A Matter of Principle* (Cambridge, Mass.: Harvard University Press, 1985), p. 191.

38. Rawls, *A Theory of Justice*, p. 408.

39. For less rigid conceptions of a liberal life, see J. L. Mackie, "Can There Be a Right-Based Moral Theory?" in *Theories of Rights*, ed. Jeremy Waldron (Oxford: Oxford University Press, 1984), p. 175: "People differ radically about the kinds of life that they choose to pursue. Even this way of putting it is misleading: in general people do not and cannot make an overall choice of a total plan of life. They choose successively to pursue various activities from time to time, not once and for all." See also Raz, *The Morality of Freedom*, pp. 370–1: "The autonomous person is part author of his life. The image this metaphor is meant to conjure up is not that of the regimented, compulsive person who decides when young what life to have and spends the rest of it living it out according to plan. . . . [Autonomy] does not require an attempt to impose any special unity on one's life. The autonomous life may consist of diverse and heterogenous pursuits. And a person who frequently changes his mind can be as autonomous as one who never shakes off his adolescent preferences."

40. Cf. Friedrich Nietzsche, *Human All Too Human: A Book for Free Spirits*, trans. R. J. Hollingdale (Cambridge: Cambridge University Press, 1986), pp. 195–6, paragraph 618: "We usually endeavour to acquire a *single* deportment of feeling, a *single* attitude of mind towards all the events and situations of life – that above all is what is called being philosophically minded. But for the enrichment of knowledge it may be of more value not to reduce oneself to uniformity in this way, but to listen instead to the gentle voice of each of life's different situations; these will suggest the

attitude of mind appropriate to them. Through thus ceasing to treat oneself as a *single* rigid and unchanging individuum one takes an intelligent interest in the life and being of many others."

41. Michael Sandel, *Liberalism and the Limits of Justice* (Cambridge: Cambridge University Press, 1982) p. 179. See also Charles Taylor, *Hegel and Modern Society* (Cambridge: Cambridge University Press, 1979), p. 157: "The self which has arrived at freedom by setting aside all external obstacles and impingements is characterless, and hence without defined purpose, however much this is hidden by such seemingly positive terms as 'rationality' or 'creativity.'"

42. A similar suggestion is found in MacIntyre, *After Virtue*, pp. 204–5: "[W]e all approach our own circumstances as bearers of a particular social identity. I am someone's son or daughter, someone else's cousin or uncle; I am a citizen of this or that city, a member of this or that guild or profession; I belong to this clan, that tribe, this nation. Hence what is good for me has to be the good for one who inhabits these roles. As such, I inherit from the past of my family, my city, my tribe, my nation, a variety of debts, inheritances, rightful expectations and obligations. These constitute the given of my life, my moral starting point. This is in part what gives my life its own moral particularity.

"This thought is likely to appear alien . . . from the standpoint of modern individualism. From the standpoint of individualism I am what I myself choose to be. I can always, if I wish to, put in question what are taken to be merely contingent social features of my existence."

43. Could I possibly know how to respect a particular other, even one immersed in mainstream Anglo culture, simply on the basis of reading Plato, Augustine, Melville, and all the other "Great Books"?

44. See Bromwich, *Politics by Other Means*, pp. 23–6, for an example.

PART III

Relativism, reason, and public education

Chapter 6

Locke and multiculturalism: toleration, relativism, and reason

SUSAN KHIN ZAW

I do not believe that a private education can work the wonders which some sanguine writers have attributed to it. Men and women must be educated, in a great degree, by the opinions and manners of the society they live in. . . . It may then fairly be inferred, that, till society be differently constituted, much cannot be expected from education.

[T]he most perfect education, in my opinion, is such an exercise of the understanding as is best calculated to strengthen the body and form the heart.

Mary Wollstonecraft[1]

I want to preface this essay with an explanation of why I have produced, for a volume on multicultural education, an essay which appears to say almost nothing about it. One reason is that I am uncertain of the usefulness of offering, from the security of the academy, theoretical criticisms of educational programs designed for much more desperate conditions than I am familiar with; I'm reluctant to comment on what's proposed for Los Angeles or Liverpool because I don't know what it's like out there. But there is also a deeper reason, given in the first of the two quotations from Mary Wollstonecraft which head this chapter. Wollstonecraft reminds us of something which it is easy to forget. Multicultural education provokes passionate debate about educational values which are felt to be deeply important (and so they are). This confers importance also on the debate about them, where theoretical issues arise (for instance about the universality of specific values) with which philosophers are likely to feel at home. But theoretical debate does harm if preoccupation with it distracts attention from the social evils from which it springs.

An educational program has to be assessed in the light of what it is for. It is usually assumed that the purpose of multicultural education

121

is to combat social ills, such as discrimination and injustice, by attacking the conditions and attitudes which give rise to or result from them – such as ignorance, disadvantage, prejudice and low self-esteem. Debate then proliferates over the real value and likely effects of the programs proposed. But if the object of multicultural education is as stated, there is a prior, and much bigger, problem. Clearly, to expect to get rid of all those evils by means of education alone is to expect a nut to crack a sledgehammer. For as Wollstonecraft says, "Men and women must be educated, in a great degree, by the opinions and manners of the society they live in" – and not just by these but even more so by the opportunities which that society offers to and withholds from them.

Unequal opportunities are to some extent products of the attitudes multicultural education tries to combat. But as long as the inequalities still exist, they will undermine whatever education puts up to counter them. Children taught to value a minority culture in the classroom will have reason to doubt or disregard their teachers if they find this valuation contradicted by, say, employment and housing practices with regard to that minority in the surrounding society. Awareness of this may lead advocates of multiculturalism to seek ever stronger educational measures in compensation; this in turn tends to polarize and embitter the educational debate, and thus to reproduce there and reinforce elsewhere the social divisions against which multicultural education was originally directed.

Thus Mary Wollstonecraft is right: "till society be differently constituted, much cannot be expected from education." Multicultural education may support but cannot substitute for more direct attacks on unequal treatment, even if it could find a form which would meet all the objections of its critics. It makes no sense unless it is seen as part of a wider endeavor – the creation of a truly multicultural society. This chapter is concerned with that wider endeavor. Its defense is especially urgent now, when formerly multicultural nations (Yugoslavia is the most bitter example) are turning to exclusion and separatism. Now more than ever we need to demonstrate that multiculturalism is not an option: it is a necessity.

However, in what follows education is not entirely ignored. As the only social enterprise where a serious attempt has been made to put multiculturalism into practice, it provides the central example of my discussion. But my interest is in its practice rather than in its theoretical justification. The focus of concern is therefore not so much whether multicultural education is a good thing, as what it would take to make it work and how to think about the kind of conflicts to which it gives rise.

MULTICULTURALISM AND LOCKE[2]

We do not have to understand new things, but by dint of patience, effort and method to come to understand with our whole self the truths which are evident.

Simone Weil[3]

Multiculturalism puts forward a social ideal: a number of culturally diverse communities harmoniously participating in the same polity, each one preserving its own cultural distinctiveness while respecting that of others. This ideal can be seen as a modern expression of the liberal values of tolerance and reason whose classic defense is Locke's *Letter concerning Toleration*.[4] There Locke defends confessional plural-ism within Christian states and denies the legitimacy of attempts to impose a Christian orthodoxy by force, even if the orthodox could know themselves to be in possession of the truth, which is impossi-ble. Dissenters are to be brought to orthodoxy not by compulsion, but by " . . . arguments: which is the only right method of propagating truth, which has no such way of prevailing as when strong arguments and good reason are joined to the softness of civility and good us-age." Similarly, multiculturalists defend cultural pluralism within the state and deplore state imposition through education of the values and practices of the dominant culture. Any resultant conflicts of val-ues between different cultural communities are to be resolved not by force and authoritative instruction but by toleration and dialogue: opposing convictions must be altered, if need be, by argument and reasoning. Multiculturalism thus inherits from Locke a strong alle-giance to toleration and commitment to reason as a method of resolv-ing disputes.

However, toleration of other cultures raises theoretical and practi-cal problems not easily amenable to Locke's solutions. First, on the theoretical side, Locke's argument was addressed specifically to inter-necine Christian strife, and is largely *ad hominem* – it appeals to fun-damental Christian values and beliefs, such as the requirement of loving-kindness and belief in a divine judge. Are Locke's arguments adaptable for use by non-Christians? Are they in any case applicable to multiculturalism, which requires toleration of much greater diver-sity than differences within Christianity?

Second, on the practical side, toleration for Locke is constituted by acceptance of separation of religious practice within the state. This is a feasible practical solution to the primarily doctrinal differences with which Locke was concerned, since effects on practice were largely confined to forms of religious observance. Sufficient areas of moral agreement remained to make it possible for people to live more or less harmoniously while attending different churches. However, attempts to practice multicultural living inevitably raise problems of conduct to which acceptance of separate practices, simple toleration, is not a solution. For the greater scope of multicultural toleration means that disagreements both cut deeper and extend into areas where practices inevitably collide. Thus intractable moral disputes may arise which nevertheless demand, at the level of conduct, a decision one way or another. Such *practical* disputes obviously cannot be resolved by the amicable agreement to disagree appropriate to tolerant doctrinal or theoretical conflict; having agreed to disagree on what to think, but finding that this leads to our getting in each other's way in practice, how are we to decide whose view is to prevail – how are we to decide what to do? Liberal multiculturalism would say, rationally; but how is reason to be brought to bear on such decisions? Locke does not address this practical question, since for him separation of confessions ensures it does not arise.

Here is a real example to illustrate the point; it comes from the British state secondary education system, much of which is explicitly committed to multicultural education. The parents of a Muslim girl in a coeducational state school asked that, after a certain age, their daughter be exempted from those parts of the curriculum which in their view involved too close physical proximity to boys. The girl herself did not wish to be excluded. The head teacher felt that the decision should be the girl's, and so on ethical grounds he was personally inclined to let her participate; however, if he did so in defiance of the parents' instructions and with their knowledge, this would probably result in their withdrawing their daughter from the school, which she would like even less. How is a decision to be reached in such a case? After one submits the moral issue to "argument and good reason" in dialogue between the contending parties, what if, despite the best rational efforts of both, neither side can convince the other – as seems all too likely? Is that the end of the role of reason? If so, how is the case to be decided – can the head teacher, who has the power to make the decision, abandon reason at that point? What does toleration of other cultures *then* require of him?

Locke could regard doctrinal difference as a private matter which need not give rise to public conflict; compulsion by the civil authority in this private sphere was particularly inappropriate, since belief cannot be compelled. But the multicultural example shows that toleration of other cultures may give rise to moral differences which cannot be regarded as of purely private significance. Possibly civil society can afford to abjure religious compulsion; but it cannot do without the public and compulsory morality expressed in law or custom. This public morality is subject to cultural variation. For Locke it was guided by the Christian ethic, on which there was at least a measure of agreement between different churches; what is to guide the enforceable public morality of a multicultural society?

These difficulties suggest that if multiculturalism, as a modern expression of liberal values, is successfully to inherit Locke's mantle, a reinterpretation or extension of his position is called for. So let us first look at his position in more detail.

Locke has three chief grounds for objecting to forcible impositions of orthodoxy. The first is a moral ground: intolerance is unchristian. Locke points out that the savage treatment then frequently meted out by Christians to Christian dissenters seems contrary to Christian charity: "I esteem . . . toleration to be the chief characteristic mark of the true church. . . . If the Gospel and the apostles may be credited, no man can be a Christian without *charity*, and without *that faith which works*, not by force, but by *love*. Now, I appeal to the consciences of those that persecute, torment, destroy, and kill other men upon pretense of religion, whether they do it out of friendship and kindness towards them or no?"[5] Religious persecution is wrong because its motives are suspect. Truly Christian zeal cannot be like this. Locke appeals directly to Scripture to bring out, and to condemn, the secular ambition implicit in attempts at religious compulsion: "*The kings of the gentiles exercise lordship over them*, said our Saviour to his disciples, *but you shall not be so*, Luke, xxii. 25. . . . Whosoever will list himself under the banner of Christ, must in the first place, and above all things, make war upon his own lusts and vices."[6] Failure to do this results in mistaking worldly desires for religious zeal: "Let them not call in the magistrate's authority to the aid of their eloquence or learning, lest perhaps, whilst they pretend only love for the truth, this their intemperate zeal, breathing nothing but fire and sword, betray their ambition and show that what they desire is temporal dominion."[7] In sum: True Christians are known by love, not hostility, towards their fellows, and do not seek temporal power over them, even when they think them in error.

Locke's other two objections to Christian fanaticism arise from epistemological considerations. Locke was skeptical of claims to religious knowledge. His conception of knowledge is Cartesian, and its paradigm of acquisition is Euclidean geometry: science is knowledge of proven truths obtained by logical derivation from self-evident premises. Scholastic efforts to achieve religious knowledge by the same means, using Scripture as the source of indubitable premises, foundered on the limitless possibilities for different interpretations of the words of Scripture, resulting in different interpreters reaching radically different and often incompatible conclusions from the same premises. Such attempts engendered rationally undecidable disputes and fuelled sectarian violence in support of many supposedly unique orthodoxies. Hence Locke, while conceding that only orthodox views could possibly have a claim to deserve imposition, insists in return that it is impossible for us to know which views are orthodox. The geometrical method cannot be used to mine knowledge of orthodoxy from the Bible because only God knows what the Bible really means. Consequently,

> [E]very church is orthodox to itself: to others, erroneous or heretical. Whatsoever any church believes, it believes to be true; and the contrary unto those things, it pronounces to be error. So that the controversy between these churches about the truth of their doctrines, and the purity of their worship, is on both sides equal; nor is there any judge . . . upon earth, by whose sentence it can be determined. . . . The decision belongs only to the supreme Judge of all men, to whom also alone belongs the punishment of the erroneous."[8]

Thus, according to Locke humans cannot give rulings on orthodoxy because such questions are beyond human knowledge and judgment. What then can reason achieve in religion? One thing it can do is demand toleration. As we have seen, Locke in effect subscribes to a kind of *de facto* Christian relativism: though there is no doubt one true Christian doctrine, its exact lineaments are only imperfectly discernible to imperfect human Christians, with the result that they have to accept Christianity's becoming to some extent all things to all churches. Toleration is a rational response to this situation. For recognizing that interpretations of Scripture can never be certain, that religious knowledge is impossible, rationally obliges one to admit that, however deep one's convictions, one may be mistaken, and others right.

The unavailability of religious knowledge has further implications for the role of reason. For it follows from this unavailability that the most reason can hope to achieve in the religious sphere are justification of belief (instead of the demonstration of truth which would constitute knowledge) and alteration of belief in others by such justifications. There is, nevertheless, a point to rational justification, and a reasonable hope of such alterations, because divergences of doctrine and practice are embedded in a matrix of shared Scriptural belief which provides a framework for rational persuasion by argument – as Locke's own argument illustrates. It is still rational *persuasion*, not proof of truth, since even agreement over interpretations of premises does not guarantee that the interpretations are correct: *both* parties may have misread Scripture. However, the reasonable Christian will hope that such mistakes will be revealed by the sincere efforts of reason, since there is presumed to be a genuine Christian orthodoxy –

a single correct interpretation of Scripture – not contrary to reason, even though both that interpretation and its correctness are (by Lockean standards) unknown and unknowable. Currently differing versions of Christian belief can thus hope to converge over time towards this one true orthodoxy, given sufficient goodwill and rationality for mutual enlightenment – that is, given toleration. For the hidden truth, if sought by reason, draws, as it were, all its different versions towards it; and any divergences from that hidden truth will, Locke assumes, leave traces detectable by reason.

Thus, Locke's argument is essentially this: if Christianity is true, toleration is required both as the expression of its central virtues and as the best means of approaching its truths – or, failing that, of achieving agreement over them. Note the conditions and assumptions that give this argument its leverage: (i) it is addressed to Locke's fellow Christians in order to change the way they handle doctrinal, not practical, disputes – in settling matters of Christian belief, toleration and reason are to be preferred to force; so (ii) shared Christian values can be appealed to; and (iii) there is an indubitable source of shared premises – Scripture; (iv) disputes are over interpretation of Scripture, and in cases of dispute there is always a right answer in the form of true doctrine, i.e., obligatory belief, though no one can be sure what belief is obligatory; and (v) true doctrine is not contrary to reason, so (vi) applying reason, rather than force, is the appropriate way to tackle disputes.

Compare now the case of multiculturalism. Do the same conditions apply, and can the same assumptions be made? Apparently not, for (i) arguments in favor of multiculturalism recommend tolerance and reason as a way of addressing practical disputes as well as differences in belief between different cultures; they are presumably addressed to fellow members of a multicultural society, including those from other cultures than the multiculturalist's, so (ii) shared values can't be assumed, and (iii) there is no mutually recognized authority to supply shared premises; furthermore, (iv) in cases of dispute, the existence of a right answer in the form of obligatory belief can't be assumed; so (v) it can't be assumed either that reason can resolve the dispute (since the object of reason is truth, but what is at issue may not be the truth of a belief), so (vi) it is not at all obvious that reason is the appropriate way to address disputes, nor tolerance the right attitude to adopt.

These are depressing conclusions for liberals – especially the last. What is to become of us all if, when threatened with serious differences, we can't urge all parties to be tolerant and listen to reason? Isn't refusal to do either precisely what characterizes liberalism's great enemy – fanaticism? If reason is no defense against fanaticism, multiculturalism is surely doomed – and probably all of us with it.

Such anxieties may suggest, in the first instance, recourse to secular adaptations of Locke. His strict separation of divine and human jurisdictions on the basis of human incompetence can be secularized by greater reliance on his distinction between the private and the public sphere. But as I have already suggested, this is of little use to multiculturalists. The distinction obviously cannot be used to justify toleration of whole cultures, since this would include toleration of their public aspects, in particular their public morality. But how can one public morality tolerate another without defeating itself? On the other hand, if the public/private distinction is used to limit the demand for toleration to toleration only of those aspects of other cultures which are private by Lockean standards – that is, to analogues of differences within Christianity – multiculturalism's moral ideal of respect for alien value-conceptions is trivialized. Multiculturalism is transformed into a substantial monoculturalism as to values, mitigated by tolerance of exotic detail: the analogue of Locke's substantial core of shared Christian belief separating into confessional diversity at the periphery. In that case, whose cultural values are to prevail? Isn't this just monocultural hegemony under another name?

At this point our situation may seem so different from Locke's that what is required is not minor tinkering with him but a bold leap away, though onto a parallel path. For there seems to be an obvious parallel between the manifest variations in Christian belief noted by Locke and the manifest variations of value-conception observable in different cultures. This makes a philosophy of cultural relativism look like the perfect rational ground for multiculturalism, the perfect substitute for Locke's skepticism with regard to religious knowledge.

It was this skepticism which made religious toleration a rational requirement. The corresponding cultural relativist argument runs as follows. Values are meaningful only within a particular culture. Therefore the conception of absolute, or culture-neutral, value is a contradiction in terms. It follows that the value-system of one culture cannot be rationally regarded as absolutely better than that of another, since no culture-neutral standpoint is philosophically available from which the values of different cultures are intelligible, let alone susceptible of impartial comparison and rational judgment by the standards of absolute value. But if reason cannot show why one value-system is absolutely better than another, imposition of monocultural value hegemony on other cultures cannot be morally justified. Reason therefore requires that each value system tolerate the others. Multiculturalism, understood as acceptance of other cultures living by their own values, thus becomes, like Locke's religious toleration, a rational requirement.

Unfortunately, this form of cultural relativism proves too much for multiculturalist purposes. Most importantly, it does not save reason; it destroys it. First, since there are no culture-neutral moral truths, a Lockean project of convergence towards them through cross-cultural exchange of reasons is not only vain – it is absurd. Second, the commitment to rational dialogue is impossible to sustain even if it aims for something less than Locke's ultimate convergence. If the reason why we have to tolerate other cultures is that we can't understand them, recourse to moral argument as a means of resolving cross-cultural disputes is pointless, for other cultures can't be expected to understand one's arguments. Since moral arguments only have leverage within one's own culture, attempts at reasoned dialogue are doomed from the start; the only possible cross-cultural dialogue is a dialogue of the deaf. It follows that in cross-cultural disagreement, moral argument can only serve to strengthen the convictions of the faithful, not to convert unbelievers. But then, instead of being an antidote to fanaticism, reason serves to encourage it. In that case the only means available for settling cross-cultural moral disputes would seem to be force, guile, or segregation. Worse still, moral objections to using these are also impossible to sustain. For if my morality can't be said to be better than yours, it can't be said to be worse, either; and in any case since your moral lights mean nothing to me, I have no option but to act according to my own lights, which provide me with moral reasons for overriding you when your moral lights don't coincide with mine.

In other words, cultural relativism, in putting moral difference beyond the reach of understanding, puts cross-cultural moral conflict beyond the reach of reason. Relativizing moral reasons to cultures transforms reason into rationalization, so that its exercise, instead of procuring agreement as Locke hoped, sharpens divisions. Finally and disastrously, in this context rational justification readily functions as a means of convincing those who wish to override others that they are right to override them. Zeal for truth becomes indistinguishable from committed rationalization, a powerful ally of lust for temporal dominion.

Cultural relativism thus has an inbuilt tendency to push Lockean toleration towards its opposite. The practical outcome consistent with it is not the multiculturalist dream of harmony in variety and resolution of conflict through reasoned dialogue, but cultural isolationism enlivened by intercultural wars of all against all.

This is a very discouraging picture of multicultural interaction. Nevertheless, it may seem all too realistic when one considers the case of the Muslim schoolgirl described above. Since this is a case of conflict of moralities, a Lockean multiculturalism would recommend that parents and head teacher seek to resolve their differences by exchange of moral arguments. In the Lockean tradition, these would take the form of logical derivations of different practical decisions about the girl's school career from more general shared moral principles. The disagreements over Scriptural interpretation which concerned Locke would here become differences over interpretation of the shared principles; and one can imagine how, in both kinds of dispute, the results of applying different interpretations to particular cases might push the parties towards one interpretation rather than another, and perhaps produce agreement. But the method cannot operate, let alone achieve agreement, if the relevant principles are not shared, as seems likely to be the case here. In that case the result of an exchange of arguments is likely to be that what to one side are good reasons are perceived by the other as bad reasons, or no reasons at all. Thus, the religious belief and cultural custom which produce the parents' request may simply look like superstition and injustice to the head teacher, while the belief in individual liberty and responsible choice which leads him to wish to respect the girl's wishes may look like irreligion and immoral license to the parents.

Moral justifications thus do seem unintelligible outside their cultural context, just as cultural relativism predicts. And if reason can achieve no more in such cases, it is impotent to resolve the conflict; it can only rationalize the conflicting views. How then is the head teacher to decide what to do?

What he in fact did was let the girl participate and lie to the parents, appealing both to the primacy of individual liberty and to utilitarianism in justification of his action, and claiming to have arrived at his decision rationally because he could produce those justifications. (I think he saw himself as the pragmatic and resourceful defender of the freedom of the individual.) In other words, he followed his own lights, relying on philosophy to support him, and ignored those of the parents. This use of philosophy looks very much like rationalization; but even if it is, it would follow from cultural relativism both that the head teacher's philosophy is culture-bound and that resort to some such local, monocultural reasons is the best he can do by way of rational moral decision-making. But one can imagine how both his decision and his reasons would have looked to the parents, and how they might have acted in consequence. Multicultural harmony is not a likely result. On the other hand, given that the head teacher really did have the moral beliefs he claimed in his justifications, wouldn't it have been immoral for him to act otherwise? Similarly for the parents. Why else do we insist on freedom of conscience? – for which cultural relativism, once again, provides a ready explanation. Hence the frequently heard comment, "Well, morality's all subjective (or relative) anyway, isn't it?"

This is an admission of the impotence of reason when things get really difficult. That admission leads inevitably towards a view of moral conflict as moral schism, in which the practical problem can only be solved by force: from the parents' point of view, the head teacher's action is simply the imposition of a local orthodoxy by force. But such a view of conflict justifies religious war: the sleep of reason breeds monsters. Isn't that exactly what we're trying to avoid when we urge warring factions to "listen to reason"?

The example illustrates why it is both so tempting and so disastrous for multiculturalists to embrace cultural relativism. The impasse between Muslim parents and head teacher simultaneously invites a cultural relativist interpretation and reveals how dangerous cultural relativism is to multiculturalism. It is dangerous because conviction of the impotence of reason in cases of deep moral disagreement, such as arises between different cultures, encourages impatience with or even distrust of mediation by reason as soon as moral passions are roused. This feeds fanaticism, and the transformation of reasoning into rationalization feeds it even fatter. I conclude that if multiculturalism is made to depend on this form of cultural relativism, it becomes both theoretically and practically incoherent. Relativist multiculturalists are no true heirs of Locke, for relativism inevitably encourages the very things Locke was fighting.

MULTICULTURALISM AND REASON: ATTENUATED CULTURAL RELATIVISM

If cultural relativism cannot claim to provide a Lockean basis for multiculturalism, what can? The problems of multicultural toleration arise from the inability to invoke any principle with the moral authority which Christianity had for Locke. To Western philosophers in the same liberal tradition, the solution that naturally suggests itself is the one provided by the history of their discipline. In moral philosophy, Kant sought to replace the authority of religion with the authority of reason; only reason could possibly lay claim to both the authority and the cultural neutrality necessary to help mediate the disputes of a multicultural society. There are some cultural products whose value is perceptible to any culture, not just to the one which produced them. The obvious examples are mathematics and science; and Cartesian reason, or logic, a component discipline of both, must be another. On the other hand, cultural relativism surely cannot be entirely wrong, or it would not be so tempting; values do vary with culture, and the multicultural ideal must recommend toleration of this variance.

This suggests the following, much attenuated, version of cultural relativism as a Lockean basis for multiculturalism. The original version overstated the mutual impenetrability of different cultures; for even individuals without a common language, from the most widely divergent cultures, can achieve some measure of understanding and communication at the level of basic human needs. (How else did explorers get fed?) If human nature is invariant, which seems a plausible assumption, some human needs must be universal, and universal needs create universal values. Now, moralities may be secularly construed as sets of rules governing human social relations, necessarily expressing at bottom the same universal human values because they answer to the same human needs (though not necessarily only to these). No doubt different moralities express such values in different ways in different cultures. Nevertheless, their rootedness in universal needs suggests the existence of a universal core human morality embedded in all culture-specific moralities, and therefore accessible to reason.

If such an underlying human morality exists, rational people within any culture should be able to extract it from their own local one by the application of reason, somewhat as scientists extract universal physical laws from the evidence of locally observable phenomena. This, and the expression of the universal morality as a set of suitably framed universal moral principles, is a task proper to rational inquiry, and especially to rational philosophy. Particular moral judgments can then be rationally arrived at, and justified, by logically deriving them from these universal principles – thus exactly paralleling in practical morality the methods of Euclidean geometry. The scheme extends an invitation to reasonable people in all cultures to join in a common rational project: identification of the culture-neutral universal moral principles, and use of these to regulate moral disputes between them. The multicultural ideal becomes a (partial) realization of this project, and thus an exercise of rationality.

The scheme also sets necessary limits to toleration: necessary because obviously, in the case of morality, one cannot be required to tolerate everything. Unrestricted toleration makes morality self-defeating, just as relativizing truth is self-refuting. A requirement to tolerate everything would thus be irrational. Hypothesizing a culture-neutral universal morality makes it possible to say that we are not required to tolerate moralities contrary to it.

However, total moral unanimity is not to be expected. Just as different Christians could interpret the Bible differently, so different cultures may interpret the same culture-neutral universal principles differently, and this may lead to differences in the particular judgments derived from them. Reason requires us to tolerate all such differences; for once moralities have been shown to answer adequately to the set of universal principles, there is no rational basis for moral choice between them. This is the grain of truth in cultural relativism. However, rational dialogue may still be possible between adherents of different tolerable moralities over how adequately each answers to the culture-neutral universal standard, and conflict may diminish as a result.

The scheme proposed by attenuated cultural relativism looks at first attractively close to Locke. In both cases the one truth can be sought in the many versions by subjecting the versions to rational criticism; the main difference is that divine authority has been replaced by the authority of Nature (in the form of presumed laws of nature connecting human needs and moralities) and Reason. It is as if Reason and Nature have become the father and mother of us all – a trope, incidentally, characteristic of the gender attributions of eighteenth-century thought, where ideas such as these originated.[9]

This gives the scheme many advantages. Appeal to nature allows us to assume the presence of a universal morality in the morality of every culture – universal because underwritten by natural law. This provides grounds for requiring toleration, while allowing individuals to concentrate attempts at articulating universal principles on their own local morality without falling under the suspicion of cultural prejudice. (Kindly Mother Nature exhorts us to love of all mankind, while assuring us we too are truly her children.) On the other hand, showing the universality of the principles consists in separating out what is local in them from what is universal. This in turn looks like just the job for reason. (Keen-eyed Father Reason distinguishes the deserving from the undeserving without fear or favor.) Furthermore, once reason has done the job, we have a decision-procedure for setting limits to multicultural toleration which seems sorely needed in practice. Operating this procedure is another job for reason, which is thus not merely saved – it has a starring role. (Father Reason delivers judgment from on high.)

Have we now solved the multiculturalist's problem? It depends on what we think that problem is. I inserted the tropes, which sit so easily on the ideas, to point out that despite the structural similarities with Locke, the scheme has acquired a rather different character. For there are also important structural differences from Locke; as indeed would be necessary, given the important differences between the multiculturalist's situation and his. And the structural differences are not helpful to tolerant multiculturalism.

Note first that Locke's insistence on the impossibility of *knowing* the one truth, which is the keystone of his case for toleration, is not matched. On the contrary, it is assumed that the one truth – the set of culture-neutral universal moral principles – *can* be known; what makes the case for toleration is that the principles do not have a unique interpretation. (Father Reason assumes ascendancy over Mother Nature, making only his own children legitimate; kindliness is to be extended only to these.) Thus, again unlike Locke, since the one true orthodoxy can be known, toleration actually depends on a weaker version of relativism. Instead of Locke's combination of interpretative absolutism with skepticism (there is one true interpretation but we can't know it), we have a combination of cognitivism with interpretative relativism (we can know the universal principles but there isn't one true interpretation of them). Because of this, reason becomes inapplicable to practical conflicts arising from differences which we have to tolerate; for these result from relativism, and are consequently rationally insoluble. The head teacher and the Muslim parents (assuming both represent tolerable moralities) are thus still in the same fix as before. They must tolerate each other; but reason can't tell them how to do this in practice. For the only way attenuated cultural relativism allows reason to resolve conflicts between tolerable interpretations is by recognizing one as in fact *less* tolerable, because less rational, than another; in which case it would presumably recommend rejecting the less tolerable interpretation and adopting the more.

Note then what this implies about the role of reason. The task of reason is now *choosing between* culturally different moralities, rather than reconciling them. Cognitivism tends towards exclusion, not toleration: if we know that something is wrong, why should we tolerate it? Father Reason, we have seen, separates and excludes. In fact, complete success in the cognitivist project – not only identification of universal principles, but also the ranking of tolerable interpretations by degree of rationality – would leave no room for toleration at all. Why should we settle for anything less than the most rational morality? That is why the new scheme has to retain an element of relativism, of moral irrationality; without this to limit cognitivism, toleration would be unnecessary. Toleration here *depends* on irrationality because its justification is that though each side has reason for its beliefs, *there is no reason* to choose one side rather than another. This reopens the relativist gate to force and fanaticism in cases like that of our Muslim schoolgirl. If there is *nothing to choose* between the head teacher's arguments and the parents', how else can the issue between them be decided *except* by force – backed up by the appropriate arguments, now even stronger because underwritten by universal morality?

Attenuated cultural relativism thus makes the position of toleration very insecure: it is, so to speak, threatened from both ends. It is threatened on its own ground by the very relativism which creates that ground, because relativism threatens reason, and the loss of reason threatens toleration; it is threatened even more by cognitivism, since cognitive success would rule it out. At the moment, the chances of cognitivism's success do not look good. But what becomes of multiculturalism if cognitivism begins to succeed – or thinks that it has? And even if it cannot succeed, should multiculturalists have to rely on cognitivism's failure for the security of toleration?

CAN THE COGNITIVIST PROJECT SUCCEED?

The cognitivist project was to extract universal moral principles from culture-specific ones by the use of culture-neutral reason, which was identified most plausibly with logic. Its chances of success do not look good because logic alone will not suffice. Comparison with the rational paradigm, Euclidean geometry, may be helpful here. Rational extraction of culture-neutral moral principles is the analogue of proving the axioms and postulates of Euclidean geometry, and we simply don't know how to construct that kind of proof for moral principles. Indeed, it is not so easy for geometry. For centuries geometers tried and failed to prove the parallel postulate (which seemed to them somewhat lacking in self-evidence) by the method of *Reductio ad Absurdum* (denying what you want to prove to see whether this leads to contradictions; if it does, this disproves the denial, and hence proves what you want to prove).

Though *Reductio* did not work for the parallel postulate, could it work for moral principles? Unfortunately not, because the most it can do is prove that a particular set of principles is *internally consistent;* the universal morality has, as well, to be *true* – which means, according to attenuated cultural relativism, that it must answer appropriately to human nature. A bit of purely local morality could be just as internally consistent as the universal morality, but thoroughly objectionable by universal standards derived from human nature. The same objection will apply to any purely logical proof. In any case, *Reductio* – and any kind of purely logical proof – seems peculiarly inapplicable to the proof of moral principles because, notoriously, "contradictions" (incompatible moral judgments about a particular case) can typically be deduced from *any* set of moral principles sufficiently general to be plausible candidates for universality. Thus by the standards of geometrical reason, systems of morality based on such sets of principles seem congenitally infected with that most heinous of logical sins – inconsistency. (Just like the sum of Scholastic interpretations of the Bible.)

If logic cannot perform the role assigned to culture-neutral reason, what about the looser, but still rational, arguments of philosophy? After all, liberal moral philosophy from Kant[10] to Rawls[11] and beyond has tried to devise alternative forms of rational argument capable of extracting universal moral principles from its local morality. But now culture-neutrality becomes a problem, since the claim of philosophical argument to be culture-neutral seems very much more doubtful than that of logic. What is required to establish universal and cross-culturally acceptable moral principles is a method of moral argument at least as authoritative and widely accepted as scientific method. No such moral method exists. The arguments devised by liberal philosophers, far from convincing all the world, don't even convince all liberal philosophers; their efficacy is itself a matter of lively philosophical dispute. (The large literature on Rawls is a case in point.)[12]

This lack of philosophical consensus on philosophical method currently vitiates any philosophical attempt to establish universal principles. For its result is that individual philosophers typically appeal to a particular type of argument, or to a particular philosophical theory of morality or value, as the ultimate guarantor of a favored set of universal principles, claiming to have made their choice of argument or theory on rational grounds – like the head teacher in our example. But since the profession as a whole cannot produce a consensus on which is the most suitable or powerful type of argument, or the best theory, individual philosophers are honor-bound to concede that they cannot expect their reasons to convince everybody – like the head teacher in multiculturalist mode.

In fact, this introduces a further, even more damaging level of relativity into the head teacher's moral position via his philosophically based argument. For not only is the argument not expected to convince the parents; it is not even expected to convince everyone in the head teacher's own culture – only those who share his philosophical predilections! In other words, it doesn't even *claim* to be worth much more than rationalization. At this point the cognitivist project collapses into *de facto* moral relativism. Indeed, if moral reason is reduced to this, we have gone beyond attenuated cultural relativism and are well on the way to moral subjectivism. In that case the parents have every right to be indignant. For from their point of view – by hypothesis, equally expressive of universal morality – the head teacher's action is *un*reasonable and high-handed imposition of not even a local orthodoxy, but a mere personal opinion. If this is the best reason can do at handling cross-cultural conflict, things don't look good for multiculturalism.

There is thus a fatal flaw in attenuated cultural relativism: namely, an intrinsic incoherence between its universalist cognitivism and its relativism, which, when it is not squeezing ever smaller the space for toleration, threatens to collapse the whole scheme into irrationalism. If reasoning one's way to a particular moral judgment consists in logically deriving it from more general moral principles, the combination of cognitivist universalism and interpretative relativism means that in a multicultural society we are bound to end up with contradictory particular judgments. Relativism licenses these contradictions. But to accept contradiction is to abandon geometrical reason, and we have no convincing substitute. This puts us in exactly the position of Locke's despised Scholastics – despised because they carried on trusting their method, even though by its own standards, since it produced contradiction, it had failed. In fact, it puts us in a worse position than theirs; for since the combination of universalism and relativism is itself contradictory, in embracing it we positively embrace contradiction, while the Scholastics could at least hope, assuming God was a logician, that with sufficient ingenuity they might eventually succeed in avoiding it. Furthermore, because we do not have the Bible to rely on, and because the reason which was supposed to replace it has turned out to be a broken reed, we cannot have their religious confidence in our moral foundations, and given the fragmented state of moral philosophy, should have as little, if not less, rational confidence.

Claims to have identified sets of culture-neutral principles should, therefore, be treated with deep suspicion. Provability in morals has been the dream of political philosophers since Plato, because if we had it, and assuming rationality all round, we could convince those who disagreed with us that they were wrong (unless of course *we* were wrong, in which case they could do the same for us). We might thus hope for rational resolutions of political conflicts deriving from moral differences by deployment of the appropriate proofs – again assuming those who disagreed with us were prepared to be rational. And if they weren't, and Reason were on our side, we could justifiably resort to force instead, secure in the knowledge that we were demonstrably right.

In other words, one of the attractions of moral cognitivism is that it can be used to justify coercion: that is the lesson of the Scholastics, whose conception of moral argument modern rationalist conceptions so strikingly resemble. A major part of Scholastic effort went into distinguishing heresy from orthodoxy, and heretics were burned. Note also that assigning the search for universal principles to pure reason would, like Scholasticism, put moral authority into the hands of a highly educated elite, because the complexity of the method proposed naturally suggests that its use is best left to those equipped with the appropriate skills. The unskilled are likely to get things wrong. But on the universal principles everything else depends. Thus cognitivism also rationalizes moral authoritarianism. In the light of all this, perhaps cognitivists too should take to heart Locke's warning that those who call in the magistrate's authority professing love for truth may in fact desire temporal dominion.

Attenuated cultural relativism, then, turns out to have surprising affinities with Scholasticism, and fails in a similar way. What should we conclude from this? That all would be well if only philosophy could come up with a convincing, culture-neutral way of establishing universal moral principles, and that we should press on with the search? Or is the whole project, like the Scholastic project, unrealistic? If it is, does this mean that the multicultural ideal is unrealistic, too, and that both should be abandoned? Consideration of what has gone wrong suggests not one of these, but a combination. Perhaps the project has failed because it is to some extent unrealistic. Perhaps cognitivism is not the right path. But abandoning multiculturalism because of the resultant difficulties with limiting toleration would be precipitate.

Note first that it is *only* the cognitivist part of the project that has failed; having hypothesized the existence of a universal human morality grounded in human needs and variously expressed in all cultures, we looked to philosophy to identify it, and philosophy has failed to come up with the goods. But it does not follow that the hypothesis which suggested the search was wrong, and it is really on that hypothesis that multiculturalism, the ideal of a tolerant multicultural society, depends. The cognitivist project of establishing a set of explicit universal principles was necessary not to authorize toleration, but to set limits to it, since tolerating everything is morally self-defeating. If we kept the hypothesis but abandoned the project as not feasible, this would strengthen the position of toleration, for it would strengthen the resemblance between our position and Locke's. Like him, we would believe in a single, but hidden, true orthodoxy – the universal morality, of which different cultures, like different churches, possess different versions; and none could claim that its version was the only truly orthodox one. Toleration would once more become rational, and on Lockean grounds. Because Locke could not know what true Christianity was, he had to respect the different sectarian versions of it; similarly, if there were no culture-neutral way of identifying universal moral principles, we would have to respect them in the form of culturally different moralities.

But then, there is reason to think the cognitivist project not feasible *even if* all moralities are ultimately grounded in human nature. A once-and-for-all, immutable, culture-neutral formulation of universal moral principles, usable for the purposes of exclusion and conflict resolution, is arguably impossible in principle.

SYSTEMATIC SKEPTICISM REVIVED

A moment's reflection reveals a huge gap between clearly universal needs and actual moralities. Basic physical needs are universal, but do not by themselves determine a morality. Even physical needs invariably acquire cultural meanings: consider the relation between sexual satisfaction and romantic love, or between hunger, fasting and dieting. And it is through these acquired meanings that physical needs relate to morality, not through their universality. Thus it is culture, not nature, that decides the moral value of need-related practices.

This suggests that physical human nature may not be what we should be interested in anyway. Perhaps what moralities answer to are, rather, what Simone Weil has called *needs of the soul*:[13] the need for liberty, for example, though Weil herself believes that the soul has more need of obedience than of liberty. (She may be right; perhaps morality as such answers to a need for obedience.) Needs of the soul (supposing they exist), if related to needs of the body, must be so in complicated and perhaps culturally varying ways. Perhaps the moral significance of physical needs varies in different cultures because what culture alters is the relation between needs of the body and needs of the soul. For needs of both soul and body can be expected to vary in relative urgency in different circumstances, and thus to find expression and satisfaction in different ways and to different degrees in different situations. For instance, Western moral philosophy has tended to assume that moral development consists in the subjection of needs of the body to needs of the soul; but this assumes that one can choose either. What if the whole society has to choose between liberty and starvation? (Consider in this connection Colin Turnbull's description of the Ik, about whom I have written elsewhere.)[14] Different cultures, with their different moralities, can be seen as different historical solutions to the problems presented by meeting varying constellations of needs in different circumstances. Cultures develop different conceptual schemes to express their special situation in the world of both soul and body. These differences are what make the moralities of other cultures unintelligible to us (as in the case of those peculiar virtues, "magnificence" and "greatness of soul," described in Book IV of Aristotle's *Nicomachean Ethics*).[15]

Now, however, a doubt arises about whether needs of the soul can be culture-neutral in the way necessary to underwrite a culture-neutral morality. For they surely are, if not created by, at the very least dependent on, the human social relations mediated by language, and thus must be shaped by language to a far greater extent than needs of

the body. We may well be such that, come what may, we are going to have needs of the soul (and hence moralities), and possibly it is the same thing in all of us which brings this about. It does not follow that we are all going to have the same needs of the soul, in the sense that a statement in my language of the needs of my soul can be translated without loss or change of meaning into your language, and my needs recognized as identical to yours. I doubt this for the same reason that I doubt that an absolutely perfect translation of literature from one language to another is possible. If needs of the soul are mediated by language, as literature is constituted by language, they cannot but be conceived differently in different cultures. Perhaps absolutely perfect translations from one language to another are possible in the case of very special and restricted subject matters, for instance mathematics and science, which develop their own technical vocabularies. But the subject matter of morality is not restricted in this way: all human life is there, finding its best expression in natural, not technical, language. Hence the humanist objection to the barbarity of Scholastic language, which bristled with technical terms called forth by the needs of argumentative rigor – as does the language of modern moral philosophers.[16]

In sum: if there are culture-neutral needs of the soul, they will of necessity be theoretical entities *explaining* any needs expressible in natural language, so that it would take a technical language (such as the language of psychoanalysis) to express them. And such a language would not be capable of expressing actual moralities, though things said in it might be (very) loosely translatable into natural language, or acquire a currency there. (Think of all the things one *can't* say in the language of psychoanalysis, and how psychoanalytical ideas get into natural language as normative, quasi-ethical terms, but not vice versa.) If needs of the soul determine moral principles, the same applies to culture-neutral moral principles. They cannot simply be a *portion* of actual moralities, which can be identified and cut out. (Indeed, the culture-neutral universality claimed by psychoanalytical theory is itself very doubtful, even within Europe. Consider Bruno Bettelheim's argument that the standard English translation of Freud traduces his meaning, transforming his deep humanism into a spurious scientism.)[17] To formulate a truly universal morality based on culture-neutral needs of the soul, then, something much more arduous and complicated is going to be needed, probably requiring collaboration between different cultures to investigate the relationships between their moralities and to develop the culture-neutral need-concepts and international technical language necessary to capture their common universal core. The best test of the universality of a

moral principle is likely to be, consistent with this naturalist meta-ethic, an empirical one: whether we can get anyone from another culture to understand it.

Clearly this new version of the cognitivist project would be enormously difficult, laborious, and probably never-ending; and even if it could be successfully completed, I doubt that the results would be of much practical use. For the generality which made the morality universal would also empty it of practical content, since to ensure culture-neutrality, its injunctions would have to be at least as unspecific and banal as the definition of justice attributed to Simonides in Book I of Plato's *Republic*: "render to each his due."[18] This is both boring (because tautological) and useless. I can know that I must render to each his due without having the faintest idea what to do.

If I am right about all of this, then cognitivist efforts to reach a definitive statement of universal moral principles – that is, efforts to select what look like the most plausibly justifiable or fundamental principles from the local morality, and then to devise ways of proving them – are misconceived; what cognitivists want to do cannot be done in this way. Perhaps that is why philosophy has not succeeded in establishing any candidate principles to general satisfaction. In that case, if we press on regardless with such efforts, our intellectual situation really does match that of the despised Scholastics; and we may wonder whether our reasons for persisting, as they did, in necessarily vain attempts, are also similar. Notice that the practical pressure for exclusion of obnoxious views is as great now as it was then, if not greater. Just as, to the medieval churchman, the unity of Christendom (or its "temporal dominion," according to Locke) was threatened by heresy, so now the cohesion of the state (or the existing power distribution within it, according to its critics) is threatened by cultural diversity. Hence cognitivism's premature success claims. These are obviously conditions in which there is great pressure on argument to perform functions it cannot fulfil; and when they are joined to strong moral convictions in a philosophical climate of effective rational subjectivism, it is easy to forget that where universal principles are concerned, legitimate practical application demands a much higher standard of proof than that worth considering in academic debate. It is not enough just to convince the powerful.

However, if the cognitivist project can't succeed, if we must give up hope of explicit universal principles to solve our practical problems, how then do we address them? How, in particular, do we set limits to toleration? And how does multiculturalism stand now – what can we still get out of the original hypothesis?

UNIVERSALITY AND PRACTICE

Note first that for practical purposes we do not in fact need anything as powerful as immutable culture-neutral universal principles (unless what we are really interested in is coercion). Consider again the original hypothesis; it said that the universal morality varies with culture because universal needs and values express themselves differently, and have different priorities, in different circumstances. In that case all we need, and can expect, in our own culture is an articulation of universal principles adapted to our own circumstances. Of course the hypothesis says we already have them. But circumstances can change, and when they do the old articulation may no longer answer to the underlying universal needs and values, whatever they are. When that happens there will be pressure for moral change from those who find that public morality does not meet those needs. One of the ways things have changed is that states now contain different cultural communities (defined as groups with distinguishable moralities) which want to hang on to more of their diversity than was formerly the case. And new circumstances create new needs – or rather, new expressions of universal needs. For instance, now that all these different cultural communities are living in the same geographical area under the same state, they *need* to find a workable way of living together and resolving their moral differences. This is a need they didn't have when they all lived in separate countries. One way of resolving these differences is by force: the group with most political power will impose its views, that is, its version of the universal morality. Another way is "good reason": trying to evolve, by collaborative efforts, a *new* public morality from all the culturally different moralities active in the state.

Though this new morality, like all moralities, must express the universal morality, it need not take an immutable, culture-neutral form; for it is going to be the morality of *our* (joint) culture ("we" being all the citizens of whatever culturally diverse state is in question). It will therefore be a morality adapted to *our* fundamental needs and situation, and hence local, as all moralities are local – and none the worse for that. Claims to offer something more should be distrusted: as Locke suggests, they are likely to be motivated by lust for dominion disguised as zeal for truth. For the universality of culture-neutral morality combined with its inaccessibility means that Locke's remark applies: "every church [or cultural variation of universal morality] is orthodox to itself: to others, erroneous or heretical. Whatsoever any church believes, it believes to be true; and the contrary unto those things, it pronounces to be error. So that the controversy between these churches about the truth of their doctrines, and the

purity of their worship, is on both sides equal; nor is there any judge
. . . upon earth, by whose sentence it can be determined." The function of the hypothesized universal morality is to encourage hopes,
not of making dominion licit, but of finding points of moral contact
with others from which a new, shared public morality might grow.
The collaborative construction of this new, shared, public morality is
the project of multiculturalism.

Note how close we are to Locke at this point: cognitivist aspirations
have been replaced by skepticism about the possibility of moral knowledge, and evangelism by toleration. For what I am recommending is
that we, as citizens of a state which is in fact multicultural even if not
(yet) multiculturalist, abandon cognitivism (in its attempts to establish
universal principles) and instead work cooperatively towards a shared
conception (or local public morality) of the hidden truth (the universal
morality). Just so, Locke recommended that his contemporaries, as
Christians, if not (yet) tolerant Christians, abandon claims to religious
knowledge (abandon attempts to establish a definitive interpretation
of Scripture) and instead work cooperatively towards a shared conception (an agreed interpretation of Scripture) of the hidden truth (the one
true orthodoxy – God's interpretation of Scripture). Just as Christians
could not know how closely their agreed interpretation corresponded
to God's interpretation, so we cannot know how closely our agreed
public morality corresponds to universal morality. But this need not
stop either them or us from believing that there is a hidden truth. It
may exist, even though it is permanently inaccessible to us. The true
orthodoxy exists in the mind of God; the universal morality is inscribed
in our nature and exists in possibility, like Fermat's proof of his last
theorem; it is a theoretical entity whose theory has not yet been
devised – as is universal human nature. For Locke, inaccessibility is a
function of the difference between the divine and the human; for us, of
the difference between nature and culture. Humans can no more
observe a universal human nature unmediated by culture than they
can see God. And their descriptions of such a human nature will be as
culture-dependent as their descriptions of God.

It may now seem, however, as if the exchange of cognitivism for
Lockean skepticism has made little real difference; this new version of
the multiculturalist project may simply look like a domestication of
the arduous and unhopeful cognitivist collaboration described earlier
with all its disadvantages. For how is it to be pursued? If culture-
neutral universal morality is unstatable, how are we to formulate a
new public morality that expresses it? What about the other element
in Lockean toleration – reason, about which nothing so far has been
said? Does it have any role in the new multiculturalist project? Can
part of this role be resolution of cross-cultural moral conflict?

We now come to the point at which I depart from Locke. What distinguishes this multiculturalist project from the earlier, arduous one is that it is *practical and not speculative;* that is, its objectives are political, not intellectual. For to settle on a public morality is to settle on what kind of a state one is to live in. Locke abjured cognitivism because a certain kind of knowledge was not to be found; one had to content oneself with reasonable opinion. However, the pursuit of reasonable opinion permitted the same methods as the pursuit of knowledge: geometrical reason could still be applied to test inter-pretations of the Bible – it just couldn't be expected to produce knowledge of the right interpretation. (Moreover, Locke did believe that *moral*, as distinct from religious, knowledge might be possible, because he thought of it as precisely *moral geometry* – the deduction of further moral truths from self-evident moral definitions or axioms.) Locke advocated toleration because it is constituted by the virtues necessary for the formation of reasonable opinion when knowledge is impossible: namely, respect for other views, open-mindedness, will-ingness to believe one is wrong, intellectual honesty, intellectual hu-mility. Pursuit of elusive truth demands these virtues as inexorably as any religion. The same qualities are also needed for the multicultural-ist project, which can incorporate a speculative element. But because this project is primarily practical, it requires special virtues of its own and must employ its own methods – the methods of practical, not geometrical or speculative, reason.

To say this is to part company with traditional moral philosophy, which has followed Locke in construing moral reason as essentially speculative rather than practical. This is true even of Kant, who thought of moral reason as *"pure* practical reason," for the require-ment of purity is a condition imported from the ideal of geometrical reason and so denatures practical reason. (In fact, "pure practical reason" is a contradiction in terms.) The object of speculative reason is *what is true*. The object of practical reason is *what to do*. Confusing speculative with practical reason is moral philosophy's great mistake. From it stem all the relativistic difficulties we encountered in trying to apply reason to conflict resolution in conditions of uncertainty.

In order to see this, we need first to distinguish two obviously different kinds of moral conflict, internal and external. Internal moral conflict is conflict within the individual; external moral conflict is conflict between individuals or groups. Philosophers have taken in-ternal conflict as the core case of moral conflict, and the paradigm example of theoretical reason, geometry, as the model for moral rea-son; external conflict is addressed by simply distributing the different geometrical arguments represented within the individual between the parties to the conflict. We have seen how this strategy reduced reason to impotence. I suggest this is because it deployed the wrong sort of reason for the purpose, and because the relation assumed between internal and external conflict was the wrong way round. Moral reason is *practical* reason, and it is *external* conflict which makes internal conflict intelligible.

INTERNAL AND EXTERNAL CONFLICT

Life sees to it that most people are familiar with internal conflict. Who hasn't at some time felt the strain of equally insistent moral demands, both of which it seemed wrong not to satisfy, even though it was impossible to satisfy both? And who, struggling to make the right decision in such a situation, hasn't longed to know how to give due weight to both demands in the process of arriving at a decision? This struggle to make the right decision is known in philosophy as *deliberation*. The desire to give due weight to both claims is the desire for *rational* deliberation: for a process which will deliver the right answer, the answer that somehow properly acknowledges both claims. This answer will in fact be *the right thing to do*. In internal conflict, reason's task is finding this action.

Philosophy has attempted to satisfy the longing for rational deliberation by construing moral reason as geometrical reason and representing the internal struggle towards the right decision accordingly: it becomes the struggle to express the insistent internal demands in terms of general moral principles, and the tracing of logical routes from them to different actions. Thus principles compel action as logic compels belief. Now, geometrical reason abhors falsity and hence contradiction, which is geometrical irrationality. It cannot view a hundred schools of thought contending as political emancipation and intellectual wealth; it must see them as error triumphant and intellectual failure, because so much contention means there must be a lot of contradiction and error about. The whole point of geometrical reason is *not* to let a hundred schools of thought contend, but to find out *who is right*; and by the same token, *who is wrong*. In morality it is hostile to toleration because toleration seems inconsistent with the primary intellectual virtue, namely *zeal for truth*. And the other side of devotion to truth is abhorrence of error.

This makes geometrical reason a tool shaped to the fanatic's hand. Thus, as we saw, when rational deliberation is construed as the application of geometrical reason, the object is *that logic block off routes to all actions but one*. Such applications, which lend themselves to enthusiasm and fanaticism when successful, deafen the ear to the voice of practical reason. When they are unsuccessful, the failure seems to suggest that there is no role for reason of any kind. We rightly find this hard to believe; for practical reason, though forgotten, is waiting in the wings. But we have only a confused awareness of it, and so we persist in thinking that our flawed efforts at geometrical reasoning must be worth more than they are. Hence the relativistic acceptance of rationalization as reasoning. But this is to mistake the understudy for the star. The star is waiting unregarded in the wings: it is practical reason.

This becomes obvious as soon as we turn our attention to external conflict. A notoriously intractable case here is Salman Rushdie's, but the conflict between our head teacher and the Muslim parents falls into the same class. Problems arise here not because of uncertainty about what to do, but because of its opposite – people with incompatible views nevertheless all think they know what should be done. Muslim fundamentalists are certain that Salman Rushdie should be killed, and liberal devotees of free speech are certain that he should not – some are certain that those prepared to shoot him should themselves be shot. Similarly, both head teacher and parents were convinced they were doing right by the girl. The problem is that because all these certainties proceed from different value systems, actions perceived by each side as virtuous are likely to inflict what one side or the other perceives as harms. In practical terms, each side is, so to speak, constantly getting in the other's way: they cannot live together. Thus the practical question is essentially a political one: what should be done about this uneasy relationship, which is so productive of social strife?

What do we expect of reason here? Note first that the conflict between Muslim and liberal fundamentalists is just the sort of case in which we wish that both sides would listen to reason, and that led Locke to urge the advantages of reason over zeal. What do we think they will hear when reason speaks? Surely, that continued practical prosecution of the conflict can only lead to multiplication of harms all round: harms which can be recognized as such by *both* sides, so that it would be *rational* for both sides to moderate their zeal, and to seek some form of accommodation. Reason, in other words, is here *practical reason*, and speaks on the basis of *universal*, rather than local, human interests or needs, which the two sides can thus have in common.

The object of practical reason is the right thing to do. Practical reason finds the right thing to do at a particular time in particular circumstances by considering possibilities in relation to objectives. Right for whom? For anyone who is pursuing those objectives. Practical reason tells you how to get there (to those objectives) from here. Philosophy has traditionally but somewhat misleadingly called this the devising of means to ends. I say "misleadingly" because the description makes the task seem straightforwardly instrumental. How much more complex and variously problematic it is will be seen if one considers, for instance, the problem of finding the right thing to do in 1995 to achieve the objective of peace and justice in what used to be Yugoslavia. The deductions of geometrical reason are trivial amusements compared to practical reason's task of finding the right thing to do in that particular case. The task is clearly not the merely instrumental one of devising means (though that is hard enough in this case). For before that can start, practical reason would have to decide *what might count* as achieving justice and peace in former Yugoslavia. Speculative reason might possibly contribute to this task, perhaps even along the lines Locke proposed, but it could not accomplish it alone; for any theoretical insights it might offer about justice and peace in general would need to be applied to Yugoslavia's current situation in particular. This would involve *envisaging concrete realizations* of the theoretical insights about justice and peace in relation to the particular circumstances of the case. This requires, not "pure reason," reason purged of empiricism, but both knowledge of particular facts and exercise of imagination; one would have to imagine what a just and peaceful Yugoslavia continuous with the currently unjust and war-torn one might look like. All this is nonetheless part of practical reason. Philosophy's historical opposition of reason to both experience and imagination is another mistake brought on by the seductions of geometry.

Having decided what concrete states of affairs would realize justice and peace in Yugoslavia, practical reason must decide which of these to aim at; and for this it must make judgments about how feasible all the various candidates are, perhaps consider how close they are to an impossible ideal situation (which it would also have to imagine), and select the best one to go for in the light of (at least) all that. This is before devising the means has even started. And in the case of Yugoslavia it is all too clear how badly we have done with devising means: perhaps partly because too little attention was paid to the crucial prior task of delineating the objective in concrete terms – the first task of practical reason, and, as I have described it, clearly a part of *moral* thinking, though made invisible by post-Kantian philosophy. In the case of Yugoslavia, instead of tackling this primary rational task, we bystanders were alternately hurried on by moral outrage and held back by self-interest. As a result we got it wrong. There is currently (1995) neither justice nor peace in Yugoslavia. Our failure illustrates what it is to allow the passions to overcome reason, and why moralists through the centuries have urged us to avoid it. I have in

147

mind here our – bystanders' – passions: feelings of moral outrage replacing practical moral reason, and local self-interest defeating recognition of the common need for peace and justice in the world.

Practical reason tried to resolve the Salman Rushdie conflict by pointing out to both sides that they had interests – universal human interests – in common. We can now understand the function of assuming a universal human nature, why the assumption is so crucial – and why it is in fact unproblematic, despite its theoretical inaccessibility. It is crucial because universal nature and needs provide the shared starting points which allow the arguments of practical reason to exert leverage across cultural barriers. The starting points of practical argument are indeed written in the book of human nature, just as the starting points of Christian argument are written in Scripture. They are also unproblematic because whatever their cultural expression, when it comes to conflict resolution, as soon as some interaction and communication is taking place, universal needs and values are usually recognizable in practice – though cultural values may well often prevent them from exerting as much leverage as reasonable people hope. Nevertheless, that such arguments are at least possible makes practical reason, in partnership with the assumption of a universal human nature, a natural reconciler; its exercise is the path of choice for conflict resolution, because it seeks out what unites people in the teeth of what divides them. That is why we urge parties to a conflict to listen to reason, and feel sure that there is a reason for them to listen to; we are as sure of this as we are sure they are human. "Listen to reason" here means "Attend to the human interests you and your opponent have in common," and thus, "Get going with a bit of practical reason." That is why we call people who intransigently insist on differences and ignore commonalities *unreasonable*. They are unreasonable because *in practice* they are refusing to admit universal truths (about needs and values); though they may admit them in theory, they are refusing to act on them.

The conception of a universal human nature does not, however, have the most important function originally attributed to it: exclusion of the intolerable. How then is this exclusion to be done, since, as we saw, one of "pure" reason's successes was showing that we cannot be required to tolerate everything? The answer is that we do not need to claim culture-neutral universality to exclude – except insofar as we claim that the existing public morality of our state, like every such public morality, has culture-neutral values embedded in it. Local moralities, including ours, will already designate some things as intolerable. Changing circumstances may make those designations themselves intolerable to those living under them. Whether and how to redefine the intolerable must then be a political, not a theoretical, decision, an inseparable part of the cross-cultural collaborative effort to formulate a new public morality which, as I suggested earlier, constitutes multiculturalism. The intention is, of course, that the new morality should incorporate universal morality. The assumptions about universal human nature allow us to say that whether it does can only be determined empirically, by whether it can itself be tolerated. Note that, as in the case of Yugoslavia, the first essential here is not theoretical understanding of local public values, and of their possible replacements (though that may help), but the recognition, and envisaging, of their present, and future, concrete realizations – or non-realizations.

On the way to the new public morality, however, conflicts are bound to arise. Our Muslim parents and head teacher are a case in point. How does practical reason deal with these in the meanwhile? The assumption here is that we are facing conflicts which are insoluble at the level of belief. That is, we cannot show those who appear to believe incompatible things that the things they believe aren't really incompatible: the solution aimed at by geometrical reason. If they are to be resolvable at all, therefore, it must be at the level of practice. Compare the resolution of differences over child-rearing in interfaith marriages. One common solution is agreement that the children be reared in one faith till they are of an age when they can decide for themselves, when they may be exposed to the other. The conflicting beliefs remain the same, but a way is found of accommodating both in practice. The two sides devise a *modus vivendi,* a way of living that accommodates the beliefs of both.

Seeking a *modus vivendi,* a stable, practically rational solution, imposes (practically) rational requirements on both sides; these are moral virtues which optimize the chances of finding a stable solution, analogous to the intellectual virtues which optimize the chances of finding the truth. The first of these is toleration, for the first essential is that both sides accept the common aim of finding a *modus vivendi;* that is, they must *want* to live together, and give up wanting to impose their will each on the other. What else is toleration? Locke's words again come appositely: He who will list himself under the banner of multiculturalism must in the first place, and above all things, make war upon his own lusts and vices. Lust for temporal dominion must be given up. Obviously those who already possess temporal dominion, or think they have a good chance of achieving it, are unlikely to want to give it up. But equally obviously, rational resolution of conflict, as distinct from war, is impossible without this relinquishment. *Thus a condition on toleration is distribution of power.* It is folly to expect toleration if power is all on one side. With this we return to our point of departure at the beginning of this chapter.

Morality and the current constitution of society are inseparable. Producing particular virtues is as much dependent on creation of the social conditions that will allow them to flourish as on individual upbringing. We are social beings. Pure individualism, no less than pure communism, asks too much of people morally.

Now, clearly practical reason cannot find a *modus vivendi* for conflicting moral views if the parties refuse outright to contemplate its possibility, refuse to tolerate the opposing view. In that case all that practical reason could offer *both* sides by way of conflict resolution would be total separation. This may not satisfy justice. But without society there is no morality, and society has been rejected by both sides: for to reject toleration is to reject commitment to finding a *modus vivendi*, and that in turn is to reject membership in a common society.

Success in actually finding a *modus vivendi* requires further virtues. A stable *modus vivendi* will likely consist in either side so moderating its behavior in the light of the other's values, without abandoning its own, as to ensure that each gets in the way of the other as little as possible. For this the two sides need to understand each other. The moral analyses conducted by geometrical reason may possibly be of some help here – to explain and clarify, even if not to convince. Setting out logical relationships is, after all, a way of spelling out what things mean; if any premises are shared, the logical relationships may also convince, so that the moralities come closer together.

However, intellectual understanding alone is not enough. Each side must also acknowledge the moral sensitivities of the other, and be prepared, so far as it can without outraging its own morality, to adjust its behavior accordingly. This is what constitutes *respecting the other's moral views*. Finding out how to adjust behavior will require a great deal of mutual understanding, a great deal of what one might call *moral translation*: trying to understand the *point* of the other side's values by reinterpreting them in terms of one's own. This will involve imaginative transposition of oneself into the other side's position, or what Hume called *sympathy* (but is often nowadays called empathy). A presupposition of efforts at sympathy is, again, the presupposition of a universal human nature. And since sympathy for profoundly alien views may be very hard, the presupposition must amount to *faith* – sometimes in the teeth of the evidence, as with Locke's faith that the Bible was not contrary to reason in the teeth of the contradictions derivable from it. Not everyone will share his view of the Bible, but I think his instincts were right; faith in the reasonableness of his religion was the only dam he could build to keep back sectarian war. Similarly, determined faith in a universal human nature, making understanding through sympathy feasible, may be the only possible dam against cross-cultural value conflict within the state. Whatever the truth about universal human nature, we cannot afford not to believe in it.

However, sympathy is not a matter of *blind* faith. On the contrary, successful exercise of sympathy will also involve exercise of the intellectual virtues, for one must not just feel for the other person – one must try to feel and see *as the other person feels and sees*, and, if success is to be achieved in the final task, *get this right*. The best evidence that one *has* got it right is success in the final task. For the final task is *envisaging a practical solution which recognizes all the moral sensitivities involved*, and if sympathy is mistaken, so will the practical solution be. As we saw in the case of Yugoslavia, however, we are not there yet. We also have to identify which of the possible solutions envisaged does the best job of recognizing the moral sensitivities, is the most feasible, coheres best with our other objectives, and so on, and devise the means of achieving it.

Apply all this now to the case of the Muslim girl, considered as a case of external conflict between the Muslim community, represented by the parents, and the (non-Muslim) school system as a whole with its matrix culture, represented by the head teacher. Separation here is a possible option in the individual case – British education law allows for education at home, under state inspection – but is not feasible in the case of the whole community; and in any case, one of the moral sensitivities involved is that, for the host culture (in the person of the head teacher), the wishes of the girl to remain in the school, and to participate fully in its activities, count for something; as does, of course, the value the school attaches to the activities. Practical reason requires that the parents acknowledge all this, and try to understand it. However, it also requires that the head teacher try to understand the parents' fears. Achievement of mutual understanding might enable the parents to value the school activities enough to cooperate in the effort to find ways of allowing their daughter to participate, while the school tries to see how to modify the organization of its activities in such a way that she could participate without offending the parents. Of course, mutual understanding may not carry the parties that far: practical reason does not guarantee solutions. The limit is always everyone's ingenuity and goodwill, as well as practical constraints. But on the other hand, this limit rarely if ever rules out the possibility of rational solutions *a priori*. And the effort to reach agreement is potentially a source of new moral insights into the strengths and weaknesses of one's own morality: comparing it with another's is, as we have seen, the only way of getting a glimpse of universal human nature. It is, moreover, a way open to anybody, not just to highly educated experts. Thus the modest aim of finding a *modus vivendi* is a step on the road to the wider political objective of achieving a shared public morality. Perhaps it is the road itself.

MORAL CONFLICT AND CONFLICTS OF INTERESTS

What exactly is this road? What in fact we have found is that practical reason solves fundamental or ineliminable moral conflicts as if they were conflicts of interests – by negotiation. This may alarm those who are accustomed to think of morality and interest as mutually exclusive, but it should not. For obviously, to someone who doesn't share it, a moral belief *is* a kind of interest – a *moral* interest, if you like. "Moral interest" may sound self-contradictory. But consider: parties with different moral beliefs are almost bound to come into conflict at the level of action. To them, it is objectively good that the world be a certain way, but the ways they want the world to be are incompatible. Now, an ordinary interest too is a relation between the good and a state of the world – only this time, *someone's* good, instead of the objective good. And just as I can be presumed to desire the states of the world which are in my interest, so our two conflicting sides can be presumed to desire that the world be the way that seems to them objectively good. So it seems quite natural to say that our two conflicting sides each *have an interest* in the world's being their way – but a *moral*, not an ordinary, interest. What makes it feel contradictory is the connection between interest in the ordinary sense and purely personal good, since by definition, what distinguishes moral good is that it is not purely personal. Room is made for moral interests, however, by the assumption that neither side can *know* what the objective good (or universal morality) is – the conflict is in fact over presumed *versions* of it.

Given that degree of rational uncertainty in morals, one can define moral interest as follows: I have a moral interest in the world's being thus and so if and only if (i) I continue to believe that it is objectively good that the world be thus and so, despite knowing that others believe otherwise, and (ii) because I believe as I do, I desire that my beliefs rather than theirs be expressed in practice. Moral interests, like ordinary interests, are thus relationships between personal desires and states of the world.

This means that for practical purposes, the ineliminable moral conflicts that give rise to conflicts of moral interest are just like the kinds of irreconcilable conflict of ordinary interest that can only be addressed by negotiation. (Other kinds are resolved by showing that what looked like a conflict of interests wasn't one really. Such cases are just like resolvable moral conflicts: a wage-cut perceived by the workers as the result of a conflict of interests between them and the management may be defended on the grounds that it is really in the interests of the workers to take a wage-cut, as otherwise the company will go under.) For the underlying assumption of negotiation is that the conflict of interests addressed *is* irreconcilable: what makes negotiation necessary is that the world and its inhabitants are locally such that what serves one party's interest, injures the other's. Just so, in fundamental moral conflict what seems virtuous to me seems vicious to you.

This brings negotiated conflict resolution within reach in the moral case, too. Theoretically unresolvable moral conflicts can, like irreconcilable conflicts of interests, be solved at the level of practice by trade-offs of moral interest between negotiating parties. In negotiation, the question is, What is each side prepared to concede in return for what? (How far towards the pro-/anti-abortion view is the anti/pro-abortionist prepared to go? How much of what I want in higher wages are you prepared to give me in return for my giving you this degree of change in working practices?) Neither side of a negotiation is prepared to sacrifice its central interest entirely – just as neither party to a moral conflict is usually willing to sacrifice its central moral interest. This irreconcilability is what makes negotiation necessary; and the result of negotiation is not elimination of conflict, but a bargain, which both sides are, for the moment, prepared to accept.

However, as I suggested above, serious and sympathetic pursuit of this moral bargain may result in moral interests becoming reconciled. This is because of the ways in which moral interest is *unlike* ordinary interest. For what has to be presumed by all parties to a moral conflict is that the moral good is in all of our interests.

THE LIMITS OF REASON

I want to finish by saying a very few words about what is probably the most important subject of all. It has to be emphasized that in morals, practical reason cannot stand alone. It cannot work without its attendant virtues, whose necessity was explained above. But I have left the primary virtue till the last.

My recipe for rational conflict resolution essentially involves trying to understand the needs of others. Practical reason will not work – will not resolve conflicts satisfactorily – unless we get this right. But we cannot understand the needs of others unless we approach them with something more than reason, something more than respect; we need as well something traditional morality has long recognized as central, but about which moral philosophy has had surprisingly little to say: namely, love. What is conspicuously lacking in Yugoslavia is not just reason: it is also love. I have no space to say more here than that love is not a feeling, that it is inseparable from moral reason, and that it is the first necessity of social cohesion. Recall Locke's insistence on the need for charity: once more, he was right. For there is a human, as well as a Christian, imperative of love, just as there is a human, as well as a Christian, imperative of toleration. (In fact, I think the Christian imperatives borrow plausibility from the human ones.) To live together harmoniously, the good of others must be at least minimally the object of all, or social strains and enmities will develop which threaten all. Loving others is taking their good as an object. But multicultural living imposes special strains, which demand a more strenuous form or manifestation of love; I have in mind something like Simone Weil's concept of *attention*.[19] Attention is what it takes to understand the stranger. Without attention, understanding of strangers is impossible, and without that understanding, multiculturalism is impossible. Hence the second quotation from Mary Wollstonecraft at the head of this chapter: "the most perfect education . . . is such an exercise of the *understanding* as is best calculated to strengthen the body and *form the heart*" (my emphasis). I read this as, The heart must be formed to love by the understanding. Love wants what is best, reason sees what is best; love cannot know what is best without reason – but reason cannot see what is best without love. It would take another essay to explain why.

NOTES

1. Mary Wollstonecraft, *A Vindication of the Rights of Woman*, vol. 5 of *The Works of Mary Wollstonecraft*, ed. Janet Todd and Marilyn Butler (Washington Square, N.Y.: New York University Press, 1989), chap. 2, p. 90.
2. I first became aware of the shape of the connection between multiculturalism and Locke from an article by Amy Gutmann and Dennis Thompson, "Moral Conflict and Political Consensus," *Ethics* 101 (October 1990): 64–88; responding to Gutmann's "The Challenge of Multiculturalism in Ethics" (private communication) further developed the ideas in this essay, and for all this I am duly grateful. However, it will be seen that my view of Locke is not Gutmann's, nor is my conception of the relationship between his arguments for toleration and multiculturalism. Her view and mine follow the same contour, but there is a great gulf between.
3. Simone Weil, *Gravity and Grace*, trans. Arthur Wills (New York: Octagon Books, 1979), p. 169.
4. John Locke, *A Letter concerning Toleration*, ed. M. Montuori (The Hague: Martinus Nijhoff, 1963), p. 37; all subsequent references to this work are to this edition.
5. Ibid., p. 7; his emphasis.
6. Ibid., pp. 7, 9.
7. Ibid., p. 43.
8. Ibid., p. 35.

9. On this see L. J. Jordanova, "Natural Facts: A Historical Perspective on Science and Sexuality," in *Nature, Culture and Gender*, ed. C. MacCormack and M. Strathern (Cambridge: Cambridge University Press, 1980); and L. J. Jordanova, *Sexual Visions* (London: Harvester Wheatsheaf, 1989).

10. I. Kant, *Grundlagen zur Metaphysik der Sitten* (*Foundations of the Metaphysics of Morals*), 1785.

11. John Rawls, *A Theory of Justice* (Oxford: Oxford University Press, 1972).

12. A collection of articles discussing and often dissenting from Rawls's *Theory of Justice* soon appeared: Norman Daniels, ed., *Reading Rawls* (New York: Basic Books, 1975). The stream of literature on Rawls has continued unabated.

13. Simone Weil, *The Need for Roots: Prelude to a Declaration of Duties Towards Mankind* (London: Routledge & Kegan Paul, 1952), pp. 3–41.

14. Colin Turnbull, *The Mountain People* (London: Picador, 1974). On the evidence of Turnbull's own descriptions of the Ik, I strongly dissent from his view of them, which (astonishingly for an anthropologist) is strikingly monocultural. See my "Morality, Survival and Nuclear War" in *Objectivity and Cultural Divergence*, ed. S. C. Brown (Cambridge: Cambridge University Press, 1984). Indeed, so strong is my dissent from Turnbull that I am moved to quote Dorothy Parker: "This book should not be tossed lightly aside. It should be thrown with force."

15. Aristotle, *Nicomachean Ethics* IV, 2–3, 1122a-1125b.

16. Humanist criticism of language was essentially moral as well as aesthetic. See Lorenzo Valla, *The Profession of the Religious and the Principal Arguments from The Falsely Believed and Forged Donation of Constantine*, trans. and ed. Olga Zorzi Pugliese (Toronto: Toronto Centre for Reformation and Renaissance Studies, 1985). Valla scorned Scholastic logic as boring as well as misleading, and initiated philological criticism of the Bible, which did not endear him to the Church.

17. Bruno Bettelheim, *Freud and Man's Soul* (London: Chatto Windus/Hogarth Press, 1983).

18. Plato, *Republic* I, 331e.

19. Simone Weil, *Gravity and Grace*, pp. 169–76.

Chapter 7

Challenges of multiculturalism in democratic education

AMY GUTMANN

How can a multicultural society educate its members for democracy? Many contemporary controversies about public schooling turn on the clash of two apparently competing educational aims: securing common values and respecting cultural differences.[1] This chapter argues that democratic education can integrate both civic and multicultural aims, and not merely in a pragmatic compromise but in a genuinely principled combination. At the outset, I describe two responses that fail to do justice to both aims. One response sets the project of civic unity against the diversifying tendencies of multiculturalism; the second puts cultural diversity above the claims of civic education. Both responses reflect significant political impulses in the United States and throughout the world, and both contain partial insights. I try to capture the partial truth in each and integrate them into a democratic conception of civic *and* multicultural education.

The second part of the chapter develops the integration by considering a test case – a recent French controversy known as the "Affair of the Scarf" or the "chador case" – that highlights one of the deepest conflicts endemic to multicultural societies. Can a conception of democratic education at least provisionally resolve conflicts between religious toleration and the other civic aims of democratic education? I show how a democratic response to this case can respect a wide range of cultural differences without sacrificing the aims of teaching a common set of civic values to all citizens.

The last part of the chapter distinguishes multiculturalism from multinationalism, and explores the even greater challenge that multinationalism poses for civic education. Despite the difference between multinationalism and multiculturalism, there is a significant parallel between the democratic responses to these two challenges, pertaining to the importance of teaching children about foreign cultures.

CIVIC EDUCATION, CULTURAL DIFFERENCES, AND MUTUAL RESPECT

Public schools in the United States once included Protestant prayers and readings from the King James Version of the Bible as central parts of the school day. Little or no effort was made to respect the diverse religious beliefs of non-Protestants. Catholic children were sometimes whipped by teachers if they refused to read from the King James Bible. In the same schools, history was taught largely without reference to, let alone understanding of, the experiences of American Indians, blacks, and women. And, perhaps more significantly, all subjects were taught to racially segregated student bodies, for whom even an inclusive, culturally respectful civics curriculum would have been overwhelmed by the civics lesson in white supremacy implicit in the way children were distributed among schools.

This traditional American model illustrates the problem with a civic education unmodified by multiculturalism. The traditional model withheld respect from different ways of life, and denigrated the contributions of minority groups and women to American civic culture. It also taught morally skewed lessons in civic virtue. When history classes exalted the contributions of the founding fathers with scant discussion of the institution of slavery, the lives of slaves, the Underground Railroad, or the contributions of African-Americans to civic understandings, public schools failed, among other things, to teach students the civic values of democratic dissent and disobedience to unjust laws. In not teaching these democratic values, schools diminished the role of dissenters and restricted the range of reasonable political alternatives that children could understand and embrace.

To cite another, not atypical example, from personal experience: The world history texts in my public school devoted as much space to the heroic acts of righteous Christians in rescuing Jews during the Holocaust as to the unaverted slaughter of millions of Jews. These texts sent an unsubtle signal, not only to me but to every student who read them, that some people count for more than others in this country. These texts also failed to convey how the historical experiences of minorities can offer American citizens a more adequate understanding of our civic values of "liberty and justice for all."

These purportedly patriotic history lessons were *repressive*. They simultaneously restricted understanding of diverse ways of life and denigrated the people who lived those lives. Repression in schooling is commonly identified with banning books and punishing teachers or students for unpopular ideas. But schooling is often repressive, and more insidiously so, by virtue of what it fails to teach. A civic

education is repressive when it fails to teach appreciation and respect for the positive contributions by minorities to a society's common culture.

An antidote to this traditional civics curriculum is education that aims to understand and appreciate the social contributions and life experiences of the various groups that constitute society. Such understanding and appreciation define one common conception of multicultural education, a conception compatible with the principles of democratic education.

Some contemporary American educators, however, defend schooling that is multicultural in a dramatically different sense. They defend schools designed primarily to sustain the separatist cultural identities of minorities and to bolster the self-esteem of students on the basis of their membership in a separatist culture. Afrocentrism is a currently controversial instance of such a separatist multicultural perspective, but the perspective is not unique to Afrocentrism or new to American education. Some fundamentalist Christian academies are designed to serve a similar if less publicly heralded and criticized purpose.

I mean by Afrocentrism not simply the teaching of black students about Africa or African history. Afrocentrism "puts Africa at the center," morally and historically. It teaches that Africa is the birthplace of humanity and the seat of the first great civilizations, from which others are derivative.[2] It teaches that medicine, science, and mathematics originated in Africa, and that African values are superior to Western values.[3]

Some of the historical revisionism in Afrocentrism possibly constitutes an important challenge to established historical understandings, but a troubling amount of Afrocentric history can at best be considered mythology and at worst fabrication. The inaccuracy of Afrocentrism is only part of what makes it problematic as an educational movement. The chief problem with Afrocentric education from a democratic perspective is not inaccuracy but *discrimination*. Its cultivation of a reverse racial mythology and sense of racial superiority makes Afrocentrism an uncivic ideology. Democratic governments cannot prevent private individuals and associations from conveying to children a sense of superiority based on race, religion, gender, or class, but they need not and ought not support schools that convey the very disrespect that democratic education should be designed to dispel.

Even if teaching students to identify with the superior contributions of their ancestors bolsters their *self-esteem* – "the favorable appreciation or opinion of oneself" – it can do so only at the cost of undercutting *mutual respect* among citizens – "a proper regard for the dignity of [a] person or position."[4] In a democracy, proper regard for

the position of citizen includes the mutual recognition that all persons, regardless of the accomplishments of their ancestors, are entitled to equal political and civil liberties, adequate opportunity to choose among good lives, and a fair chance to compete for scarce social offices.

Public schooling in a democracy need not forswear the aim of increasing the self-esteem of minority students or women. I have argued only that public schools should not try to increase self-esteem by discriminatory means, such as crediting to particular groups of students the superiority of their ancestors. This aim is to be distinguished from recognizing and respecting the identification individuals make with particular cultures. This identification is something that public schooling can support, as a way of respecting students with different cultural identifications, and also as a way of recognizing the multitude of cultural opportunities that are open to all students as members of a multicultural society. Imagine a curriculum in which the achievements of Africa and Africans, ancient and modern, are given due place alongside the treatment of other continents and peoples, and in which the links – causal, cultural, and emotional – between the history of Africa and the history of African-Americans are made plain. Such a curriculum taught to *all* students puts multicultural education in service to democratic values, not in opposition. Such a curriculum supports rather than subverts one of the most basic lessons of democratic education: that all individuals, regardless of their cultural identifications, have equal civic standing, and are not rightly honored, or dishonored, or otherwise judged by the acts of their ancestors.

For schools to cultivate a sense of self-esteem that is sustainable alongside mutual respect among citizens, they have no alternative but to help every student succeed academically. Schools can teach students to appreciate themselves as accomplished individuals by helping them become accomplished learners. That educational task is a lot harder than teaching students to identify with their ancestors, which may explain why attempts to increase self-esteem through group identification vary inversely with the educational success of American schools. Educational success entails learning something that is worthy of being publicly honored as knowledge and (moral, empirical, or analytical) understanding.[5] The fact that educational success, like self-esteem, is achieved by individuals does not mean that its attainment must be a solitary endeavor. Some of the most successful teaching occurs in cooperative and diverse learning groups. But self-esteem and educational success, understood as compatible with treating people as equals, cannot be acquired by group identification.

We have now identified two mistaken responses to the apparently competing educational aims of securing common values and respecting cultural differences: the traditional American civics curriculum that imposed a unity of view false to the pluralism of American life and disrespectful of many of its citizens, and a separatist curriculum that educates by exclusion, fostering a sense of superiority among some students at the cost of disparaging others. Neither response promotes mutual respect.

Teaching mutual respect is a crucial aim of democratic education. Mutual respect is a public good as well as a private good in a democratic society. It expresses the equal standing of every person as an individual and citizen, and it also enables democratic citizens to discuss their political differences in a productive way, first by understanding one another's perspectives and then by trying to find fair ways of resolving their disagreements. Schools can teach mutual respect in at least two ways that avoid pitting civic aims against multicultural aims to the detriment of both.

First, schools can create curricula that recognize the multicultural heritage of the United States as everyone's resource, belonging not only to all of us but also to future immigrants and generations to come. In addition, there is a civic as well as a purely intellectual reason for schools to teach about cultures that are presently foreign to the United States. This is a country of immigrants, and if it is to remain a haven for political and economic refugees, we need to respect cultures that are not presently represented within our borders. Recognition of foreign cultures cannot of course be comprehensive. But then, cultivating a relatively deep appreciation of only a few foreign cultures may well be more effective than conveying a superficial familiarity with many.

Cultural inclusiveness in a curriculum is not enough to teach students the civic virtue of mutual respect, nor is it the toughest task now facing most schools. There is a second, more pedagogically (and politically) demanding way in which schools can support mutual respect among citizens. They can teach students how to engage together in respectful discussions in which they strive to understand, appreciate, and, if possible, resolve political disagreements that are partly rooted in cultural differences. Mutual respect that rests only on recognition of cultural diversity is an incomplete democratic virtue. Recognition needs to be accompanied by a willingness and ability to deliberate about politically relevant disagreements.

A culturally diverse citizenry dedicated to deliberation strives for reciprocity in political relationships. It seeks agreement on public policies that are justifiable (as far as possible) to all citizens who are bound by them. Reciprocity is not a goal likely to be fully realized. Rather, it is an ongoing aspiration, constitutive of democracy under-

stood as a political ideal. By teaching the skills and virtues of deliberation, schools can contribute to bringing a democracy closer to its own
ideal.

There are ways of approaching, if not completely realizing, the
educational aims of inclusive multiculturalism and morally informed
deliberation. We can find examples of promising practices in existing
schools, including non-elite public schools. Deborah Meier's pioneering District 4 in East Harlem and California's statewide history curriculum offer different models of an inclusive multicultural curriculum.
Neither model is perfect, but both are far better than anything that
has gone before them. Meier's school is successful both by traditional
measures (increased reading and mathematical achievement scores)
and non-traditional measures (integration of a multiracial student
body).

One of the best illustrations of teaching the virtues and skills of
morally informed deliberation comes from an account of an American
history class in a Brooklyn high school, where students were asked
whether it was moral for the United States to drop the atomic bomb
on Japan:

> The lesson was taught in a Socratic manner. Bruckner [the teacher]
> did not lecture. He asked questions and kept up a rapid-fire dialogue
> among the students. "Why?" "How do you know?" "What does this
> mean?" . . . By the time the class was finished, the students had cov-
> ered a great deal of material about American foreign and domestic
> politics during World War II; they had argued heatedly; most of them
> had tried out different points of view, seeing the problem from different
> angles.[6]

An inclusive multicultural curriculum encourages students who
identify with different cultural groups to respect each other as equal
citizens, regardless of the accomplishments of their ancestors, and to
take different points of view seriously when thinking about politics.
The very practice of morally informed deliberation requires students
to accord each other the mutual respect and moral understanding that
are too often lacking in contemporary politics. Teaching mutual respect among citizens in both these ways is a central aim of civic
education in a multicultural democracy. Bolstering self-esteem by
group identification is not, not because self-esteem is unimportant or
unsupportable by education, but because the self-esteem that is compatible with mutual respect among citizens must be earned by individual students (working cooperatively or alone), rather than acquired by means of group identification. Just as a civic education
unmodified by multiculturalism represses cultural differences, so too
a multiculturalism uninformed by civic values discriminates among
citizens on the basis of their group identities. Schools can meet the

challenge of multiculturalism by linking common civic values with uncommon cultural appreciations.

DEMOCRATIC MULTICULTURAL EDUCATION AND "THE AFFAIR OF THE SCARF"

In the first section, I criticized two common approaches to the challenge of multiculturalism in a democratic society. One response speaks in the voice of a transcendent universalism, the other in the voice of a separatist particularism. But both speak misleadingly in these voices, in that they fail to do justice to the important values that universalism and particularism represent. A common civic education can, and should, express universal values, but it cannot completely transcend particular cultures. Education can and should help sustain a diversity of cultures, but not at the expense of universalist values such as equal liberty, opportunity, and mutual respect among citizens.

Easier said than done, a critic might reply. The proposed democratic integration of multiculturalism and civic education has yet to confront one of the most formidable challenges of cultural difference within democracy, that which involves religious conviction. To meet this challenge, consider a controversy in which the aims of civic education seem to be at odds with an inclusive multiculturalism committed to accommodating religious freedom.

In 1989, three Muslim adolescent girls went to their local public high school in Creil, France, wearing chadors, head coverings that are associated with orthodox Islam. French public schools are, by law and centuries-long tradition, secular. A 1937 law prohibits the wearing of religious symbols, or at least conspicuous religious symbols, in government-run schools. (Parents may send their children to private schools that teach religion, but these schools charge tuition and many families cannot afford them.) Citing the 1937 law, the principal of the high school, a Catholic of Martinican origin, told the three students that they must remove their chadors in class. When they refused, the principal, supported by the school's teachers, forbade the girls to attend class.[7]

Controversies like this one pose perhaps the toughest challenge of multiculturalism to a universalist conception of civic education. The chador case divided not only French society, but French socialists, who consider themselves as universalist as anyone. Although the socialists could unite in criticizing reactions like those of the conservative newspaper *Le Point*, whose headline read "Should We Let Islam Colonize Our Schools?" and the right-wing politician Le Pen, who urged the repatriation of all immigrants who had arrived in France since 1974, they were bitterly divided among themselves. Some socialists found themselves allied with conservatives in defending the 1937 law, while others proclaimed it unjust.[8] The debate among socialists helps demonstrate why transcendent universalism is inadequate as a public educational philosophy, and points us to a more defensible way of posing and provisionally resolving such problems.

Socialists who supported the 1937 law argued that the veil is "a sign of imprisonment that considers women to be subhumans under the law of Islam" and should therefore not be admitted by a public educational system committed to teaching gender equality. In opposition to the law, Prime Minister Michel Rocard said that "tolerance must be put before principle." We might say that religious toleration itself is a universal principle to be considered alongside the principle of teaching gender equality.[9] Invoking universal values alone therefore does not resolve the conflict, since religious toleration and gender equality – principles at the core of this moral conflict and many others – both are universal. (To say a value is universal does not of course mean that it *is* universally accepted but only that it *should* be by all people who find themselves in similar social and political circumstances.)

Even after we reject appeals to an exclusionary nationalism, the question therefore remains: If French public schools are committed to universalism, which universal value should take priority in the case of conflict? Should universalists agree with Mme. Mitterand, who took the position that public schools should tolerate all religious symbols, even those that express gender inequality, because teaching religious toleration takes priority over teaching gender equality? Or should they side with Gisele Halimi, a founding member of a prominent anti-racist organization, *SOS-Racism*, who argued that distinctively public (or civic) values rather than private (or personal) values should be taught in public schools? The social equality of men and women is a public value, Halimi argued. The chador is "a humiliating form of dress" symbolizing gender subordination and therefore has no legitimate place in public schools.[10] Each argument invokes universal values, but they support conflicting conclusions.

The indeterminacy of universalism is not a sufficient reason to abandon it, unless particularism carries with it better moral arguments. Does particularism get the better of universalism in this conflict? A great attraction of particularism is that it offers religious parents effective access to schools that reflect their religious perspectives. Divide the French school system into streams, particularists argue, and give every major cultural group the effective opportunity to shape the schooling of its own children. The French government could authorize each major community, including secularists, to run its own publicly subsidized schools. French secular schools could remain strictly secular, while orthodox Catholics, Muslims, and Jews (among other groups) could send their children to subsidized schools committed to reinforcing their particular communal values. If the government subsidizes separate schooling for each group, then no group needs to compromise its particularist values for the sake of a common civic education.

Although the particularist response would require a radical restructuring of French education, it cannot be rejected on grounds that its values are foreign to French social understandings. Asked about the situation of orthodox Jewish students in France who wish to wear yarmulkes, Sabine Roitman of the Representative Council of Jewish Institutions in France responded that "Jewish students have had little trouble with the issue, because those who want to wear yarmulkes generally attend private religious schools."[11] What about the fact that many parents, like those of the Muslim girls, cannot afford the private schools of their choice? Particularists also have a reasonable response to this challenge: they can defend public subsidies for all schools, religious as well as secular.

Something is still missing from particularism that democratic integration with universalism can provide. A major weakness of this particularist response to religious diversity is its neglect, or downplaying, of the government's role in regulating the schools that it subsidizes. The particularist response turns out to be indeterminate when it comes to specifying what constitutes legitimate state regulation of schools so as to ensure that they adequately educate future citizens. It is this aim of educating future citizens that justifies massive state subsidies of schooling. So particularism cannot escape the question, What may citizens reasonably expect of schools as a condition of their receiving public funding and accreditation? The relative silence of particularism in response to this question sustains the worry that separatist schooling is not designed to promote the civic values that justify public funding of schooling in the first place.

Unless schools serve civic purposes that citizens can share, why should their support not be left at least primarily to parents and private associations? In response to this challenge, some particularists recognize that all streams of schooling should be publicly regulated to the extent necessary to ensure that they promote civic educational purposes. This recognition opens the door to giving precedence to democratic principles (such as the teaching of toleration and mutual respect across cultural differences) over particularistic purposes. Particularism, so modified, is far more defensible, but it no longer can claim the attraction of avoiding controversies over the content of civic education by ceding to each religious group its own autonomous sphere of schooling. Nor is it easy to distinguish this kind of particularism from a universalism that recognizes the value of religious diversity.

The problems of unregulated particularism are the mirror-image of those confronting a universalism that tries to transcend particularist cultures. While transcendent universalism expects too much uniformity in the content of public schooling, separatist particularism expects too little. By minimizing state regulation, particularism forsakes a commitment to teaching the public values that constitute mutual respect among citizens, even though these values can be justified to (almost) all citizens.

Public schools are the primary institution by which a democratic society educates future citizens, preparing them to share in responsible self-government. Teaching the elements of responsible self-government – which include toleration, racial and sexual nondiscrimination, and deliberation on politically relevant issues – is therefore a major reason for mandating and publicly subsidizing schooling for all children. These and other lessons in liberty, opportunity, and deliberation are essential to public schooling in liberal democracies, or aspiring liberal democracies. The very attraction of some culturally segregated schools to some people – their ability to preempt political disputes that are generated by cultural diversity – stems from a serious democratic defect. Such schools neglect teaching some of the public values that are central to democratic education, in particular, deliberation among a culturally diverse citizenry.[12]

Suppose we grant that teaching students the values of basic liberty, opportunity, and deliberation is a primary purpose of public education. We must still wonder whether any conception of education that recognizes this purpose can find a way of resolving the chador case and similar conflicts that pit civic education and cultural diversity against each other. Is there a way of resolving the conflict between religious freedom and a civic education that aims to educate children for the rights and responsibilities of citizenship, where religious beliefs apparently conflict with the aims of civic education?

We cannot defer as a matter of principle to religious freedom regardless of its claims against civic education, as does a particularism unmodified by civic values. Nor can we defer as a matter of principle to a civic education that would expel religious dissenters, regardless of the content of their claims against civic education, as would one version of the universalism represented by the French left – a transcendent universalism that is unmodified by particularist values. This kind of universalism in effect denies that religious freedom, like freedom of conscience more generally, is a basic liberty, necessary to the integrity of persons as we know them.

Public schools have a responsibility to teach and practice religious toleration as *part* of civic education. Both a universalism that respects particular values and a particularism that respects civic values can recognize this responsibility. The critical question remains, To what extent can schools teach and practice religious toleration without sacrificing the other civic values that support basic liberty, opportunity, and mutual respect among citizens? A conception of democratic education directly confronts this question in the face of challenges like the one posed by the chador case.

We can begin to answer the question by recognizing that there are principled limits to the religious freedom that the law must respect, and therefore also limits to the religious practices that a public school must tolerate. (Insisting on wearing a chador is not the same as insisting on being taught in classes that are segregated by religion, gender, ethnicity, or race.) We need to determine the substantive limits of religious toleration in a particular context of public schooling and therefore to consider in the chador case whether the wearing of conspicuous religious symbols, especially religious symbols of gender inequality, in a public school classroom exceeds those limits.

Clearly we can locate religious practices that lie beyond the legally protected realm of religious freedom and toleration. The legally protected realm excludes religious practices that conflict with other basic democratic rights and are themselves less valuable than the particular rights with which they conflict. Examples of religious practices that may be outlawed in order to protect more valuable rights are ritual human sacrifice and the denial of essential health care to children.

In harder cases where rights conflict, we encounter more uncertainty. These conflicts must be resolved, at least provisionally, but they cannot be even provisionally resolved without our rendering some substantive judgment, which will not be neutral among particular ways of life. The position of deferring either to established religious practices or to established state policy is not morally neutral, nor does liberal democracy establish a presumption in favor of either position. We have no better alternative than to assess the conflict as carefully as we can and at the most specific level that public policy can handle. We cannot legitimately counterpoise teaching gender equality against protecting religious freedom in its entirety. Instead, we need to focus on the specific aspects of gender equality and religious freedom that are at issue – the school's obligation to teach students, regardless of their religion or gender, to associate as civic equals in the classroom, and the students' freedom to wear conspicuous religious symbols to school, including those that are commonly associated with gender subordination. We now must ask, Is there any way to reconcile these two apparently conflicting values? If not, which value is the more important to secure in this context?

If we recognize the school's dual responsibility – to teach the civic equality of men and women, and to respect individuals regardless of religious differences insofar as these differences are consistent with civic values – we can develop an alternative way of viewing the conflict, one that is overlooked by both particularism and universalism in their usual, unmodified forms. The alternative consists of a principled integration of the two perspectives. The liberal democratic values that give public schooling its primary social purpose guide the integration. Schools should tolerate the religious difference represented by the chadors without acquiescing in the gender segregation and subordination that often accompanies this dress in religious practice outside schools. The French public schools could have made an educational opportunity out of the girls' wearing of the scarves in school in order to express a democratic commitment to educate all students, regardless of their gender and the religious convictions of their parents.

Schools can teach these democratic lessons in different ways, but the way in which the French government recently resolved the chador controversy is not one of them. In September 1994, the government reversed an earlier ruling by the *Conseil d'Etat* that would have allowed the wearing of chadors in public schools. Under the new policy, students are not permitted to wear "ostentatious religious signs" in the classroom, and chadors, not surprisingly, count as ostentatious signs. Crucifixes and yarmulkes, on the other hand, are considered discreet and are therefore permitted. Thus, Catholic boys and girls who wear crucifixes or Jewish boys who wear yarmulkes will be welcome within French public schools, while Muslim girls who insist on wearing chadors will not.

The previous ruling by the *Conseil d'Etat* had been more defensible on democratic grounds, though it too fell short of a full integration of particularism and universalism. The wearing of religious symbols, the *Conseil* had said, is permissible so long as it does not involve one of the four P's – "pressure on others, provocation, propaganda, or proselytism."[13] The ruling raised a critical question concerning moral responsibility in an educational context: What if the wearing of chadors provokes some students to taunt the girls? The ruling suggested that discipline may be directed to the girls rather than the taunters. Yet this way of resolving the problem of provocation would be unjust to the girls, who should not be held responsible for the uncivil behavior of students who fail to respect their right to religious freedom.

Educators should be able to distinguish such uncivil behavior from another kind of reaction among students, which would be fully consistent with democratic education. The wearing of chadors might provoke criticism among some students for being a symbol of women's second-class citizenship. This criticism, in turn, might provoke the Muslim girls to respond with a defense of their tradition. These forms of civil provocation might be discomforting to all parties, but such discomfort is not unwelcome to democratic education. While multiculturalism informed by democratic principles encourages us to understand the value that different ways of life have for people who live them, it also exposes every way of life to civil criticism.

The democratic rationale for opening schools to the display of religious difference, along with other kinds of cultural difference, is therefore not to protect each particular way of life from criticism or even from erosion in the face of legitimate social pressure.[14] The rationale is rather to encourage citizens to understand and to evaluate politically relevant differences among ways of life. Because some ways of life are more open to criticism and change than others, reflection on politically relevant differences is bound to be more unsettling to some students and citizens than to others, but the non-neutrality of a democratic education is a virtue as well as a necessity. Non-neutrality is a necessity because an educational program would be empty of substance (and perhaps even form!) were it to rest upon neutrality among different conceptions of the good life. Non-neutrality, more interestingly, is a virtue because citizens should not collectively support an educational system that is neutral between those ways of life that respect basic liberty, opportunity, and deliberation, and those that do not. A liberal democracy should take its own side in arguments about teaching the skills and virtues that are constitutive of its own flourishing.

Among the various responses in France to the chador case, the one that best reflects the democratic aim of integrating particularism and universalism was that of Souad Benani, a spokesperson for *Les Nanas Beurs*, an organization of women of North African descent. "As Arab feminists of Muslim culture," Benani said, "we believe that fundamentalism in all its forms is dangerous and the scarf is oppressive. But it should not be used as a pretext to exclude twelve- or thirteen-year-old girls from school when it is precisely these secular schools that should offer them the opportunity to learn, grow, and make their own choices."[15] Informed by a larger conception of democratic education, this response does not simply defer to the religious beliefs of Muslim parents or students, nor does it claim to be transcendent in its universalism. Its guiding principles – which include basic liberty and opportunity for all individuals, and their effective freedom to deliberate as civic equals about collective choices – are arguably universal for our world as we now know it, but these principles are also importantly open-ended in their content. Not only will their implications vary with the facts of particular societies, something all universalists and particularists can acknowledge, but the principles themselves are also legitimately subject to interpretation by the ongoing public deliberation that democratic education ideally supports.

The principles of democratic education do not comprehensively specify what constitutes a *good* education independently of particular cultures, life projects, and democratic deliberations. Democratic education rejects the separatist strand of particularism, which would give up on the project of educating all children for the rights and responsibilities of citizenship, regardless of their familial culture. But it respects the widest range of cultural differences compatible with teaching those rights and responsibilities. These differences include cultural practices that you or I may judge wrong or of lesser value than competing practices but that we can still recognize as reasonable for those who adopt them.

The response of democratic education to the Muslim girls embraces the partial truths in both particularism and universalism. It does not force the girls to give up wearing chadors in class, but it does expose them to a public culture of gender equality in public school. This exposure gives them reasons why women should view themselves as the civic equals of men, and it opens up opportunities (to pursue a career or hold public office, for example) that are not offered by their families and religious communities. By opening up such opportunities to all children, democratic education may lessen the likelihood that certain kinds of cultural practices will perpetuate themselves. This effect is justifiable; civic education should not try to perpetuate cultural practices apart from their value to individuals and the principles that constitute the society of which they are a part.

Some critics suggest that this position of partial accommodation is little more than a pretense of accommodation with ways of life that dissent from liberal democratic orthodoxy. "Funny-hat liberalism," it is sometimes disparagingly called.[16] Why? Because the price paid by orthodox Muslim parents for accepting the accommodationist position of democratic education may be a drastic weakening of the hold of their religious convictions and inherited way of life on their children.

The critics have a point, but it is quite partial. They are correct in suggesting that democratic education does not grant illiberal ways of life nearly all that they claim for themselves, nor even all that they may need in order to perpetuate themselves. Democratic education does not even give them all they might legitimately expect of public schooling in a society that knew no other way of life but their own. But democratic education does not claim to support any cultural way of life on its own terms, or even to the extent necessary to guarantee its survival. Nor should it. Cultures do not have a "right to survival" as such.[17] People have rights to religious freedom, along with other freedoms and opportunities, that place demands on democratic education. As we have seen, however, the right to religious freedom has principled limits. Among those limits are the right of children to be educated for full citizenship in a democratic society, and the responsibility of publicly supported schools to secure that right for students, even when it conflicts with religious commitments of their parents.

Moreover, the critics' disparagement of accommodating the wearing of chadors in public schools is not true to the experience of the Muslim parents and the girls themselves. As far as the critics or we can tell, the Muslim parents and their children strongly preferred the earlier accommodation by the *Conseil d'Etat* to the more recent banning of chadors, and for good reason. The parents argued for the right of their children, *dressed in accordance with their religious convictions,* to be educated as future French citizens within the public schools. They did not argue for their right to be *religiously* educated, as Muslims, in public schools. The critics may think that insistence on religious education in publicly subsidized schools is the only consistent position available to Muslims or any other truly religious parents. Many religious parents reasonably believe otherwise, and it is their willingness to draw some line of separation between civic education and religious education that permits any religiously pluralistic democracy effectively to pursue liberty and justice for all.

The critics are therefore correct in claiming that the earlier ruling did not provide the Muslim girls with a public education that conformed to their religious convictions, but mistaken in suggesting that public education should be judged by its capacity to conform to the religious convictions of citizens. No system of public education could justifiably strive to satisfy the religious beliefs of a diverse citizenry. Publicly subsidized education should serve distinctively civic purposes, which can be shared by a diverse citizenry, not distinctively religious purposes, which legitimately divide them.

Democratic education respects religious differences in many noncomprehensive ways, among them, by accommodating the wearing of religious symbols that conform to the religious convictions of students and their parents. Democratic education also expects citizens, whatever their religious beliefs, to honor a non-comprehensive set of civic responsibilities, which includes allowing their children to be educated for full democratic citizenship. Democratic education is in this sense a principled integration of universalist and particularist values, and it can be recognized as such by a religiously diverse citizenry who are willing to share a society on mutually justifiable terms.

MULTINATIONALISM AND EDUCATION

Not all persons are so willing to share a society. The unwillingness to share a society on mutually justifiable terms is sometimes rooted in a kind of cultural diversity that we have yet to consider: multinationalism as distinct from multiculturalism. How does a multinational society differ from a multicultural one? A multicultural society contains many cultures whose members typically overlap and willingly interact with each other in significant ways. A culture is a human community (larger than a few families) that is historically associated with common ways of seeing, doing, and thinking about things.[18] A multinational society, by contrast, is composed of two or more "peoples" who share a language, history, and territory, and either enjoy or aspire to enjoy as much political autonomy for themselves as practical circumstances permit.[19] Not every nationality has its own state, but most if not all aspire to the greatest possible degree of political autonomy from other nationalities.

By this understanding, the vast majority of contemporary societies are multicultural. This is an important, although unstartling, truth. Some contemporary societies, but far from all, are also multinational. A nationality, by definition, is not morally committed to sharing a sovereign society with any other nationality on democratic terms. That aspiration would transform the nationality into a culture. (There are, to be sure, gradations between nationality and culture, but I focus here on the defining difference of multinationalism because it poses a distinct challenge for democratic education.) The United States is more distinctively multicultural than it is multinational. The former Soviet Union, in contrast, was as distinctively multinational as it was multicultural. Belgium is distinctively bi-national as well as multicultural. Thus, not all contemporary societies are multinational or multicultural to the same degree, and the degree makes a difference: the political challenges and therefore the educational challenges of multiculturalism and multinationalism are different.[20]

The logic of a nationality is to seek its own sovereign society. Out of necessity, however, nationalities sometimes seek a *modus vivendi* with other nationalities by demanding separate, semi-autonomous spaces within a sovereign multinational society. A consistently democratic resolution would be to establish separate sovereign, democratic societies for groups who are adamantly opposed to sharing a society on terms of equal citizenship, but who would honor the democratic sovereignty of other societies, thereby making it possible for all individuals to share as political equals in some decent democratic society.[21]

A second alternative, worthy of serious consideration in cases where sovereignty for each nationality is not possible, is for a sovereign society to support an educational system that is divided into national streams, each of which tries to teach not only its own distinctive national values but also a shared set of civic values, including toleration and mutual respect for national (and other collective and individual) identities unlike their own. This educational path is a pragmatic, but not unprincipled, compromise between democratic values and nationalist sentiments. It supports the separation of various nationalist communities within a sovereign society, but it does not guarantee survival rights to any community. Those communities that cannot survive the teaching of toleration and mutual respect among diverse communities may deteriorate over time. A society of diverse nationalist communities that can thrive with the teaching of toleration and mutual respect may be relatively stable, perpetuating itself as a multinational society over time. Or such a society may gradually transform itself from a multinational into a multicultural society, where shared citizenship and multicultural opportunities open to all citizens, regardless of their national origins, become more robust unifying elements than political recognition and respect for separate nationalities.

The practicality of this second, principled path of multinational integration depends on the presence of enough people who are willing to support an educational system that does not teach antagonism among diverse national (ethnic, religious or racial) groups. In multinational societies that are beset by entrenched historical animosities, a democratic education that tries to discourage antagonistic national identities is anathema to most members of every nationality. The first path of democratization – division into separate sovereign or quasi-sovereign societies – is typically the first choice of disadvantaged nationalities within a bi-national or multinational society because they have little reason to trust majorities to teach the toleration and mutual respect necessary to putting democratic education even minimally into practice. But territorial division of already existing sovereign societies presents notoriously difficult practical problems, making the first path no more promising than the second.[22]

Whichever path a particular society takes, it cannot identify democratic education with the educational practice of perpetuating *hostile* nationalistic identities. This all-too-common educational practice needs to be distinguished from cultivating a sense of national particularism or patriotism alongside respect for the liberty and opportunity of all individuals, regardless of their nationality, religion, race, ethnicity, gender, or class origins. The worry about dividing schooling within a society into nationalistic streams parallels the problem that attends the inescapable division of schooling among sovereign societies: will the division of students and curricula by nationality carry with it a message of nationalistic superiority and disrespect for the rights of outsiders? Or can the division be made compatible with a mutual concern for creating a world in which people combine particularistic loyalties with universalistic values? Education in a multinational society, like education in a multicultural society, need not sacrifice the universal to the particular. All national groups within a multinational society can teach respect for a robust set of human rights, such as those articulated in the United Nations Declaration of Human Rights, that are due all people regardless of their nationality. A democratic multinational education would teach universal values as well as particular ones within an educational system that was segregated by non-antagonistic nationalities.[23] The problem with this conception is that nationalities are more often mutually antagonistic than respectful of each other's particularities. Were they respectful of each other's particularities, they would probably feel less of a need to segregate the education of their children by nationality.

This problem of reconciling multinationalism with democratic education parallels a problem of multiculturalism that we have yet to address. Must the division of schooling by sovereign societies also carry with it, implicitly if not explicitly, a message of nationalistic superiority and neglect of outsiders? The division of schooling by states more often than not carries this message, but is it because the division is inherently suspect? I think not. The problem lies elsewhere than in the division of education by sovereign societies. It lies in the nationalistic content of the education itself.

The challenge of reconciling democratic education with separate sovereign societies is therefore importantly different from the challenge we just posed of reconciling multinationalism with democratic education. In the case of multinationalism, separate national identifications among adults create the demand for educating children in separate nationalist streams within a single society. The demand for educating children in separate sovereign societies would exist even if all adults identified themselves not primarily as members of this or that society, but as equal persons committed to the aim of establishing liberty and justice for all other persons, wherever they happen to reside. The demand for educating children within a sovereign society makes moral sense if only because each sovereign society is a major political actor in bringing about better or worse conditions for its own citizens as well as other people who are also significantly affected by its policies. We know of no better way of enabling individuals to help bring about justice for all on a global scale than to educate children as citizens of necessarily separate democratic societies. The problem, then, is not to abolish the sense of patriotism that attends education for democratic citizenship, but to educate children within a democratic society to be as concerned with pursuing justice for all people as a theory of liberal justice demands.

Democratic education should try to teach students not only about their shared citizenship but also about their shared humanity with all individuals, regardless of their citizenship.[24] The same values that support the commitment to using public schools to develop a shared sense of citizenship among all citizens, regardless of their more particular identities, also support a cosmopolitanism compatible with patriotism. Whereas empowering children as democratic citizens cultivates patriotism, conveying concern for all human beings, regardless of their citizenship, cultivates cosmopolitanism. Patriotism and cosmopolitanism complement each other, both practically and morally speaking. Multicultural societies whose citizens care for each other establish the kind of social security that encourages citizens to care about people who live beyond their borders. Multicultural societies whose citizens care about people who live beyond their borders support the kind of patriotism that eschews parochialism and injustice. The aim of developing in all citizens a sense of shared humanity as individuals, regardless of our particular citizenship, does not take us beyond democratic education. Quite the contrary, this broad educational aim follows from the most basic democratic commitment to treating all people as equals.

Is this aim, the cosmopolitan core of democratic education, utopian? It certainly can be difficult to educate children to extend their concern to the least advantaged citizens of their own society, especially when those citizens differ in religion, ethnicity, or race, so it is easy to understand why the cosmopolitan aim of democratic education appears utopian. In light of our limited generosity, we would perhaps become cynical about the desirability of helping anyone close to home, were we taught that we are citizens of the world, above all else. But democratic education does not claim that we are citizens of the world. We are citizens of our own societies, ideally publicly educated and politically empowered as such, but we must not therefore be educated to care only for members of our own societies.

Whereas educating children for world *citizenship* misrepresents the political aim of a democratic education, teaching children to care only for their fellow citizens misrepresents its moral content. Because there is no world polity to be a citizen of, it is all the more important that democratic education seek to develop in all students a sense of shared humanity, not citizenship, with concomitant responsibilities to people who live beyond their national borders. This commitment of democratic education does not presuppose either unlimited generosity or the existence (or even potential) of a democratic world polity. It presupposes only that we have moral obligations as citizens and as individuals that extend beyond national boundaries, and that we can also learn something important about our own lives by learning about the lives of culturally and geographically distant people.

Recognizing the need to teach children about foreign countries and cultures is consistent with giving greater attention to the history, cultures, and politics of our own country than we do to any other. There are at least three reasons that justify a greater (but not exclusive) focus on our own country that are worth mentioning.

The first and most basic reason is that particular cultures and politics would not thrive were people to take an equal interest in, and feel an equal commitment to, every existing culture and politics on the face of the earth. Cultures and politics are like friendship and love in this limited respect. They require particularistic commitments on the part of individuals, but those commitments – at least in the case of culture and politics – should be consistent with respecting the rights of all people and securing their capacity to enjoy similar benefits. Because most people do not enjoy the benefits of even the imperfect system of liberties and opportunities available to United States citizens, it is particularly important that we learn about foreign cultures, politics, and people.

A second reason why schools may concentrate on domestic cultures and politics, especially in the early years of schooling, is that children often learn to respect other human beings by first learning to respect people who are close and familiar to them. It is important, however, that the focus broaden over the years, and perhaps never be exclusively on one's own country, so as to begin cultivating even in young children the capacity to identify with members of other societies.

A third reason for focusing in far more detail on the politics of the students' own country is that this is primarily – but again not exclusively – the politics that they must enlist to help people not only within but also beyond their national borders. There are of course less local forms of politics, but these are typically less effective in enlisting the political energies of ordinary people, and not primarily because education fails to familiarize people with these political possibilities. Most people want to live their lives on a local, rather than global, level. There is much that they can do to further the cause of global justice on this level, provided they learn how to be effective citizens of their own society.

These three reasons explain why public schooling in the United States, for example, may rightly focus *more* on national (including state and local) history, culture, and politics than on the history, culture, and politics of every other country. But the three reasons do not together justify the neglect of world history and politics beyond national boundaries that has characterized public schooling in the United States. If public schooling teaches respect and understanding only of already familiar people, it teaches too little to satisfy the fundamental democratic ideal of treating *all* people as equals, an ideal which informs a moral commitment to democracy at the national level. If schooling fails to familiarize students with the various means of improving the world that extend beyond their national government, it deprives citizens of a complete sense of their political power and the opportunities to create a better world for themselves and other people.

In this significant sense, multinational and multicultural education, at their democratic best, share similar aspirations, even if the means of achievement vary with local contexts and conditions. Teaching respect for basic human rights is necessary but insufficient to satisfy either democratic ideal, because democratic education also requires teaching the virtues and skills of citizenship among people who share the same sovereign society. But teaching the virtues and skills of a shared citizenship is also insufficient if schools do not count among those virtues moral responsibility toward, and intellectual curiosity about, people who happen to live in other societies. An adequate educational response to the challenges of both multiculturalism and multinationalism therefore combines respect for individuals who have particularistic identities with cultivation of common values among those individuals.

This integration is unlikely to take hold without lessons in democratic deliberation, lessons which invoke universal and particular values that are central to democratic self-government and also cross national boundaries. The history class in Brooklyn where students were asked to discuss the morality of dropping the bomb on Hiroshima is a good example of such a lesson in democratic deliberation. It demonstrates that democratic education need not be parochial or uncosmopolitan even when it is particular in its focus and provisional in its precepts. Quite the contrary, only when children are educated for a deliberative citizenship that is informed by multiculturalism and committed to treating all individuals as equals, regardless of their nationality, can we begin to reconcile civic education with cultural diversity.

NOTES

1. When speaking of public education or public schooling, I include all publicly subsidized and publicly accredited institutions that satisfy a mandatory schooling requirement, whether they are actually controlled by public or private organizations. Accredited private schools in the

United States and public schools in Great Britain, for example, are all part of the public education systems of those countries.

2. See Molefi Kete Asante, *The Afrocentric Idea* (Philadelphia: Temple University Press, 1987), p. 170; Molefi Kete Asante, *Afrocentricity: The Theory of Social Change* (Buffalo, N.Y.: Amulefi, 1980), p. 45.

3. Asante, *Afrocentricity*, p. 45; *African-American Baseline Essays*, rev. ed. (Portland, Oreg.: Portland Public Schools, 1990). Asante oscillates between the view that African values are superior for people of African origin, just as Western values are superior for people of European origin (*Afrocentricity*, p. 54; *The Afrocentric Idea*, pp. 62, 180), and the view that African values are superior to Western values (*Afrocentricity*, pp. 9–10; *The Afrocentric Idea*, p. 170).

4. These definitions are taken from the *Oxford English Dictionary*. My discussion here draws on two more general comparisons of self-esteem and self-respect, those of David Sachs, "How to Distinguish Self-Respect from Self-Esteem," *Philosophy and Public Affairs* 10 (Fall 1981): 346–60; and Michael Walzer, *Spheres of Justice* (New York: Basic Books, 1983), pp. 272–80.

5. What is worthy of being publicly honored is not the same as what schools have traditionally taught. Gender discrimination, for example, is not worthy of being publicly honored, despite the fact that many public schools have long taught this lesson.

6. Diane Ravitch, *The Schools We Deserve: Reflections on the Educational Crises of Our Times* (New York: Basic Books, 1985), p. 288.

7. *New York Times*, November 12, 1989, p. 5, and December 3, 1989, p. 17. The various news stories raise an important issue: whether the parents of the adolescents gave them the option of deciding on their own whether to wear chadors in class or whether the parents decided on their behalf. According to the news accounts, the girls' fathers were committed to their wearing chadors in school. The accounts say nothing about the commitments of their mothers or the girls themselves except by implication.

8. *New Statesman and Society*, December 15, 1989, pp. 13–14. According to this report, Le Pen claimed that repatriation "would go a long way to solving . . . the problems of law and order, drugs, AIDS and the Paris traffic jams"! For a sociological interpretation of the controversy, see David Beriss, "Scarves, Schools, and Segregation: The *Foulard* Affair," *French Politics & Society* 8 (Winter 1990): 1–13.

9. *New York Times*, November 12, 1989, p. 10.

10. Ibid.

11. *Washington Post*, October 23, 1989, p. 12.

12. I discuss deliberation in the context of a conception of democratic education in *Democratic Education* (Princeton, N.J.: Princeton University Press, 1987), pp. 50–2. A detailed discussion of the values of basic liberty, opportunity, and deliberation as constitutive of deliberative democracy can be found in Amy Gutmann and Dennis Thompson, *Democracy and Disagreement* (Cambridge, Mass.: Harvard University Press, 1996).

13. *The Guardian*, December 1, 1989, p. 38. For the most recent ruling of the French government, see Youssef M. Ibrahim, "France Bans Muslim Scarf

in Its Schools," *New York Times*, September 11, 1994, p. 4; and Lynn Terry, "French Girls Expelled for Wearing Islamic Head Scarves," transcript of *Morning Edition* (National Public Radio), November 1, 1994.

14. Compare the perspective of Charles Taylor in *Multiculturalism and "The Politics of Recognition"* (Princeton, N.J.: Princeton University Press, 1992), pp. 25–37. Taylor suggests that democratic governments should be committed to securing the survival of cultural communities into the future insofar as their survival is consistent with respect for basic individual rights.

15. *The Guardian*, November 23, 1989, p. 38.

16. For a critique of the disparagement of liberal toleration conveyed by the term "funny-hat liberalism" and a discussion of the chador case, see Anna Elisabetta Galeotti, "Citizenship and Equality: The Place for Toleration," *Political Theory* 21 (November 1993): 585–605.

17. Compare Charles Taylor, "The Politics of Recognition," in *Multiculturalism and "The Politics of Recognition,"* esp. pp. 58–9.

18. See Jeremy Waldron, "Multiculturalism and mélange," Chapter 5, this volume. A culture is not only a set of behavior patterns but also a set of social standards, which can change over time. See R. LeVine, "Properties of Culture: An Ethnographic View," in *Culture Theory: Essays on Mind, Self, and Emotion*, ed. R. A. Shweder and R. A. Levine (Cambridge: Cambridge University Press, 1984), p. 67. See also Clifford Geertz, "The Impact of the Concept of Culture on the Concept of Man," in *The Interpretation of Cultures* (New York: Basic Books, 1973), p. 44. Compare Richard A. Shweder, *Thinking Through Cultures: Expeditions in Cultural Psychology* (Cambridge, Mass.: Harvard University Press, 1991).

    For an important discussion of the ways in which individual freedom depends on membership in a culture, see Joseph Raz, "Multiculturalism: A Liberal Perspective," in *Ethics in the Public Domain: Essays in the Morality of Law and Politics* (Oxford: Clarendon Press, 1994), pp. 155–76. I regret that Raz's essay appeared too late to be discussed in this essay.

19. This is a working definition, which will do for our purposes. For a more extensive discussion of nationalism and an illuminating critique of alternative understandings, see Yael Tamir, *Liberal Nationalism* (Princeton, N.J.: Princeton University Press, 1993).

20. For an illuminating discussion of the political implications of multinationalism, especially in the Canadian context, see Will Kymlicka, "Three Forms of Group-Differentiated Citizenship in Canada," in *Democracy and Difference: Changing Boundaries of the Political*, ed. Seyla Benhabib (Princeton, N.J.: Princeton University Press, 1996). Kymlicka notes that although the United States contains national minorities, it is, with few exceptions, not a multinational state. He does not discuss the implications of multinationalism for educational policy, except to oppose allowing national minorities to pull their children out of school before the legally mandated age for all children.

21. Honoring the sovereignty of other decent democratic societies is a necessary but not sufficient condition for honoring the rights of all individuals. We also need to consider potentially more demanding obligations such as

resource transfers to poorer societies for the sake of providing a decent life for the most disadvantaged individuals. A discussion of the source and nature of these obligations is far beyond the scope of this essay.

22. For a far-ranging examination of the practical and principled problems of dividing territory to establish national sovereignty, see Allen Buchanan, *Secession: The Morality of Political Divorce from Fort Sumter to Lithuania and Quebec* (Boulder, Colo.: Westview Press, 1991).

23. The teaching of respect for human rights is always a moral imperative, but it is also often a prudent public policy, and therefore need not be utopian in many multinational contexts. In the absence of teaching respect for human rights, nationalist suspicions and hatreds are likely to be inflamed, preventing the establishment of even minimally peaceful and cooperative relations among national groups.

24. Martha Nussbaum's comments on an earlier version of this essay focused on the importance of educating children above all for world citizenship, an aim she identifies as "cosmopolitan." Democratic education, as I understand it, is cosmopolitan in its commitment to furthering liberty and justice for all individuals, regardless of their nationality. But democratic education does not claim in the name of cosmopolitanism that children must be educated above all to be citizens of the world. Anthony Appiah puts it well when he writes that "We should . . . as cosmopolitans, defend the right of others to live in democratic states of which they can be patriotic citizens; and, as cosmopolitans, we can claim that right for ourselves" ("Loyalty to Humanity," *Boston Review* [October/November 1994], p. 10). For an extended discussion of democratic education and cosmopolitanism, see the special issue of the *Boston Review* dedicated to this topic, October/November 1994, pp. 3–34.

PART IV
Teaching history

Chapter 8

Multiculturalism and history: historical perspectives and present prospects

GARY B. NASH

The furor in the popular press over multiculturalism in the schools has left many parents concerned about the history their children are taught. Some parents, especially among ethnic and racial minorities, feel that school history remains a narrow, Eurocentric course of study. Other parents worry that multicultural approaches to history are divisive and unscholarly. The concerns on both sides might be moderated by a better understanding of contemporary historical scholarship and a recognition of the potential strengths of school lessons informed by that scholarship.

This essay has two purposes. The first is to describe how far the writing and teaching of history have already moved away from the male-oriented, Eurocentric, and elitist approaches that were dominant for so long at all levels of the American educational system. It is important to acknowledge this because new calls for change often ignore what has already occurred in the rethinking and rewriting of history, and, as a result, sometimes prescribe irrelevant or misguided formulas. My second purpose is to show how multicultural approaches enhance, rather than diminish, the quality of historical analysis in the classroom.

REIMAGINING THE PAST

Among contemporary academic historians, there is widespread agreement that American history – whether in school textbooks, college courses, museum exhibits, or mass media – has been presented in a narrow and deeply distorted way. In the 1930s, when he was writing *Black Reconstruction*, W.E.B. Du Bois wrote, "I stand at the end of this writing, literally aghast at what American historians have done to this field. . . . [It is] one of the most stupendous efforts the world ever saw to discredit human beings, an effort involving universities, history, science, social life, and religion."[1] Few white historians would have agreed with Du Bois at the time; it was their work, after all, that he was attacking. But a half-century later, the white president of the Organization of American Historians, Leon Litwack, concurred with Du Bois's assessment. In his 1987 presidential address, Litwack charged that "no group of scholars was more deeply implicated in the miseducation of American youth and did more to shape the thinking of generations of Americans about race and blacks than historians."[2]

Such charges of miseducation can be readily confirmed by looking at a few of the most influential American history textbooks. For example, David Muzzey's various histories, probably the most widely used throughout the nation from the 1930s through the 1950s, made African-Americans largely invisible, suggesting, as Frances Fitz-Gerald has written, that slaves "appeared magically in this country at some unspecified time and had disappeared with the end of the Civil War."[3] Slavery, as Muzzey presented it, was a political problem for white men to worry about; but slaves and free blacks were neither a social group with their own history of struggle and survival nor an economic and cultural force that helped shape American society.

Though most school historians followed Muzzey in making slaves and free blacks disappear, a few college textbooks, beginning in the 1930s, introduced Africans in America as a distinct people with their own history. But these same books also suggested that, through a fortuitous combination of European and African cultural characteristics, the slaves turned out to be contented workers: European masters, coming from enlightened cultural stock, were generally considerate of their slaves; and Africans, coming from retrograde cultural stock, were pleased to trade barbaric Africa for the civilized European colonies in the Americas. Oliver Chitwood, publishing his college textbook on American history in 1931 and leaving it virtually unchanged through the 1960s, offered a typical portrait:

> Generally, when the master and slave were brought into close association, a mutual feeling of kindliness and affection sprang up between them, which restrained the former from undue harshness toward the latter. . . . We find that there were always some brutal masters who treated their black servants inhumanely, but they were doubtless few in number. . . . Good feeling between master and slave was promoted in large measure by the happy disposition or docile temperament of the Negro. Seldom was he surly and discontented and rarely did he harbor a grudge against his master for depriving him of his liberty. On the contrary, he went about his daily tasks cheerfully, often singing while at work. . . . The fact that he had never known the ease and comforts of civilization in his homeland made it less difficult for him to submit to the hardships and inferior position of his condition. In this respect, the

American Negro was better off than the slave of ancient Rome, who was often the intellectual equal and sometimes the superior of his master.[4]

Chitwood's message for college undergraduates took some time to percolate down to the precollegiate textbooks, but at least as early as 1947 it had appeared in *My Country*, a fifth-grade textbook published by the state of California. For years thereafter, thousands of children learned about slavery and slave life from these passages:

> The Negroes were brought from Africa and sold to the people of our country in early times. After a while there came to be thousands and thousands of these Negro slaves. Most of them were found in the southern states. On the southern plantations, where tobacco and cotton and rice were grown, they worked away quite cheerfully. In time many people came to think that it was wrong to own slaves. Some of them said that all the Negro slaves should be freed. Some of the people who owned slaves became angry at this. They said that the black people were better off as slaves in America than they would have been as wild savages in Africa. Perhaps this was true, as many of the slaves had snug cabins to live in, plenty to eat, and work that was not too hard for them to do. Most of the slaves seemed happy and contented.

For slave children especially, life was full of amusements:

> Perhaps the most fun the little [white] masters and mistresses have comes when they are free to play with the little colored boys and girls. Back of the big house stand rows of small cabins. In these cabins live the families of Negro slaves. The older colored people work on the great farm or help about the plantation home. The small black boys and girls play about the small houses. They are pleased to have the white children come to play with them.[5]

The biases reflected in such textbooks were also visible in accounts of African history generally. Du Bois would surely have been dismayed if he had read one of the most popular textbooks in Western Civilization courses in the 1960s, where the much-honored British historian Hugh Trevor-Roper magisterially proclaimed that to study the African past would be to inquire into "the unrewarding gyrations of barbarous tribes whose chief function in history . . . is to show to the present an image of the past from which, by history, it has escaped."[6]

Similar mental constructions prevailed in regard to Native American history. In 1958, introducing Douglas Leach's history of King Philip's War in 1676 – the bloodiest Indian war of the seventeenth century in North America – Samuel Eliot Morison instructed readers how to view both colonial/Indian relations and the decolonization movements in the Third World after World War II: "In view of our recent experiences of warfare, and of the many instances today of backward peoples getting enlarged notions of nationalism and turning ferociously on Europeans who have attempted to civilize them, this early conflict of the same nature cannot help but be of interest."[7]

Embedded in the controlling idea that European/Native American relations involved the confrontation of savagery and civilization lay the idea that conflict between higher and lower cultures was inevitable and that the outcome was foreordained. Muzzey's books, the history primers for millions of American children for two generations, declared, "It was impossible that these few hundred thousand natives should stop the spread of the Europeans over the country. That would have been to condemn one of the fairest lands of the earth to the stagnation of barbarism."[8] Dozens of other books followed the same basic formula. They placed the responsibility for historical events on impersonal or super-personal forces, eliminating the notion of individual or group responsibility; what happened, and the way it happened, were seen as the result of forces that no human being could control. As Isaiah Berlin tells us, historical explanations that stress inevitability are the victor's way of disclaiming responsibility for even the most heinous chapters of history. Once inevitability has been invoked, "our sense of guilt and of sin, our pangs of remorse and self-condemnation, are automatically dissolved. . . . The growth of knowledge brings with it relief from moral burdens, for if powers beyond and above us are at work, it is wild presumption to claim responsibility for their activity or blame ourselves for failing in it. . . . Acts hitherto regarded as wicked or unjustifiable are seen in a more 'objective' fashion – in the larger context – as part of the process of history."[9]

The paradigmatic shift in the writing of history is far from complete, but some of those who currently protest about Eurocentric or racist history take little account of how resolutely the present generation of historians have challenged older conceptualizations. Academic historians, most of them detached from what is occurring in primary and secondary education unless they have children of their own in the public schools, are often puzzled by the furor over the question of "Whose history shall we teach?" because they have watched – and participated in – wholesale changes in their own discipline during the past thirty years. African and African-American history, women's history, and labor history are taught in most colleges and universities; Asian-American, Hispanic-American, and Native American history are taught in many. These courses are built on a solid foundation of scholarship produced by the current generation of historians.

African-American history provides an instructive example. Even fifteen years ago, John Hope Franklin, author of the leading textbook in African-American history, wrote of "a most profound and salutary change in the approach to the history of human relations in the United States." He noted that as a result of this change, "the new Negro history has come into its own."[10] Since 1977, this blossoming of black history has continued unabated. In compiling a bibliography of African-American history covering just the period from 1765 to 1830 for the forthcoming *Harvard Guide to Afro-American History,* I prepared references for more than 200 books and more than 1,200 articles published since 1965. The proliferation of scholarship on the period after 1830 is vastly greater. When the *Harvard Guide* is completed, it will list thousands of books, articles, and doctoral dissertations on African-American history and race relations – an enormous outpouring of scholarship that has wrought fundamental changes in the basic contours and emphases of American history.

In women's history, the amount and range of scholarship, and the variety of sophisticated courses based upon it, is equally impressive. The biannual Berkshire Conference of Women's Historians draws hundreds of historians together and serves as a showplace of exciting new research. So, too, younger scholars, building on the work of a few old hands, are creating the knowledge required for a thorough understanding of the history, literature, art, music and values of Hispanic-Americans, Native Americans, Asian-Americans, and other groups. It is a measure of how the historical profession has changed that so many of the book prizes awarded by the Organization of American Historians in recent years have gone to books about the role of racial groups and women in the making of American society.

In the current atmosphere of heated debate, it is worth reflecting on why and how such wholesale change has occurred in the writing of history. Three developments have intersected to cause a major transformation. First, and largely forgotten in the current debate, is the change in the recruitment of professional historians – the people who do historical scholarship, teach at the collegiate level, and write the textbooks used in the schools. Before World War II, professional historians were drawn almost exclusively from the ranks of white, male, Protestant, and upper-class American society. From the perspective of such professionals, it was entirely fitting that they should be the keepers of the past because they believed that only those of the highest intellect, most polished manners, and most developed aesthetic taste could stand above the masses and look dispassionately at the annals of human behavior. Ordinary people, in the view of these guardians of history, were ruled by emotion; only the wealthy and educated could transcend this weakness and achieve disinterested rationality. Pitted against this thoroughly dominant group since the early nineteenth century was a small number of women, African-

Americans, and white radicals who worked without much recognition as they tried to create alternative histories.

As Peter Novick has pointed out, small cracks in the fortress of historical scholarship began to appear in the 1930s, as Jews struggled for a place in the profession. When Richard Leopold, who would emerge as a major historian of diplomacy, applied for his first teaching job, his graduate mentor at Harvard observed of him, "of course a Jew, but since he is a Princeton graduate, you may be reasonably certain he is not of the offensive type." Bert Lowenberg was described in a letter of recommendation as follows: "by temperament and spirit . . . [he] measures up to the whitest Gentiles I know."[11]

Not until after World War II would more than a handful of Jews gain admission to the historical profession. By that time, the GI Bill was opening the doors of higher education to broad masses of Americans. This enormous expansion, which created a majority of the college campuses existing today, rapidly enlarged and diversified the historians' guild. Religious barriers continued to fall, and class barriers began to fall as well, though not without creating consternation in many quarters. In 1957, at a time when the growth of American universities demanded thousands of newly trained professors, George Pierson, the chairman of the history department at Yale, observed in a letter to the university president that while the doctoral program in English "still draws to a degree from the cultivated, professional, and well-to-do classes . . . by contrast, the subject of history seems to appeal on the whole to a lower social stratum." Pierson complained that "far too few of our history candidates are sons of professional men; far too many list their parent's occupation as janitor, watchman, salesman, grocer, pocketbook cutter, bookkeeper, railroad clerk, pharmacist, clothing cutter, cable tester, mechanic, general clerk, butter-and-egg jobber, and the like." Five years later, Carl Bridenbaugh, the president of the American Historical Association, lamented what he called "The Great Mutation" that he believed was undermining the profession. "Many of the younger practitioners of our craft, and those who are still apprentices, are products of lower middle-class or foreign origins, and their emotions not infrequently get in the way of historical reconstructions."[12]

The notion that lower-class and foreign-born backgrounds disabled apprentice historians by conditioning them to substitute emotion for reason was revived when racial and gender barriers began to fall in the 1960s. The historical profession had for many decades included a small number of notable women and African-Americans, and an occasional Native American, Hispanic-American, or Asian-American. But women began to enter the profession in substantial numbers only in the 1960s, and the number of historians belonging to racial minority groups has increased only gradually since that time. Charges that emotions outran analytic insight were again heard from members of the old guard, none of its members more vocal than Oscar Handlin, whose Jewish background had nearly prevented his entry into the profession a generation before.[13] But by the late 1970s, the old guard had been overwhelmed, and social historians had surged forward to displace the traditional emphasis on male- and elite-centered political and institutional history and on intellectual history that rarely focused on the thought and consciousness of people who were not of European descent.

Given these changes in the composition of the profession – by 1990, more than 35 percent of all graduate students in the humanities were women – it is not surprising that new questions have been posed about the past: questions that never occurred to a narrowly constituted group of historians. The emphasis on conflict rather than consensus, on racism and exploitation, on history from the bottom up as well as from the top down, on women as well as men, is entirely understandable when we realize that people whose histories have never been written are now challenging the dominant paradigms by recovering those histories. Step by step, new historians (including many white males) have constructed previously untold chapters of history and have helped to overcome the deep historical biases that afflicted the profession for many generations.

The dramatic period of protest and reform that occurred in the 1960s and 1970s helped to sustain and strengthen this transformation of historical scholarship. The struggles of women, people of color, and religious minorities to gain equal rights spurred many historians to ask new questions about the role of race and gender relations in the nation's history and to examine racial minorities, women, and working people as integrally involved in the creation of American society. These historians, who were often participants in the social protest movements, were not breaking new ground altogether; for many decades, reaching back to the early nineteenth century, pioneering individual scholars had tilled the fields of women's and minority history, and the events of the 1930s had sparked interest in labor history. But the professional colleagues of this avant-garde offered little appreciation of their work, and certainly their efforts to recover the history of women, people of color, and the working classes rarely found a place in textbooks used at the primary, secondary, or even collegiate level. The importance of the protest movements of the 1960s and 1970s was to legitimize the work of those who had been regarded as cranky radicals and who, in the immediately preceding years of the McCarthy witch-hunts, had often been hounded out of the academy entirely.

Other developments fueling the change in the writing of history have been the decolonization of the Third World and the growing interdependence of nations. The liberation movements that erupted after World War II were accompanied by the emergence of intellectuals who began to reconstruct the past of what Eric Wolf calls "the people without history." Both in Third World countries and in the West, scholars began to insist on the integrity of the cultural practices and the venerable histories of indigenous peoples. In the United States, such efforts were yoked – often uneasily – to area studies programs established by the Ford Foundation, most notably the African studies centers established at a number of major universities. In the public schools, this development has fostered an awareness of the importance of studying the histories of many cultures and of teaching world history rather than simply the history of Western civilization. The internationalization of economic, political, and cultural affairs has driven home to historians and teachers that a Eurocentric history that measures all progress and renders all historical judgments on the basis of the experience of one part of the world will not equip students for satisfactory adult lives in the twenty-first century.

The profound changes in the way history is written have not occurred without internal dissent and controversy. In the period from the 1930s to the 1950s, opposition to a reconceptualized history was usually expressed with reference to the unsuitability of the "outsiders" entering the profession. In contrast, the current debates within the historical profession focus more directly on the kind of history that is being written. Opponents see the new "social history" – that is, the history of women, laboring people, people of color, and religious minorities – as creating a hopelessly chaotic version of the past, in which no grand synthesis is possible and all coherence is lost. Yet the overarching themes and the coherence of earlier histories were only possible as long as scholars emphasized the experience of dominant groups in American society and grounded all historical generalizations in the Western experience. The contribution of the social historians is precisely to show that the sense of coherence achieved by earlier scholarship will not hold up when we broaden our perspectives and start thinking about the history of all the people who constitute American (or any other) society. The new scholarship has, for example, not only provided an immensely enriched understanding of the history of women and the family but in the process obliged all historians to rethink the allegedly coherent paradigms for explaining the past that were derived from studying primarily the male experience. Likewise, the new scholarship on the black experience suggests the validity of Du Bois's assessment of the history presented to his generation and has fostered more adequate reconstructions of that experience.

Some of the opposition to the new history stems simply from resistance to change or discomfort with the loss of old paradigms. For example, historians used to arguing about Turner's frontier thesis – that the frontier was a crucible of democratic ideas and institution-building, a place where democratic values were continuously replenished – may find it painfully unsettling to consider the westward movement from the perspective of the Lakota or Cheyenne who watched the wagon trains appearing from the east; or from the vantage point of Mexican ranchers and miners of the Southwest who found themselves demographically and politically overwhelmed by the arrival of land-hungry settlers; or through the eyes of Chinese contract laborers brought to the Pacific slope in the 1870s to build levees and railroads. For each of these groups the "frontier movement" was anything but heroic, anything but the westward "march of democracy."

The new history, in paying close attention to gender, race, and class, emphasizes that historical experiences have varied with the position and power of the participants. This insight makes it harder to tell a simple or unified story about such eras or movements as "The Jacksonian Age of the Common Man," the "Progressive Era," or the post-1945 "Affluent Society." The challenge of a history built upon consideration of alternative experiences and perspectives goes beyond simply incorporating notable women or people of color into traditional narrative themes; it forces the invention of genuinely new story lines, based on the diverse experiences of the entire society under investigation. This challenge, while liberating historians from simplistic and biased formulas about the past, also raises real perplexities about the prospects of wresting any kind of general unity out of multiple and conflicting perspectives. If, for example, older historical accounts achieved a spurious unity by taking the experiences of certain men as the unspoken measure of historical significance, redress doesn't come simply from incorporating into a revised story the newly recognized and acknowledged experiences of women, since the category of "women" dissolves in turn into multiple and conflicting perspectives arising out of racial, economic, regional, and other differences. As one leading feminist historian describes this "seemingly intractable" problem: "What is the conceptual link for women's history . . . among what seems to be an infinite proliferation of different [women's] stories . . . ? [I]s there a common identity for women and is there a common history of them we can write?"[14] If the sin of the old history was to impose a false unity on diverse experiences and perspectives, the problem for the new history is to give voice to the diversity without reducing history to Babel.

HISTORY IN THE SCHOOLS

To what extent has the presentation of history in the public schools reflected the developments in historical scholarship? In 1979, reviewing American history textbooks for schoolchildren from the early twentieth century forward, Frances FitzGerald concluded that "[t]he texts of the sixties contain the most dramatic rewriting of history ever to take place in American schoolbooks."[15] In FitzGerald's view, one of the largest changes was in the textbooks' new presentation of the United States as a multiracial society – a signal revision which she attributed less to the influence of new historical scholarship than to the pressure exerted by school boards in cities with a high percentage of black and Hispanic students. Yet FitzGerald admitted that by the late 1970s, textbooks were far from cleansed of Eurocentric bias and represented a "compromise . . . among the conflicting demands of a variety of pressure groups, inside and outside the school systems" – a compromise "full of inconsistencies" (among which, she noted, was an almost absolute ban on any discussion of economic conditions, social and economic inequality, and violence and conflict in American life).[16]

Why was it that the flowering of social history in the universities, which made such important gains in breaking through Eurocentric conceptualizations of American history and world history, made only limited gains in bringing a less nationalistic, white-centered, hero-driven, and male-dominated history to the schools? There are several ways of explaining its relatively minor impact. First, most social studies teachers had only a smattering of history in their own undergraduate education – generally, just a few courses, or a minor at best. Second, most teachers attended colleges and universities where the new scholarship was only palely represented. The 1970s were years in which new faculty appointments were few, especially in the state universities where most teachers are trained. Third, the books used in the schools, though often produced by professional historians, only cautiously incorporated the new social history of women, laboring people, and minorities. Publishers who catered to a national market were far more timid than university presses about publishing history that radically revised our understanding of the past, especially the American past. Thus, by the early 1980s, the textbooks in United States history for the secondary schools reflected far less of the new scholarship than textbooks written for college survey classes.

The changes in the schools, limited as they were, stimulated controversy among ordinary Americans. In the early 1970s, Jules Feiffer captured the disgruntlement of the man in the street in a cartoon where a white laborer in a hard hat complains: "When I went to school I learned that George Washington never told a lie, slaves were happy on the plantation, the men who opened the West were giants, and we won every war because God was on our side. But where my kid goes to school he learns that Washington was a slaveowner, slaves hated slavery, the men who opened the West committed genocide, and the wars we won were victories for U.S. imperialism. No wonder my kid's not an American. They're teaching him some other country's history." Feiffer's cartoon suggests that an elitist, male-dominated, Eurocentric history appealed to the white working class because, while they were largely excluded from it, that history more closely represented their values and self-image than it did those of women or people of color.

Controversies about teaching history in the schools continue, and the pace of change in reforming the history curriculum has accelerated. Multicultural curricula, "stressing a diversity of cultures, races, languages, and religions," and eliminating "ethnocentric and biased concepts and materials from textbook and classroom," have been adopted by school systems throughout the United States.[17] California has implemented an explicitly multicultural history-social science curriculum, and many other states and individual school districts are following the same path, though with many variations.

While many people worry that multiculturalism leads to bad history, in fact the new curricula are more likely to enrich our historical understanding. This is especially true with respect to events which are already familiar and recognized as critically important. The American Revolution, for example, has been a staple part of the history curriculum for the last two centuries, and yet that curriculum has seldom communicated its complexity and significance.

Almost all textbook discussions of the Revolution have passed over the experiences and the contributions of large groups in colonial society, or simply homogenized all colonial Americans into one undifferentiated mass (except, of course, for the Loyalists, who are usually pictured as those too timid or too self-interested to join "the glorious cause"). Thus, the popular understanding of the Revolution is based mostly on the great-man theory of history. Washington, Jefferson, John and Samuel Adams, Franklin, and a few other political and military leaders occupy center stage. Precious few ordinary figures even wait in the wings. Students have little idea of what the Revolution meant to the one-fifth of the population that was black, of how Native Americans were caught up in the Revolution, of the significance of female revolutionary experiences, or even of how the revolutionary aspirations of white male Americans differed from class to class and region to region.

Because the Revolution is taught primarily as a war for independence, with little attention paid to the "war at home," the struggle to redefine the nature of social relations and politics in the new nation, which was carried on much more systematically (and at times more ferociously) than the war itself, is almost entirely obscured. Hence, most textbooks present the Revolution in a two-dimensional manner, avoiding its complexity, robbing it of its radical force, and underplaying the contingency of its outcomes.

Tellingly, virtually all treatments of the Revolution used in the schools ignore the complicated process of drafting state constitutions. Casting themselves into a state of nature after renouncing the English charters and law under which their societies had been functioning, the Americans began anew, deciding just what kind of laws, political structures, and constitutionally protected liberties they wished to enshrine and by what means they should create these new governmental arrangements. The recent immigrant Thomas Paine captured some of this challenge in his widely read *Common Sense:* "We have it in our power to begin the world over again. A situation similar to the present has not happened since the days of Noah until now. The birth day of a new world is at hand."[18] Ten weeks before the Declaration of Independence, Paine made his point more directly: "The answer to the question, can America be happy under a government of her own, is short and simple, viz. As happy as she please; she hath a blank sheet to write upon."[19]

This was the opportunity, but it was also the problem. If the sheet was now blank, people did not agree about what to write on it. United in their desire to begin anew, they were at the same time divided by region, class, religion, ethnicity, and a keen sense of their various historical experiences in the colonial period, in relation both to the mother country and to each other. They brought different agendas to the bargaining table, different notions of how to redefine American society. In some states it took nearly the entire course of the war for all the participants to frame their demands and negotiate agreements, and even then knotty unresolved questions carried over into the postwar period.

Why has the American Revolution been sanitized in the textbooks, emptied of all drama except that which flows from the battle of David against Goliath? One reason, perhaps, lies in the assumption by textbook writers that the civic education of children is best accomplished through showing the nation's past – and especially its birth – in untarnished, heroic terms. However, such stainless-steel versions of our Revolution are not likely to nurture active citizenship or encourage the moral, political, and social inquiry that is indispensable in a living democracy. Frederick Douglass's words are worth remembering in this regard: "Those who profess to favor freedom and yet deprecate agitation are men who want crops without plowing up the ground, they want rain without thunder and lightning. They want the ocean without the awful roar of its many waters."[20]

A more realistic view of the American Revolution is more likely to inculcate a commitment to democratic principles – and to promote understanding amid the current culture wars – than the simplistic great-man view of the Revolution offered in most schools today. And a more realistic view cannot help but be a more inclusive multicultural view – with "multicultural" understood to refer to differences in class, gender, and religion as well as in race and ethnicity.

The Revolution is an epic example of how people at many levels of society, in many regions, from different backgrounds, and of different and often conflicting points of view, take part in a historical transformation. Nearly all the colonists were involved in the Revolution in one way or another. Almost all had to make difficult choices, decide what freedom was worth, and personally calculate whether the revolutionists promised the kind of freedoms they were willing to die for. In few eras have so many been eager to participate in the making of their own history and the reshaping of the society under which they and their children would live. Some saw more of their agenda for America accomplished than others. Some suffered keen disappointment but drew upon Revolutionary principles, as they understood them, to continue their struggles after the war. Nearly all were drawn into the civic process in one way or another and became part of an often disorderly but also exhilarating campaign not only to win a war but to define the future of the American republic.

If the Revolution is presented as a multilayered, complex, and often contradictory struggle, students discover that their nation was born not only through a war against England but through a fascinating negotiation among different groups, from both sides of the conflict, over what kind of American society would emerge if military victory were achieved. Students can understand how the Revolution divided neighbors, families, churches, and social and occupational groups. Seeing that the nation was born not in unity but in controversy may give them greater insight into contemporary arguments swirling around them. I do not know whether the mythic Revolution comforts students today, but surely the nation's birth will seem more real if they are led to explore how people at the time, in all their varied stations, experienced it – as an event that was, by turns, terrifying and exhilarating, heroic and mundane, divisive and binding.

Why, for example, should it be forgotten that at critical moments,

artisans and shopkeepers in Philadelphia led the revolutionary agitation against English policies, pushing their social superiors along the
road to independence? Why are students, and citizens generally, not
aware of the radical state constitution drafted by the Pennsylvania
convention – a constitution that appalled moderates like John Adams
because it gave the vote to propertyless white males, emasculated the
executive's role, and created a unicameral legislature?

Moreover, while understanding the Revolution as a social and political upheaval within white, male society, we need also to understand it through the eyes of women, African-Americans, and Native
Americans. None of these groups were of one mind and none had a
unified experience during the Revolutionary era. But within each
group, the Revolution had profound effects, and each group profoundly affected the course of the dual struggle for American independence and for a redefined America.

For African-Americans, the Revolution offered a new opportunity
to overthrow the abominable system of chattel slavery. Drawing upon
white rhetoric regarding inalienable rights, they petitioned for their
freedom, and some attempted to enlist in the American cause. Along
with white allies, they pointed out the gross inconsistency in white
Americans' arguing against English oppression while continuing to
oppress so many thousands of their fellow human beings. And when
it became clear that the Revolution would bring no general emancipation, they seized the moment, whenever it presented itself, to liberate
themselves. Especially important was the British offer of freedom to
slaves reaching British lines. This stratagem changed the entire character of the war, especially in the South, where the white revolutionists found themselves fighting the British, Loyalist neighbors, and
escaping black slaves who were engaged in what amounted to the
largest slave insurrection in American history. Among the results of
the black American Revolution were new pressures to abolish slavery
in the North and the southern border states; the exodus of slaves who
had fought for the British, first to Nova Scotia and from there to West
Africa, where they figure among the founders of Sierra Leone; and the
creation of a free black leadership cadre in the North that established
the churches, schools, fraternal organizations, and mutual aid societies
that sustained the emerging free black communities from Charleston to
Boston and kept abolitionism alive in the post-revolutionary decades.

For some 200,000 Native Americans living between the Atlantic
Ocean and the Mississippi River, the Revolution was also a time "to
try men's souls." Like most black Americans, most Native Americans
concluded that their revolutionary goals could best be achieved
through fighting against the side that proclaimed the equality of all
human beings and for the side that the Americans accused of tram-

pling on their natural, irreducible rights. The logic of nearly 200 years of contact with European settlers dictated the choice, for it was the colonial subjects of the King who most threatened Indian autonomy, while it was the royal power that before the Revolution had attempted to protect Indian land and political sovereignty through the Proclamation Line of 1763.

In the end, the Indians who fought alongside the Americans – among them the Catawba, Oneida, and Stockbridge peoples – were losers of the Revolution no less than those who sided with the British. Their efforts won them little protection from land-hungry settlers and speculators after the war. But this does not gainsay how importantly they affected the course of the military conflict; it does not alter the fact that they too were motivated by the desire for life, liberty, and the pursuit of happiness; and it goes some way towards explaining why their plight awakened at least some in the revolutionary generation to argue for a change in the course of Indian-European relations, so as to ensure that the new republic acted in accordance with the principles enunciated in the Declaration of Independence. Nor can we ignore the fact that in the postwar era – when the movement for independence turned into a movement of national expansion – the wartime experience of Native Americans led to new attempts at pan-Indian resistance against the invasion of their homelands west of the Appalachian mountains.[21]

Though our history books have underplayed the role of women in the revolutionary era, it is clear that in their capacity as market-goers and consumers, American women were crucial to the conduct of boycotts against British goods in the years leading up to the war. The success of nonconsumption pacts depended upon the colonists' swearing off tea and substituting homespun cloth for English textiles. From Georgia to Maine, women began spinning yarn and weaving cloth, turning every fireside, as John Adams recalled after the war, into "a theatre of politics."

Nor can the American military victory be understood without thinking about the role of women in providing the necessary food for armies on the march, in raising money to support the war effort, in caring for the wounded and dying, and even in providing emotional support and inspiration that sustained soldiers on the battlefields and campgrounds. At the same time, women were deeply involved in redefining family relationships, as well as social relationships more broadly. As male leaders talked about England's intentions to "enslave" the Americans and its callous treatment of its colonial "subjects," American women began to rethink their own domestic situations. The language of protest against England reminded many American women that they too were badly treated "subjects" of their husbands. Abigail Adams's clarion call to her husband John to "not put such unlimited power into the hands of the Husbands," and her warning that women would not "hold ourselves bound by any Laws in which we have no voice or Representation," are but two of many examples in which a woman pressed forward to write upon the blank sheet Tom Paine had described – to take part in the process of redefining America.[22]

The stirring of consciousness about the political rights of women did not lead to radical change during or just after the war (although women in New Jersey did briefly obtain the franchise). The "daughters of liberty" were more successful in defining new roles for women as guardians of public virtue and as nurturers of children whose character would determine the fate of the new nation. In this sense, women assumed a vital civic role, even if they were largely excluded from formal politics. The "republican mother" – understood to be rational, competent, and educated – would raise children capable of acting responsibly in a system unprecedented in the scope it gave to political participation. If Tocqueville was correct in the 1830s in attributing the superiority of the Americans to the quality of their women, then a good measure of this superiority can be traced back to the emergence of capable republican women during the revolutionary era.

SEPARATE GROUND AND COMMON GROUND

Except among what might be called white and black racial fundamentalists, who so far have had only limited influence on curricular change in the schools, there is little argument about the desirability of including people of all classes, colors, and conditions in our accounts of how history unfolds. Such inclusion is simply an element of sound historical analysis. Nor is there much doubt that children will find history more compelling and relevant when they recognize that people of their religion, color, region, ethnic background, or class played active roles in the making of American society. But even as they discover the historical relevance of gender, race, religion, and other categories that help shape their identity, students also need to discover the common humanity of all individuals, and to realize that many of the most important lessons of history can be learned by studying themes and movements that cross racial, ethnic, religious, gender, and class lines. Once more, the American Revolution, understood as the struggle of people of all kinds to seize the separation from England as the opportunity to "begin the world over again," offers vast scope to lessons in category-crossing.

Whatever their origins and characteristics, we should hope that all students will find in history inspiring figures of different colors, genders, and social positions. Why should the lives of Harriet Tubman and Ida B. Wells be relevant only to young African-American women? Likewise, what student can fail to gain wisdom from studying the trial of Anne Hutchinson or the Lincoln-Douglas debates? Who cannot draw inspiration from the courage and accomplishments of Black Hawk, John Brown, Elizabeth Blackwell, A. Philip Randolph, Louis Brandeis, or Dolores Huerta? W.E.B. Du Bois knew that the history he was taught was wildly distorted and used as an instrument of white supremacy. But he also knew that he had benefited greatly from reading the great writers of many cultures: "I sit with Shakespeare and he winces not. Across the color line I move arm in arm with Balzac and Dumas, where smiling men and welcoming women glide in gilded halls. . . . I summon Aristotle and Aurelius and what soul I will, and they come all graciously with no scorn nor condescension. So, wed with Truth, I dwell above the Veil."[23]

The veil of which Du Bois wrote was the color line, and he is only one of a long line of brilliant black scholars who drew sustenance from all parts of humanity. Ralph Ellison, growing up in Macon County, Alabama, remembered that he "read Marx, Freud, T. S. Eliot, Pound, Gertrude Stein, and Hemingway. Books which seldom, if ever, mentioned Negroes were to release me from whatever 'segregated' idea I might have had of my human possibilities."[24] C.L.R. James, the Trinidadian historian and author of *Black Jacobins* – still after a half-century the most important book on the Haitian Revolution – writes movingly of his education in the classics of English literature in the schools of Trinidad. As an adult, James came to recognize "the limitation of spirit, vision, and self-respect which was imposed on us by the fact that our masters, our curriculum, our code of morals, everything began from the basis that Britain was the source of all light and leading, and our business was to admire, wonder, imitate, learn."[25] But James went on to read and learn from French and Russian literature and to find an authentic voice of his own, much enriched by his cosmopolitan education. His accomplishments are a reminder that a curriculum organized around only one vantage point for learning, whether English, European, or African, will limit both the vision of our students and the scope of their achievements.

In 1979, looking at the progress of multiculturalism in its earlier stage, Frances FitzGerald expressed concern that the new social history would splinter into a bundle of fragmented group histories. Such an outcome, she wrote, would suggest that "Americans have no common history, no common culture and no common values, and that membership in a racial cultural group constitutes the most fundamental experience of each individual. The message would be that the center cannot, and should not, hold."[26]

In some urban schools today, one group boycotts another group's ethnic festivities and racial tensions flare when one holiday is celebrated over another, confirming FitzGerald's fear that ethnic pride might increase ethnic divisiveness.[27] Thus, her question about what holds us together, whether we have a common culture, is all the more relevant. The debate within historical scholarship about endlessly proliferating perspectives and the lack of coherent themes may not be definitively resolved, but the task of raising children to be members of a decent, thriving society does require giving them something in common. This requirement, however, doesn't mean supplying students a history free of conflict and strife. As the example of the Revolution suggests, it was out of such conflict that an enduring set of institutions and a new political language emerged.

The social, political, and philosophical ideals articulated during the Revolution have never been fully realized, and yet these ideals have been reference points for virtually every social and political struggle carried out by women, religious minorities, labor, and people of color. Our entire history can be read as a long, painful, and often bloody effort to bring social practice into correspondence with these lofty goals. In his classic study of race relations, Gunnar Myrdal focused on the central contradiction of a democracy that would not extend equal rights to Jews, black Americans, and other "outsiders." But at the same time, Myrdal recognized that such disadvantaged groups "could not possibly have invented a system of political ideals which better corresponded to their interests."[28] That our history is one of struggle – and that the struggle continues – is no argument against the ideal of a common political culture. It is only a reminder of an agenda still waiting to be completed, of what the African-American historian Vincent Harding has poignantly called "wrestling toward the dawn."[29]

NOTES

1. W.E.B. Du Bois, *Black Reconstruction: An Essay Toward a History of the Part Which Black Folk Played in the Attempt to Reconstruct Democracy in America, 1860–1880* (New York: Harcourt, Brace, 1935), pp. 725, 727.
2. Leon Litwack, "Trouble in Mind: The Bicentennial and the Afro-American Experience," *Journal of American History* 74 (1987): 326.
3. Frances FitzGerald, *America Revised: History Schoolbooks in the Twentieth Century* (Boston: Little, Brown, 1979), p. 83.
4. Oliver Perry Chitwood, *A History of Colonial America* (New York: Harper Brothers, 1931), pp. 351–2.

5. Quoted in Gilbert Sewall, "Textbooks Past and Present," *American Educator* (Winter 1991): 18.

6. Hugh Trevor-Roper, *The Rise of Christian Europe* (New York: Harcourt, Brace and World, 1965), p. 9.

7. Douglas Edward Leach, *Flintlock and Tomahawk: New England in King Philip's War* (New York: Macmillan, 1958), p. ix.

8. David Saville Muzzey, *A History of Our Country* (Boston: Ginn, 1937), p. 36.

9. Isaiah Berlin, *Historical Inevitability* (Oxford: Clarendon Press, 1954), pp. 39–40.

10. John Hope Franklin, "The New Negro History," in *Race and History: Selected Essays, 1938–1988* (Baton Rouge: Louisiana State University Press, 1989), p. 46.

11. Peter Novick, *That Noble Dream: The 'Objectivity Question' and the American Historical Profession* (Cambridge: Cambridge University Press, 1988), p. 173.

12. Quoted in Ibid., pp. 366, 339.

13. Oscar Handlin, *Truth in History* (Cambridge, Mass.: Harvard University Press, 1979), passim.

14. Joan Scott, "Women's History," in *New Perspectives on Historical Writing*, ed. Peter Burke (University Park, Pa.: Pennsylvania State University Press, 1992), p. 57.

15. FitzGerald, *America Revised*, p. 58.

16. Ibid., p. 109.

17. Robert K. Fullinwider, "The Cosmopolitan Community," *Journal of Social Philosophy* 27 (Fall 1996): 5ff.

18. Thomas Paine, *Common Sense and Other Political Writings*, ed. Nelson F. Adkinds (Indianapolis: Bobbs-Merrill, 1953), p. 51.

19. Thomas Paine, "The Forester's Letters," #3, in *The Complete Writings of Thomas Paine*, ed. Philip S. Foner (New York: Citadel Press, 1945), vol. 2, p. 82.

20. Quoted in Litwack, "Trouble in Mind," p. 336.

21. For a more extended treatment, see Gary B. Nash, "The Forgotten Experience: Indians, Blacks, and the American Revolution," in *The American Revolution: Changing Perspectives*, ed. William Fowler and Wallace Coyle (Boston: Northeastern University Press, 1979), pp. 27–46.

22. Abigail Adams to John Adams, March 31, 1776, in *Adams Family Correspondence*, ed. H. Butterfield Lyman (Cambridge, Mass.: Harvard University Press, 1963–73), vol. 1, p. 370. For more extended treatments of women's roles and experiences in the Revolutionary era, see Alfred F. Young, "The Women of Boston: 'Persons of Consequence' in the Making of the American Revolution," and Linda Kerber, " 'I Have Don . . . much to Carrey on the Warr': Women and the Shaping of Republican Ideology after the American Revolution," in Harriet B. Applewhite and Darliene G. Levy, *Women and Politics in the Age of the Democratic Revolution* (Ann Arbor: University of Michigan Press, 1990), pp. 181–258; and the essays in *Women in the Age of the American Revolution*, ed. Ronald Hoffman and Peter J. Albert (Charlottesville: University Press of Virginia, 1989).

23. W.E.B. Du Bois, *Souls of Black Folk: Essays and Sketches*, in *Writings*, ed. Nathan Huggins (New York: Library of America, 1986), p. 438.

24. Quoted in Jim Sleeper, *The Closest of Strangers: Liberalism and the Politics of Race in New York* (New York: W. W. Norton, 1990), p. 234.

25. C.L.R. James, *Beyond a Boundary* (London: Hutchinson, 1963), pp. 38–9, 70, passim.

26. FitzGerald, *America Revised*, p. 104.

27. "Multiculturalism: Building Bridges or Burning Them?" *Los Angeles Times*, November 30, 1992, p. 1.

28. Gunnar Myrdal, *An American Dilemma: The Negro Problem and Modern Democracy* (New York: Harper & Brothers, 1944), p. 13.

29. Vincent Gordon Harding, "Wrestling Toward the Dawn: The Afro-American Freedom Movement and the Changing Constitution," *Journal of American History* 74 (1987): 31.

Chapter 9

Patriotic history

ROBERT K. FULLINWIDER

History will never be restored as a subject of value unless it is detached from vulgar utilitarianism; it should not be expected to infuse morals or patriotism.

Diane Ravitch[1]

Education for Democracy: A Statement of Principles, issued in 1987 by the American Federation of Teachers, the Educational Excellence Network, and Freedom House, exhorted the nation to "a special effort to raise the level of education for democratic citizenship."[2] It expressed the "fear that many young Americans are growing up without the education needed to develop a solid commitment to those 'notions and sentiments' essential to a democratic form of government."[3]

What curricular reforms can serve this special effort? "We regard the study of *history* as the chief subject in education for democracy," declared *Education for Democracy*, reflecting a growing movement to re-establish history as a vital part of the school curriculum.[4] In the same year, *What Do Our 17-Year-Olds Know?*, by Diane Ravitch and Chester Finn, made national headlines with its findings that students are dismally ignorant of historical facts; the Bradley Commission on History in the Schools issued its preliminary report urging increased historical studies; and California, under the guiding hand of Diane Ravitch and Charlotte Crabtree, rewrote its social studies curriculum to require three years of world history and three years of U.S. history between grades five and twelve.[5] In 1989, the National Commission on Social Studies in the Schools, a joint project of the American Historical Association, the Carnegie Foundation for the Advancement of Teaching, the National Council for the Social Studies, and the Organization of American Historians, likewise urged substantial teaching of world and national history from early grades on.[6]

It seems plausible that a renewal of civic education should be built around solid instruction in history, especially national history. From the time it first entered the school curriculum in our country, teaching history was linked explicitly to "the cultivation of good citizenship."[7] It continues to be so linked today. *One Nation, Many Peoples: A Declaration of Cultural Interdependence*, the 1991 New York report on multiculturalism and the social studies, framed its first concern in these words:

> Despite growing attention to the need for preparing young people to participate in the world community, the United States continues to be deeply involved in nation-building. The common school is generally viewed as one of the principal vehicles for building in our young people the attitudes, knowledge, skills, and understandings essential to continuing national cohesion and viability. The teaching of the nation's history, our national traditions and values, and a common loyalty are purposes commonly accepted as appropriate to the social studies.[8]

Although the New York report sparked criticism for its proposals about ethnicity, race, and multiculturalism, no commentators objected to this leading premise.

How does teaching history, especially national history, serve the aim of "nation-building"? Clearly, in a democracy, an informed citizenry is better than an uninformed one, and school history supplies important facts about past social conditions and their contemporary effects. It also creates a framework for continued learning after school. Historical learning provides more than useful information; it fosters a *sense* of history, which in turn provides perspective and distance on immediate affairs and aids in balanced judgment. In these ways, historical knowledge contributes to citizenship, and thus to "nation-building."

Still, these and other effects of historical studies seem secondary to a special outcome history purportedly underwrites: a sense of identity. As Michael Kammen, a member of the Bradley Commission, observes, "[i]t has become commonplace to say that one sound reason for studying history is to enrich the understanding of identity. . . ."[9] Indeed, the Bradley Commission report itself emphasized that history can "satisfy young people's longing for a sense of identity, and of their time and place in the human story," and the Commission recommended extensive study of history in the schools: "American history to tell us who we are and who we are becoming; the history of Western civilization to reveal our democratic political heritage and its vicissitudes; world history to acquaint us with the nations and people with whom we shall share a common global destiny."[10]

There is considerable plausibility to the idea of history as shaper of identity. We make sense of our lives through stories. Indeed, understood in a certain way, stories *constitute* identities. Alasdair MacIntyre insists that "man is in his actions and practice, as well as in his fictions, *essentially* a story-telling animal."[11] This is so because we "cannot characterize behavior independently of intentions, and we cannot characterize intentions independently of the settings which make these intentions intelligible both to agents themselves and to others."[12] And these settings ultimately have the form of narratives: "I can only answer the question 'What am I to do?' if I can answer the prior question 'Of what story or stories do I find myself a part?'"[13]

Our lives are best conceived as narratives within narratives. Though all of us seek to extend our own stories in ways unique to us, because our personal stories are embedded in larger stories we are only partly the authors of our own. The structures of significance from which our personal narratives draw are already fixed and only partly malleable to our desires and intentions.[14] We inherit our identities just as we inherit our hair color – our identities are given by the ongoing stories into which we find ourselves born. Moreover, our defining commitments – our moral identities – also arise from the roles, expectations, limitations, and duties we inherit, whether we assume them as our own or resist and react against them.

Because stories are so important in our self-understanding, school history naturally suggests itself as a vehicle for shaping political identity.[15] *National* history tells children of the "great deeds and high purposes" of their predecessors and locates them as "participants in an unfinished story."[16] It makes them bearers of a heritage – a "precious inheritance," in the words of *Education for Democracy*.[17] It reminds children that the opportunities and well-being they now enjoy resulted from the hard work and sacrifices of earlier generations, grounding a sense of "gratitude to the past and responsibility for future generations."[18]

I call such history "patriotic history." Its purpose is not merely to inform but to elicit commitments, to inculcate values, *to create citizens*.

Even in a society largely homogeneous in class and culture, and roughly agreed on the interpretation of its past, the project of patriotic history may be open to challenge. Objectors could protest, as Diane Ravitch does, against subordinating historical studies to "vulgar utilitarianism." History, they might argue, ought not be enlisted to "infuse morals or patriotism."

In a society like our own, characterized by great heterogeneity and riven by political struggles among groups trying to achieve certain kinds of social recognition and acquire increased economic opportunity, patriotic history becomes the focus of greatly intensified discord. Edmund Gordon and Francis Roberts, the co-chairpersons of the New York committee that issued *One Nation, Many Peoples,* described in an afterword the conflicts within the committee itself:

> Some of us were shocked by the depth of feelings about diverse renditions of history. Some of us who are comfortable in the belief that the history we know is valid were offended by the assertion that much of that history is incomplete or false. Some of us who feel that the standard histories have excluded or misrepresented important players found it difficult to assert our claims dispassionately. In the views represented by some of us, it appears that much of the dominant or traditional information available to us is viewed with doubt, skepticism and distrust because it does not fit comfortably with the experiences of some, while for others it is simply counter-intuitive. Deciding what to teach under such existential circumstances confronts us with problems of monumental complexity. Even more problematic for the teaching and learning of history and social studies is the ease with which information, ideology and belief become commingled in the minds of people whose interests are at stake – sometimes so much so that these concepts, despite their differential order, came to be interchangeable one for the other. Although we were generally in agreement that histories tend to reflect the interests and perspectives of those who write them, there was a ubiquitous undercurrent of concern for the recognition of historical and other truth.[19]

Composing a patriotic history "confronts us with problems of monumental complexity," say Gordon and Roberts. How should educators and interested citizens address these problems? Can their complexity be reduced? Is the issue truth versus ideology, interest versus interest?

These questions are too large to be tackled in the short span of this chapter. Here, I carve out a small but core issue, the legitimacy of patriotic history. I explore the case for patriotic history sympathetically. I argue that educators are rightly concerned to offer students a "usable past" that encourages the development of desirable civic attitudes and commitments. I consider and deflect objections to patriotic history by Arthur Schlesinger, Jr., and Jurgen Habermas. Finally, I illustrate some of the shoals Historian–Educators must navigate in composing patriotic history.

A USABLE PAST

That night when the Boss and I called on Judge Irwin in the middle of the night and when, burning the road back to Mason City in the dark, the car hurtled between the black fields, he said to me, "There is always something."

And I said, "Maybe not on the Judge."

> *And he said, "Man is conceived in sin and born in corruption and he passeth from the stink of the didie to the stench of the shroud. There is always something."*
>
> *And he told me to dig it out, dig it up, the dead cat with the patches of fur still clinging to the tight, swollen, dove-gray hide. It was the proper job for me, for, as I have said, I was once a student of history. A student of history does not care what he digs out of the ash pile, the midden, the sublunary dung heap, which is the human past. He doesn't care whether it is the dead pussy or the Kohinoor diamond. So it was a proper assignment for me, an excursion into the past.*
>
> Robert Penn Warren, *All the King's Men*[20]

Patriotic history proceeds on the premise that children need a common, "usable past" if they are to be formed as citizens willing to make the sacrifices necessary to support and improve the nation's political institutions. Is patriotic history a concession to the "vulgar utilitarianism" Diane Ravitch would have us deplore? Is the search for a "usable past" a misuse of history?

The criticisms in Arthur Schlesinger, Jr.'s widely read little book, *The Disuniting of America: Reflections on a Multicultural Society*, might lead us to think so. Schlesinger argues that writing or teaching history as a means of "defining national identity" turns history "into a weapon," and

> [h]istory as a weapon is an abuse of history. The high purpose of history is not the presentation of self or the vindication of identity but the recognition of complexity and the search for knowledge.[21]

"Honest history calls for the unexpurgated record."[22] History should be "disinterested intellectual inquiry," not "manipulated" as an "instrument of social cohesion and political purpose,"[23] and our schools should teach it "for its own sake."[24]

History for its own sake, disinterested, noninstrumental: patriotic history is none of these, so it seems to stand condemned. But the force of Schlesinger's argument fades the moment we make it more precise. To announce *the* purpose of history implies "history" means only one thing and the historian has only one role. But the historian can play many roles, in some of which disinterest would be a vice, not a virtue. Consider these three roles and the aims that animate them: the Historian–Scholar, the Historian–Educator, and the Historian–Public Citizen.

Scholarship, let us grant, is indeed subservient to one imperative only, "disinterested truth-seeking." Whatever the Historian–Scholar finds in the sublunary dung heap of the past, whether it is the dead pussy or the Kohinoor diamond, its being there – its truth – is a sufficient reason for him to exhume it, *no matter what the consequences.* That, I take it, is the meaning of being *disinterested.*

But an Educator may not ignore consequences. The Educator's task is to tutor the young toward a certain end, and every tool must be measured by its efficacy for that end. The Historian–Educator, whose tool is history, is no exception. Similarly, the Historian–Public Citizen, by whom I mean the historian who aspires to give public discourse a theme or story or guiding vision as a means of clarifying public purpose, likewise concerns herself with the effects of her engagement. Whatever the relation of the Historian–Educator and the Historian–Public Citizen to truth and truth-seeking, it is, and must be, an *interested* relation.

We can see this quite clearly by looking at one of the educational outcomes aimed for in the California History–Social Science Framework: through studying history, students "should recognize that ideas and actions have real consequences – that history, in other words, is not simply the ebb and flow of impersonal forces but is shaped and changed by the ideas and actions of individuals and governments."[25] Now, aiming to produce such "recognition" makes educational sense. If young people were to think their own actions can make no difference to the larger world, why would they act in it rather than resign themselves to it? Why would they exude public energy rather than public apathy? How would they be good citizens within democratic institutions requiring active participation?

But how shall the Historian–Educator convey this important lesson in agency to eighth graders, say? Certain kinds of historical approaches and perspectives clearly don't lend themselves very well to incitement to action. The long-term perspective of Fernand Braudel's *The Mediterranean and the Mediterranean World in the Age of Philip II*, for example, reduces events and actions to "no more than the foam on the sea of history," a sea really governed by large and remote structural forces.[26] Such a perspective may be the best one for certain scholarly purposes. Indeed, historians might argue that it is *the* best perspective for scholarship, all things considered, since it gives the best vantage point for achieving real historical understanding. But it is clearly not the best perspective for encouraging civic activism in students through belief that their actions can make a difference in the world.

The same is true of religiously and philosophically based views of history whose bent is fatalistic or pessimistic. For example, a view like Heidegger's, which characterizes our own times as deeply nihilistic and traces the cause of this nihilism to those very Enlightenment notions of liberty and autonomy that underlie our democratic practices, does not provide a very usable past for encouraging students to trust in their own actions and in the actions of democratic governments.[27] Whatever we may think about the ultimate truth of such views, the educational aim posited by the California Framework requires telling the human story with a different slant.

The same considerations apply to historical content as well as historical perspective. The educator must select with an eye toward desired effect. Schlesinger declares that "[h]onest history calls for the unexpurgated record." Let us concede that the Historian–Scholar rightfully holds nothing back, however horrible. But does this rule apply to the Historian–Educator? What if the unexpurgated record undermines rather than promotes the aim posited in the California Framework? Isn't the Historian–Educator going to have to provide a rather artful and selective packaging of the contents of the ash pile, the dung heap which is the human past, if eighth graders are to take from their historical studies optimism about their institutions, hope for a brighter future, and faith in their own efforts? Auschwitz and Hiroshima, world wars of extraordinary destructiveness, mass starvation, totalitarianism, slavery, colonialism, the obliteration of civilizations, barbarism at every turn – all of these and more must be conveyed to students in a way that fortifies their resolve and encourages their industry, not sickens and unnerves them.

The history teacher in the California classroom has an *interest*: to instill a sense of efficacy in students. This interest is ulterior to historical truth. Of course, the teacher has other educational aims as well. Indeed, one of them, we may suppose, is to implant in her students a love of truth. *But this interest, too, is ulterior to historical truth.* There is no guarantee that historical truth supports lessons in the love of truth. A comprehensive survey of the human ash pile may reveal that lies have served most human interests better than truth has. Implanting the love of truth in students would then call for an adroitly blinkered tour through the ash pile. Every educator must keep her eye on her ulterior purpose.

Schlesinger himself writes with an ulterior purpose. *The Disuniting of America* is not a disinterested look at the past. In it, Schlesinger wears the hat not of Historian–Scholar but of Historian–Public Citizen. He means to warn fellow citizens against certain false views of history not simply because they are false but because they are dangerous. They threaten our national cohesion; they stretch bonds "sufficiently fragile already."[28] The proper account of our past, on the other hand, strengthens the "common purpose" that holds us together. It reinvigorates the American Creed. It reminds us of the "marvelous inheritance" bestowed upon us, that we might better commit ourselves to preserve and sustain it. Truly, the proper account of our past can "above all . . . give a sense of national identity," Schlesinger announces at the end of his book, forgetting his earlier warnings about history as weapon.[29] *The Disuniting of America* is itself a prime example of patriotic history – history told for effect, history told not simply to inform but to elicit and strengthen commitments to national unity.

Schlesinger can so easily conflate the Scholar/Educator/Public Citizen into one undifferentiated Historian and speak of *the* purpose of history because he does not imagine truth and good purpose coming apart. Accurate history is always good for us. Accurate history makes us better citizens. Accurate history teaches the California lesson: "Properly taught, history will convey a sense . . . of the ability of individuals and peoples to overcome obstacles."[30] This faith that more accurate history is more civically useful history keeps Schlesinger from noticing and addressing the possibility that the Historian–Scholar and the Historian–Educator may face diverging imperatives. Schlesinger looks at American history through the eyes of an optimist, self-confessedly so.[31]

This same faith animates another recent contribution to the multicultural lists, Ronald Takaki's *A Different Mirror: A History of Multicultural America*.[32] While Schlesinger is a wary observer of multicultural history, Takaki is an enthusiastic proponent. *A Different Mirror* tells the stories of Irish, Jewish, Japanese, Chinese, and Mexican immigrants to the United States as well as the stories of African-Americans, Native Americans, and indigenous Hispanics – people transported to this country as slaves or incorporated by conquest or expansion. Their stories are told from their own perspectives and through the voices of common people.

Takaki offers two reasons why such a multicultural telling should be incorporated into any larger history of America. First, such enlarged history is more accurate.[33] Second, it has the power, by allowing different groups to understand one another, to help a divided and fractious people "to get along" (in Rodney King's words).[34] Greater accuracy and mutual understanding go hand in hand.

Each of the groups in Takaki's story endures oppressions and hardships – slavery, discrimination, dispossession, exploitation, hostility. Yet each struggles for its place in the American sun. Though victimized, members of these groups are not victims: they act for themselves, defying stereotypes of passivity and docility.[35] By the sweat of their brows, they build American agriculture, industry, transportation. By their challenges and strikes, they broaden legal rights for themselves and all workers. By their "resistance against racial borders and distances," they appropriate and advance "America's principle that 'all men are created equal.'"[36]

The apogee, at least symbolically, of this story of struggle by different groups comes with World War II. There we find contributing to the war effort Navajo signal units and Cherokee pilots; Chinese airplane builders; Japanese infantrymen; Mexican rail laborers and artillerymen; and black defense workers and tankers.[37] There we find all of America's groups fighting "A War for Democracy," "*Fighting as One People.*"[38] There we find a vital "lesson . . . forged in the crucible of America's multicultural history," a lesson teaching, in the words of Franklin Roosevelt, that "Americanism is a matter of mind and heart"; it "is not, and never was, a matter of race or ancestry."[39]

This is the same lesson Schlesinger wants us to learn from history.[40] Takaki's multicultural story no less than Schlesinger's traditional account provides a past usable for patriotic purposes: for creating citizens. Takaki's story emphasizes the importance of agency even in the most oppressive circumstances. It conveys the dignity of common people, who quietly struggle under difficult conditions and who, in large and small ways, refuse to submit passively to abuse, discrimination, and exploitation. Takaki tells a story to inspire readers to take up the uncompleted project of "nation-building" (to use the words of *One Nation, Many Peoples*), the uncompleted project of making "Americanism" truly a matter of heart and mind rather than race or ancestry.

Takaki, like Schlesinger, is an optimist. In his view, we "have nothing to fear but our fear of our own diversity."[41] Embrace our multicultural story, learn from and accept each other, and we will be a stronger society for it.

Optimism about "accurate history" – faith that it will make us better rather than worse – is not something the historian accidentally stumbles across in the sublunary dung heap; it is not something that ineluctably jumps out at us if we sift there long enough. It is something the historian *brings* to the telling of history. Optimism may be a vice in the Historian–Scholar, or at least it may not be a virtue; but in the Historian–Public Citizen and the Historian–Educator surely it *is* a virtue. The Public Citizen and the Educator have an *interest* – in the present case, to teach and encourage a sense of efficacy and to define the project of "getting along together" that the rising generation of citizens ought to take up and advance. This interest shapes their accounts of the past into a patriotic history intimating to students and citizens the *potential* for effective action in the future. The Historian–Educator and Historian–Public Citizen need a faith in progress.

PATRIOTISM

The difference [between altruism and patriotism] is that patriotism is based on identification with others in a particular common enterprise. I am not dedicated to defending the liberty of just anyone, but I feel the bond of solidarity with my compatriots in our common enterprise, the common expression of our respective dignity. Patriotism is somewhere between friendship, or family feeling, on one side, and altruistic dedication on the other. The latter has no concern for the particular: I am inclined to act for the good of anyone anywhere. The former attach me to particular people. My patriotic allegiance does not bind me to individual people in this familial way; I may not know most of my compatriots, and may not particularly want them as friends when I do meet them. But particularity enters in because my bond to these people passes through our participation in a common political entity. Functioning republics are like families in this crucial respect, that part of what binds people together is their common history. Family ties or old friendships are deep because of what we have lived through together, and republics are bonded by time and climactic transitions.

Charles Taylor[42]

That Schlesinger proves not to be an effective critic of patriotic history but rather a practitioner of it doesn't mean patriotic history is immune to objection. Critics may still think it misdirected. They may take my propositions about constructing a "usable past" as casting the Historian–Educator or Historian–Public Citizen in a role too similar to that of a propagandist.

Patriotic history induces citizens to shoulder the burdens of defending and reforming particular institutions by telling a story that connects citizens to those institutions as *theirs*. Why couldn't citizens, instead, be prompted to support particular institutions simply because they are good, simply because they embody certain attractive principles? Patriotic history would then be unnecessary for creating civic responsibility. This is the possibility seemingly offered by Jurgen Habermas.

In 1986, the West German *Historikerstreit* ("Historians' Controversy") threw that country's intellectual community into a furious tumult centering on historical re-interpretations of German history in the Nazi era. Coming to terms with the recent past has, of course, not been an easy process for Germans. West German historians began only after about 1958 to study the Nazi period thoroughly. West German citizens in general exhibited little relish for looking backwards, and in the 1950s and 1960s, students were taught "next to nothing" about World War II and the concentration camps.[43] In 1982, after thirteen years of rule by the Social Democratic Party, the conservative Christian Democratic Union under Helmut Kohl assumed power. Part of Kohl's desire as Chancellor, reflecting broader conservative sentiment, was to create a more "positive historical consciousness" for West Germany.[44] He supported the creation of museums in Berlin and

Bonn devoted to the German past and, of course, conceived the visit to Bitburg Cemetery by President Reagan on the 40th anniversary of V-E day – a ceremony meant to symbolize Germany's full partnership with the West and "symbolically . . . wipe away the last residues of moral probation under which the Federal Republic still labored."[45]

Among some German historians and intellectuals, the matter of "German guilt" became a topic of intense discussion, and in June 1986, Ernst Nolte, philosopher/historian and author of the well-known 1963 book *Three Faces of Fascism*, published an article in the *Frankfurter Allgemeine Zeitung* called "The Past That Will Not Pass Away." Nolte argued against the thesis that the Nazi extermination of Jews was "unique." He claimed that "everything the National Socialists later did – with the sole exception of technical procedures of gassing" – had already been done by the Soviet Union in the 1920s and 1930s. Thus, Nolte argued, it was necessary to ask: "Did the National Socialists carry out . . . an 'Asiatic' deed only because they regarded themselves and their kind as the potential or real victims of an 'Asiatic' deed? Wasn't the 'Gulag Archipelago' more original than Auschwitz? Wasn't class murder by the Bolsheviks logically and actually prior to racial murder on the part of the Nazis?"[46] The question, of course, was meant as an answer. The point for Nolte of putting and answering the question was not merely to set the historical record straight; recognizing the context of Auschwitz would, he hoped, dispel the "myth of absolute evil" that stood as a barrier to German identity.[47]

During the same period, Michael Sturmer, another conservative historian, was writing a series of essays on the need for historians to provide for West Germans a usable past.[48] Sturmer, too, lamented the Germans' "obsession with their 'guilt'" and emphasized the need for a nation to have a positive sense of identity.[49] The "fall of God and the decline of Religion," Sturmer wrote, has deprived individuals of the traditional framework for defining their "personal or collective place in time and space."[50] Without a religious foundation of values, a people must turn to its own history as a source of meaning. Historians should aid this turn by providing a usable past.[51] That is, they should assume the role of what I have called the Historian–Public Citizen.

Nolte's and Sturmer's arguments, contentious as they are, might have remained the objects of intramural historical debate but for the interjection of Jurgen Habermas, Germany's best-known contemporary philosopher. In July 1986, Habermas published in *Die Zeit* a broadside against Nolte, Sturmer, and a third historian, Andreas Hillgruber. Hillgruber's *Two Kinds of Downfall*, published that year, joined together two separate essays, one on the destruction of European

Jews and the other on the destruction of the Third Reich. The second, longer essay caused Habermas to lump Hillgruber with Nolte and Sturmer. In that essay Hillgruber defends the German Army's tenacious resistance on the Eastern Front in 1944–45, even though it prolonged Hitler's reign and the destruction of the Jews, by arguing that the historian "must identify himself with the concrete fate of the German population in the East and with the desperate and sacrificial exertions of the German Army . . . which sought to defend the population from the orgy of revenge of the Red Army, the mass rapine, the arbitrary killing, and the compulsory deportations."[52]

Habermas's harsh attack on the three historians, "Apologetic Tendencies,"[53] ignited a furious controversy on all sides about "historical revisionism" and the proper use of history. As Habermas characterized the controversy, one side had a "functionalist understanding of the public use of history" while the other side, his own, opposed "this kind of 'politics of history'" and advocated "enlightenment."[54] The "bad side" wanted to make use of history to support a national identity rooted in an acceptable past,[55] while the "good side" eschewed identity "centered on national identity"[56] for one that embraced universal principles of right. The conservative side wanted a national identity founded on a "past that one can approve of"[57] while Habermas wanted a "post-conventional identity"[58] founded on a "constitutional patriotism,"[59] rooted in the "universalist value orientations of democracy"[60] and "human rights."[61] Habermas thought West Germany needed a "sober political identity [that] has detached itself from the background of a past centered on national history."[62]

Habermas's characterization of the two sides presents a distinction between a civic education that attaches us to our institutions because they exemplify some external standard of excellence and a civic education that attaches us to our institutions because they are ours. If there is a patriotism cut free of national history, a patriotism attached to abstract principles, then we needn't start down the path of "patriotic history" as I've characterized it. We needn't get into doubtful quarrels about creating a usable national past. We needn't pose a choice between universalist outlook and particularist attachment.

But Habermas doesn't actually succeed in articulating a patriotism that doesn't depend on particular traditions. His patriotism needs its own usable national past, a "past one can approve of." Habermas differs with his opponents not on the need for an acceptable past but on what that acceptable past need be. West German "constitutional patriotism" turns out not to leave national history and culture behind at all. Its ties to universal principles "have to be nourished by a heritage of traditions that is consonant with them. . . . [T]he abstract idea of the universalization of democracy and human rights forms the hard substance through which the rays of national tradition – the language, literature, and history of one's own nation – are refracted."[63]

The universal principles of right that Habermas lauds are embedded in a particular constitution – West German Basic Law – and it is this particular constitution West Germans are loyal to. And there is a story behind that embedding that must be told in the right way.

Our life, says Habermas, is the product of "familial, local, political, and intellectual traditions . . . a historical milieu that made us what we are today. None of us can escape this milieu, because our identities, both as individuals and as Germans, are indissolubly interwoven with it."[64] Now, one unavoidable fact about those traditions is that they made possible Auschwitz, "not by contingent circumstances but intrinsically."[65] It consequently falls to Germans to keep alive the memory of Auschwitz as the unique evil it was. Thus, Nolte's comparison of the Holocaust with Soviet crimes is to be rejected. Germans are the inheritors of their traditions, according to Habermas, but the way they critically appropriate and continue those traditions is up to them.[66] Critically appropriating and continuing those traditions means finding something in them acceptable even in the face of Auschwitz.

But here is the daunting challenge. No matter how much garden-variety barbarism there is in a nation's past, usually some good can be found in it, something in its traditions that endures and transcends the barbarism. It may require some imaginative reworking, some strategic forgetfulness, to get the story of the past to be "acceptable," but usually it can be done without great violence to the truth. However, what happens if an event like Auschwitz lies across the past, an event so uniquely awful it threatens to *annihilate* all past value, achievement, and good? What remains to nourish even the most abstract constitutional patriotism? What is there to appropriate and carry forward in any way?

This is the apparent sticking point the conservative German historians mean to overcome by their "revisionism." Who is a German? The story they want to tell goes something like this. A German is someone whose culture and history stretch over centuries. The period 1933–45 stands over that history as a horrible and troubling time, not in any way to be glossed over or downplayed. But the horrible events of 1933–45 must be seen in context, seen as partly a reaction to Bolshevism and the vast exterminations by Stalin. Moreover, both Bolshevism and National Socialism can be viewed as extreme reactions to the dehumanizing tendencies of secular modernism.

This interpretation "normalizes" 1933–45 by fitting it, and its admitted horrors, into the longer history of German and European history. There is much in that longer history that constitutes a "past one can approve of," and the hope of the conservative interpretation is to bracket the events of 1933–45 in a way that leaves some of those elements of the longer past alive for appropriation and use in German identity. If the events of 1933–45 are not bracketed somehow, if Auschwitz literally annihilates all the value in the past, then what hope is there for a German identity?

Habermas offers a different interpretation to overcome the same sticking point. A German, on this interpretation, is one who appropriates 1933–45 in a particular way, not by fitting it, however awkwardly, into a continuous German story, not by "normalizing" it in some way, but by keeping "alive, without distortion . . . the memory of the sufferings of those who were murdered by German hands" and by affirming what followed the end of the Third Reich as a "new beginning" dedicated to constitutional democracy and human rights.[67] It is only by keeping the memory of Auschwitz alive as absolute evil, and defining future German identity in opposition to it, that Auschwitz is prevented from annihilating the worth of all German traditions. The very project of living against Auschwitz from 1945 on, while creating a healthy democracy and free, open political life, constitutes a "past one can approve of," and one that lets elements of older traditions be retained and appropriated.

The contest between Habermas and his conservative opponents is not, then, a contest between a "functionalist" versus "nonfunctionalist" view of history. Habermas needs a usable past for his form of patriotism as much as his opponents need one for theirs. Habermas's "constitutional patriotism" is not (in the terms Charles Taylor set out above) "altruistic dedication" to a set of universal principles. It is a readiness to identify with particular political institutions. The identity-sustaining allegiance to the principles embodied in those institutions rests not just on the general character of the principles as principles of right but on the specific, always-remembered, duty-defining fact that they "were violated in an unprecedented way" in 1933–45.[68] German constitutional patriotism arises out of a specific shared mission, a mission in which each German citizen can find his dignity affirmed and reflected.[69]

INTERESTED TRUTH: TWO LESSONS

The Historian–Educator and the Historian–Public Citizen are interested rather than disinterested partisans of the truth. They reconstruct usable pasts for students and citizens. They write and teach with an eye to effect.

Although American historians in writing for the eighth grade do not have to navigate around the Third Reich and Auschwitz as German historians do, they have in slavery (and its aftermath), as well as

in the displacement and extermination of the Indians, their own considerable challenges to interpretation and composition. Stories about
racial and ethnic conflict, which abound in the American past and
present, invariably risk controversy. We may imagine that the "depth
of feelings" Gordon and Roberts noted among the members of the
New York committee had to do largely with "diverse renditions" of
the story of race and ethnicity in American history, and not different
interpretations of the value of the gold standard.

How shall the patriotic historian proceed in the face of such depth
of feeling? Within the debate about multicultural history, two ubiqui-
tous watchwords – "accuracy" and "inclusiveness" – seem to offer
guidance. Both Schlesinger and Takaki, from different vantage points,
endorse more accurate, more inclusive history. *One Nation, Many
Peoples* follows suit, proposing that the history taught in New York
classrooms be "based on up-to-date scholarship" and be "culturally
inclusive." "This inclusivity," it goes on to say, "should incorporate
opposing opinions and divergent interpretations."[70]

Accuracy and *inclusiveness* are like mom and apple pie: no one can
oppose them in the abstract. However, neither do they offer much
guidance to the patriotic historian. The mechanical application of the
two standards would result in stories neither multiculturalists nor
anti-multiculturalists would accept. It would make histories mindless.
The patriotic historian cannot escape the need to impose a particular –
and controversial – interpretation on the past. In composing her accurate and inclusive story, she has to distinguish between *real* and *spurious* accuracy, *genuine* and *specious* inclusiveness. And how will she do
this except by reference to the usable past she has in view? Two
lessons in American history illustrate what I mean.

In 1991, the adoption by California of the Houghton Mifflin Social
Studies textbook series occasioned impassioned debate in some school
districts, as critics charged that the series distorted or misrepresented
the experiences of various minority groups.[71] One charge the critics
didn't make, however, was that the account of Martin Luther King,
Jr., in *A More Perfect Union*, the eighth-grade text in the series, omitted
important facts.[72] In a 620-page book covering the whole of United
States history, it is quite understandable that Martin Luther King gets
no more than a few lines. The text's authors had to be very selective in their account of King. They describe King's charisma from
the pulpit, his doctrine of non-violence, and his moving "I Have a
Dream" speech delivered in 1963 before the Lincoln Memorial.[73] They
do not refer, however, to his multiple infidelities or his plagiarism of
others' writings in his doctoral dissertation.

Some facts get included, some omitted. What is the principle of
selection? It might be argued that the second set of facts have no

bearing on King's leadership in the Civil Rights Movement, and thus have no place in a brief passage where the only issue is that of leadership. The principle of selection is material relevancy. But this answer won't quite do. Though the second set of facts doesn't bear on King's leadership, it does bear on the *greatness* of his leadership. And his greatness is at issue in the text as well as his leadership, for children naturally infer that men who do great things are great men. That inference is allowed to stand – indeed is encouraged – by the brief passages about King in *A More Perfect Union*. And the real point of omitting the second set of facts is not to upset or complicate that inference. Indeed, were a textbook deliberately to include the second set of facts along with the first, people would justly accuse it of trying to discredit King.

Not all men and women who do great things are great persons. In some cases their personal failings or misconduct so dishonor them as to obscure all their achievements.[74] In other cases, an individual's failings and misconduct, even of a serious nature, can leave untouched the greatness of his accomplishments and of his own person. There is no simple correspondence between doing good and being good. Assessments of achievement and greatness can involve many complications. It is precisely these complications that we fear may overwhelm or disorient eighth graders reading a text describing Martin Luther King, and that justify omitting the second set of facts.[75]

In leaving out those facts, however, did the authors of *A More Perfect Union* write "less accurate" history? They certainly omitted some of that "latest scholarship" *One Nation, Many Peoples* favors. Even so, adding the second set of facts, because of its effect, would have brought only a spurious, not a real, accuracy to the text. Martin Luther King, Jr., is now an American icon. The successful political struggle to establish a national holiday for him fixes his name in the American pantheon alongside Washington, Lincoln, and Jefferson. Whatever the true significance of his role in the Civil Rights Movement in comparison to that of other leaders and participants, his name is shorthand for that movement and its aspirations. Since history texts will invariably associate the Civil Rights Movement and King, to include in the necessarily brief compass of King's deeds his plagiarism and infidelity would have the effect of discrediting not only King but the Movement. The King depicted in *A More Perfect Union* and similar texts, on the other hand, leaves to children a vital legacy, a movement for racial justice and human dignity to be carried further toward completion by new generations. The King of "I Have a Dream" lets students never forget the upwelling of hope embodied in the Civil Rights Movement. The King of "I Have a Dream" bequeaths to students a usable past.

Not only did the authors of *A More Perfect Union* reject a spurious accuracy, they also rejected a specious inclusiveness. They did not offer "opposing opinions and divergent interpretations" of King. They did not tell the story of King from "multiple perspectives."

As one of its principal recommendations, *One Nation, Many Peoples* declares that the "social studies should be taught from multiple perspectives." Too often, it tells us, history has been taught from only one or a few points of view. For example, typically the "story of the western United States is told as one of westward expansion, assuming the perspective of the migrating Easterners and disregarding the native men and women already there or the long-established Hispanic influence and settlements in the West."[76]

Arthur Schlesinger agrees: "Of course history should be taught from a variety of perspectives. Let our children imagine the arrival of Columbus from the viewpoint of those who met him as well as those who sent him."[77] Here we seem to have a potential pedagogical solution to teaching history in the face of disagreement about the meaning of the past: teach history from "multiple perspectives"; teach our disagreements.[78]

It is, indeed, often quite illuminating to be aware of, and see from, different perspectives. Taking account of other perspectives can lead us to revise our own, or to construct a preferred perspective that ours and others should answer to. At other times matters can simply be left in the air: we can note that Group A believes one thing, Group B another thing, and leave it at that.

But noting that there are different views can also, in the right context, prejudice a particular view rather than leave everything in the air. Were *A More Perfect Union* to add to its account of Martin Luther King that *some people think* he was a philandering, plagiarizing opportunist while others think he was an American hero, the effect would be much the same as simply itemizing the charges as a list of facts. The effect would be to cast doubt in eighth graders' minds about the greatness of King.[79] The effect would be to make this piece of the past less "usable" for many students. *A More Perfect Union* wisely eschewed "multiple perspectives" about King.

It eschewed "multiple perspectives" about another "usable past" as well. *One Nation, Many Peoples* complains that New York's "K–6 syllabi . . . focus on celebrations such as Thanksgiving and Columbus Day without examining other perspectives than those of Europeans, such as the perspectives of Native Americans."[80] We can easily agree with both *One Nation, Many Peoples* and Arthur Schlesinger that Columbus can, and ought to be, looked at from many perspectives. Columbus plays no vital role in the moral economy and civic understanding of eighth-grade students. He is essentially a place-marker: after him the

Spanish, French, Dutch, Portuguese, and English came to America. That he might be demoted from a courageous, far-sighted hero to a rapacious plunderer if we look at him not from the perspective of Europe but of aboriginal America is of little consequence.

But consider the second example *One Nation, Many Peoples* joins to Columbus: Thanksgiving. How should *it* be treated? Quite possibly New York's K–6 syllabi do offer objectionable renderings of Thanksgiving, but here is what eighth graders would have learned were they reading *A More Perfect Union:*

> The Pilgrims struggled through the terrible winter of 1620–21 at Plymouth, half of them dying in the process. They did not seek contact with Indians, whom they feared and mistrusted. When spring came, they had run out of food and were too weak to begin planting.
>
> Just as the Pilgrims' situation was getting desperate, Samoset, a Pemaquid Indian, made his appearance. To the Pilgrims' astonishment, he spoke some English, which he said he had learned from English fishermen. He made his tribe's peaceful intentions known and introduced them to Squanto, an Indian who had been enslaved in Spain and had spent two years in England. Squanto showed the colonists where to fish and hunt and taught them to plant native crops such as corn, beans, and squash.
>
> After the 1621 harvest, the Pilgrims wanted to give thanks to God . . . [who] they felt had provided them with plentiful crops. Consequently, they invited their Indian neighbors to a common feast of "thanksgiving," as the colony's governor, William Bradford, proclaimed it. The peaceful relations between the Pilgrims and the Pemaquids lasted for years, and Americans have continued to celebrate Thanksgiving to this day.[81]

Now, how or why would *One Nation, Many Peoples* want to augment this story with another "perspective"?

Some critics, of course, complain about *false accounts* of Thanksgiving. Michael Dorris, a writer of Modoc ancestry, recalls (in an essay entitled "Why I'm Not Thankful for Thanksgiving") his son bringing home a school handout with the caption "[The Pilgrims] served pumpkins and turkeys and corn and squash. The Indians had never seen such a feast!" and retorts: "On the contrary! The *Pilgrims* had literally never seen 'such a feast,' since all foods mentioned are exclusively indigenous to the Americas and had been provided, or so legend has it, by the local tribe."[82] Apart from egregiously false depictions, critics may also protest accounts that "glorify the Pilgrims" and "marginalize" the Indians,[83] but the story in *A More Perfect Union* does neither.

What, then, are the perspectives *A More Perfect Union* omits? Perhaps these comments by one multiculturalist supply a clue: "as Americans, we commemorate holidays such as Thanksgiving, a celebration of ancestral survival . . . , but the reduction of Native Americans to second-class status which facilitated ancestral survival is not acknowledged."[84] If this spurious linking of Thanksgiving with the history of depredations against Native Americans is the missing perspective, then *A More Perfect Union* does well to omit it. The story recounted in *A More Perfect Union* lets students respond directly to the simple decency, humility, harmony, and peaceableness reflected in the first Thanksgiving and memorialized in subsequent ones. There is no need to sabotage that response by inserting into Thanksgiving a *mea culpa* for reducing "Native Americans to second-class status." On the contrary, the Thanksgiving of *A More Perfect Union* pictures the cross-racial comity that might have been and that might yet be if students commit themselves to it. It supplies students a very "usable past."

The "multiple perspectives" approach recommended in *One Nation, Many Peoples* can't serve as an uncritical, unrestricted, across-the-board policy for writing or teaching history. In Takaki's *A Different Mirror*, for example, though many different perspectives get attention, many others don't. Indeed, if he had allowed equal time to perspectives from which the struggles of ordinary Chinese, Japanese, Jewish, African-American, Irish, and Native American men and women had no significance, Takaki would have undermined his own project. His story of multicultural America would have ceased to be a story. It would have degenerated into gibberish. No historian, not even the Historian–Scholar, can write a story in which all perspectives get equal time and no perspective dominates. Certainly, the Historian–Educator cannot, if she is to supply a usable past.[85]

CONCLUSION

When Diane Ravitch advises us to detach history from a "vulgar utilitarianism," it is not clear whether she means the emphasis to fall on "vulgar" or on "utilitarianism." If the latter, I have argued that her advice is not sound. The Historian–Educator necessarily uses history instrumentally. The Historian–Educator has interests. A truly told history must nevertheless be truly told in a way that promotes those interests. On the other hand, if Ravitch means to condemn "vulgar" instrumentalism, then nothing argued in this chapter makes patriotic history fall under her condemnation.

Identity has many dimensions, to be sure, some of them quite unattractive, and putting history to work promoting identity might lead to objectionable forms of history. On some accounts of collective identity, for example, "every identity is the affirmation of a difference, the determination of an 'other' that is going to play the role of a 'constitutive outside.'"[86] Upon this Other we project negative attributes, defining our own group by contrast. In the context of this account, we could think of patriotic history as the marking off of national identities, defining our own nation in contrast to the inferior, deficient, backward, vicious, or perverse qualities of others. Worse, in serving as the handmaiden of nationalism, patriotic history "creates a mythic land in which people understand themselves and each other" and "legitimates attacks on people [within] whose lives are different."[87]

Similarly, patriotic history might be thought to serve national pride. Just as multiculturalists argue that children must see in their schoolbooks their own culture and attractive representatives of their own racial or ethnic group in order to achieve "self-esteem," so we might see patriotic history as designed to make citizens "feel good" about being Americans. But, of course, many forms of pride are vices rather than virtues. In a quite common form of conceit, we congratulate ourselves as though the accomplishments of our ancestors reflected credit on us. We bask in their reflected glory, which patriotic history limns for us.

But the core idea of identity I have seized upon in this chapter is not essentially connected to puffed-up pride or national chauvinism or denigration of the Other. The core idea has to do not with *pride* but with *duty*: what projects over time, begun by others, am I duty-bound to take on (or resist)? Our answers to that question fix our moral identities. It is *that* identity – moral identity – around which I build my sympathetic account of patriotic history.

Patriotic history, as I've described it, seems clearly required by the California Framework, Diane Ravitch's own handiwork. The object of the social studies, the Framework tells us, is to help students "develop a keen sense of ethics and citizenship," so that they might "*care* deeply about the quality of life in their community, their nation, and their world."[88]

Students need a usable past, I've suggested, a past in which they can find values and projects to take as their own legacies. As heirs, they define their own lives around goals and commitments that build on what came before. Their moral and political identities reside in making "more perfect" the unions and Union they are a part of. There must be, then, something perfectible in those unions. The role of Historian-Educators is to tell stories that let the "something perfectible" be revealed and carried forward.

NOTES

1. Diane Ravitch, "The Plight of History in American Schools," in *Historical Literacy: The Case for History in American Education*, ed. Paul Gagnon (New York: Macmillan, 1989), p. 68.

2. *Education for Democracy: A Statement of Principles – Guidelines for Strengthening the Teaching of Democratic Values* (Washington, D.C.: American Federation of Teachers, 1987), p. 7.
3. Ibid., quoting Tocqueville.
4. Ibid., p. 17 (emphasis added).
5. Diane Ravitch and Chester E. Finn, Jr., *What Do Our 17-Year-Olds Know? A Report of the First National Assessment of History and Literature* (New York: Harper & Row, 1987); Bradley Commission on History in the Schools, "Building a History Curriculum: Guidelines for Teaching History in the Schools," in *Historical Literacy*, ed. Gagnon, pp. 16–47; *History-Social Science Framework for California Public Schools* (Sacramento: California Department of Education, 1988).
6. *Charting a Course: Social Studies for the 21st Century* (Washington, D.C.: National Council for the Social Studies, 1989).
7. Statement by the NEA's Committee on the Social Studies, quoted by Clair Keller, "National History and Citizenship Education," Institute for Philosophy and Public Policy Working Paper (College Park, Md.: University of Maryland, 1987), p. 13. See also the foreword to Richard E. Thursfield, ed., *The Study and Teaching of American History* (Washington, D.C.: National Council for the Social Studies, 1946), p. viii; James Howard and Thomas Mendenhall, *Making History Come Alive* (Washington, D.C.: Council for Basic Education, 1982), pp. 2, 14–6; Roy F. Nichols and Arthur C. Bining, "The Role of History," in *Education for Citizen Responsibilities*, ed. Franklin L. Burdette (Princeton, N.J.: Princeton University Press, 1942), p. 62.
8. New York State Social Studies Review and Development Committee, *One Nation, Many Peoples: A Declaration of Cultural Interdependence* (Albany: New York State Education Department, June 1991), p. vii.
9. Michael Kammen, "History Is Our Heritage: The Past in Contemporary American Culture," in *Historical Literacy*, ed. Gagnon, p. 149.
10. Bradley Commission, "Building a History Curriculum," in *Historical Literacy*, ed. Gagnon, pp. 22, 24.
11. Alasdair MacIntyre, *After Virtue* (Notre Dame, Ind.: University of Notre Dame Press, 1981), p. 201 (emphasis added).
12. Ibid., p. 192. See also Jerome Bruner, *Acts of Meaning* (Cambridge, Mass.: Harvard University Press, 1990), p. 33.
13. MacIntyre, *After Virtue*, p. 201. Bruner concurs: see *Acts of Meaning*, p. 35 and throughout. See also Owen Flanagan, *Varieties of Moral Personality: Ethics and Psychological Realism* (Cambridge, Mass.: Harvard University Press, 1991).
14. Bruner offers this image: "When we enter human life, it is as if we walk on stage into a play whose enactment is already in progress – a play whose somewhat open plot determines what parts we may play and toward what denouements we may be heading" (p. 34). Michael Sandel in *Liberalism and the Limits of Justice* (Cambridge: Cambridge University Press, 1982) makes MacIntyre's point in terms of moral identity: "to have a character is to know that I move in a history I neither summon nor command, which carries consequences nonetheless for my choices and conduct" (p. 179).

15. "[H]istory has generally played a more fundamental role than literature in the creation and maintenance of national identities. A democratic public culture cannot survive without broad commitments to democratic ideas, traditions, and freedoms that come in part from a knowledge of history. Public debate requires a shared vocabulary that emerges from the historical experience and language of people who acknowledge some common values or principles or founding events." Lloyd Kramer and Donald Reid, "Introduction: Historical Knowledge, Education, and Public Culture," in *Learning History in America*, ed. Lloyd Kramer, Donald Reid, and William L. Barney (Minneapolis: University of Minnesota Press, 1994), p. 4.
16. Walter Lippmann, *Essays in the Public Philosophy* (Boston: Little, Brown, 1955), p. 137.
17. *Education for Democracy*, p. 21.
18. Thomas Pangle, *The Ennobling of Democracy: The Challenge of the Postmodern Age* (Baltimore: Johns Hopkins University Press, 1992), p. 164.
19. *One Nation, Many Peoples*, p. 31.
20. Robert Penn Warren, *All the King's Men* (New York: Harcourt Brace Jovanovich, 1982), p. 157.
21. Arthur M. Schlesinger, Jr., *The Disuniting of America: Reflections on a Multicultural Society* (New York: W. W. Norton, 1992), pp. 46, 72.
22. Ibid., p. 93.
23. Ibid., p. 47.
24. Ibid., p. 137.
25. California Framework, p. 4.
26. Fernand Braudel, *The Mediterranean and the Mediterranean World in the Age of Philip II*, trans. Sian Reynolds (New York: Harper and Row, 1972). I take the "foam on the waves" image as well as the characterization of Braudel from Peter Burke, "Overture: The New History, Its Past and Its Future," in *New Perspectives on Historical Writing*, ed. Peter Burke (University Park, Pa.: Pennsylvania State University Press, 1992), p. 4.
27. I take my account of Heidegger from Hubert Dreyfus and Harrison Hall, "Introduction," in *Heidegger: A Critical Reader*, ed. Hubert Dreyfus and Harrison Hall (Oxford: Blackwell, 1992), pp. 1–25.
28. Schlesinger, *Disuniting of America*, p. 18.
29. Ibid., pp. 11, 27, 131, 137.
30. Ibid., p. 137.
31. Ibid., p. 18.
32. Ronald Takaki, *A Different Mirror: A History of Multicultural America* (Boston: Little, Brown, 1993).
33. Ibid., pp. 6, 426.
34. Ibid., pp. 5–6, 427.
35. Ibid., pp. 116 (slaves resisted through malingering and rebellion), 187 ("Mexican workers demonstrated they were capable of defying stereotypes of docility and submissiveness"), 200 ("Chinese farm laborers did not passively accept what their employers offered them"), 207 ("contrary to the stereotype of Chinese passivity, the Chinese fought discrimination"), 257 ("Japanese workers were not passive victims of exploitation"),

261 (Japanese engaged in "day-to-day cultural resistance"), 295 (the power to strike against the shirtwaist industry "had to come from the people themselves"), 325 (the "labor militancy" of Mexican farm workers "contradicted and challenged stereotypes of Mexican passivity"), 346 (blacks "refused to be victimized by southern police abuse" by migrating north), 402 (pressure to end segregation "would have to come not from judicial pronouncements, but from a people's movement for civil rights").

36. Ibid., p. 374.
37. Ibid., pp. 383–4, 386, 389, 392–3, 395ff.
38. Ibid., p. 378 (emphasis added).
39. Ibid., p. 374.
40. Schlesinger, *Disuniting of America*, p. 37.
41. Takaki, *A Different Mirror*, p. 427.
42. Charles Taylor, "Cross-Purposes: The Liberal–Communitarian Debate," in *Liberalism and the Moral Life*, ed. Nancy L. Rosenblum (Cambridge, Mass.: Harvard University Press, 1989), p. 166.
43. Richard J. Evans, *In Hitler's Shadow: West German Historians and the Attempt to Escape from the Nazi Past* (New York: Pantheon Books, 1989), p. 11.
44. Ibid., p. 18.
45. Charles Maier, *The Unmasterable Past: History, Holocaust, and German National Identity* (Cambridge, Mass.: Harvard University Press, 1988), p. 10.
46. Quoted in Ibid., p. 30.
47. Ibid., p. 42.
48. Comments by Charles Maier in *The Unresolved Past: A Debate in German History*, Proceedings of the Wheatland Foundation Conference, ed. Gina Thomas (London: Weidenfeld and Nicolson, 1990), p. 5.
49. Quoted in Evans, *In Hitler's Shadow*, p. 103. See also Sturmer, in *The Unresolved Past*, ed. Thomas, p. 16 (quoting Helmut Schmidt).
50. Sturmer, in *The Unresolved Past*, ed. Thomas, p. 15.
51. Maier, in Ibid., pp. 5–6.
52. Quoted in Maier, *The Unmasterable Past*, p. 21.
53. See Jurgen Habermas, *The New Conservatism: Cultural Criticism and the Historians' Debate* (Cambridge, Mass.: MIT Press, 1989), pp. 212–28.
54. Habermas, "Closing Remarks," in *The New Conservatism*, p. 247.
55. Habermas, "Apologetic Tendencies," in *The New Conservatism*, p. 214.
56. Habermas, "Historical Consciousness and Post-Traditional Identity," in *The New Conservatism*, p. 257.
57. Ibid., p. 250.
58. Habermas, "Apologetic Tendencies," p. 227.
59. Habermas, "Historical Consciousness," p. 261.
60. Ibid., p. 254.
61. Ibid., p. 256.
62. Ibid., p. 257.
63. Ibid., p. 262.
64. Habermas, "On the Public Use of History," in *The New Conservatism*, p. 233.
65. Ibid.
66. Habermas, "Historical Consciousness," pp. 251, 263.

67. Habermas, "The Public Use of History," p. 233; "Historical Consciousness," p. 267.
68. Habermas, "Remarks from the Romerberg Colloquium," in *The New Conservatism*, p. 210.
69. Taylor, "Cross-Purposes," p. 165 (citizens seeing their dignity affirmed and reflected in the laws as a condition of patriotism).
70. *One Nation, Many Peoples*, p. 12.
71. See Paul Hemp, "Houghton Mifflin's Textbook Troubles," *Boston Globe*, June 25, 1991, p. 37, and Robert Reinhold, "Class Struggle," *New York Times Magazine*, September 29, 1991, p. 26.
72. Beverly J. Armento, Gary B. Nash, Christopher L. Salter, and Karen K. Wixson, *A More Perfect Union* (Boston: Houghton Mifflin Company, 1991).
73. Ibid., pp. 601–3.
74. Richard Nixon no doubt went to his grave in dread that eighth graders would for all time to come know him only for Watergate. That dread would not have been unrealistic. Nixon gets mentioned two times in *A More Perfect Union*, once in a section entitled "American Indians Make Gains," where the text notes that Nixon appointed Indians to the top twenty positions of the Bureau of Indian Affairs (p. 604), and the other in a sidebar to a section on Andrew Johnson, which describes Nixon's resignation in the face of impeachment proceedings for the Watergate coverup (p. 386).
75. Indeed, the complications thrown up by the recent revelations of King's plagiarism seem to have unnerved some sophisticated adult scholars writing in a recent symposium in the *Journal of American History* 78 (June 1991). One offers the thought that King's lifting the words of others was actually to his credit, a "part of his resistance" to "academic commandments about language" and the ideas of "Great White Thinkers," through which resistance King "began the process of creatively translating into print the [black] folk procedures of voice merging and self-making" (Keith Miller, "Martin Luther King, Jr., and the Black Folk Pulpit," p. 121). Another resists the view that "if King's flaws are revealed, we must reassess his stature," but, evidently finding the resistance hard, further opines that the academic practice of "documenting sources" is "keyed to the ownership, possession, private-property ethos that drives so much of Western cultural nationalism," in contrast to the community-based standards of African-American culture (Bernice Johnson Reagon, " 'Nobody Knows the Trouble I See'; or, 'By and By I'm Gonna Lay Down My Heavy Load,' " p. 117). A third offers the unsupported speculation that King persisted in his plagiarism because he "sensed instantly the racial double standard of his professors" for failing to penalize his initial "transparent legerdemain" and decided to "repay their condescension and contempt in like coin" (David Levering Lewis, "Failing to Know Martin Luther King, Jr.," p. 85).
76. *One Nation, Many Peoples*, pp. 19, 18.
77. Schlesinger, *Disuniting of America*, p. 15.
78. *One Nation, Many Peoples*, pp. 2–3. See also Gerald Graff, *Beyond the*

Culture Wars: How Teaching the Conflicts Can Revitalize American Education (New York: W. W. Norton, 1992).

79. Eighth graders can understand that great figures have flaws. Indicating that he had flaws like all other humans, great and small, need not discredit Martin Luther King for students, especially if the flaws are not described in brutal detail. But such an account *already* operates from within the received perspective on King provided by the text of *A More Perfect Union*. To present the "other perspective" requires conveying King's failings not as character "flaws" but as character-revealing traits.

80. *One Nation, Many Peoples*, p. 19.

81. *A More Perfect Union*, p. 29.

82. Michael Dorris, "Why I'm Not Thankful for Thanksgiving," *Interracial Books for Children Bulletin* 9 (1978): 9.

83. James W. Loewen, "The Truth about the First Thanksgiving," *Monthly Review* 44 (November 1992): 21.

84. Nitza M. Hildago, "Multicultural Teacher Introspection," in *Freedom's Plow: Teaching in the Multicultural Classroom*, ed. Theresa Perry and James W. Fraser (New York: Routledge, 1993), p. 103.

85. In respect to "usable pasts," the California History–Social Science Framework is noteworthy for the emphasis it puts on history as "a story well told" (4).

86. Chantal Mouffe, *The Return of the Political* (London: Verso, 1993), p. 2.

87. Richard Sennett, "The Identity Myth," *New York Times*, January 3, 1994, p. 17. See also Richard Sennett, "Narrative as Knowing" Symposium, *Yale Journal of Criticism* 5 (1992), pp. 179–82.

88. California Framework, pp. 2–3 (emphasis added).

PART V

Teaching literature

Chapter 10

Multicultural literature and civic education: a problematic relationship with possibilities

SANDRA STOTSKY

Recent discussions of multiculturalism and public education have focused primarily on the question of how our national history ought to be represented, and on whether different perspectives on that history can be integrated within a curriculum that fosters a common civic identity. In contrast, little critical attention has been paid, from the standpoint of civic education, to the influence of multiculturalism on the K–12 literature arts curriculum. To judge from articles in professional journals in education, presentations at professional conferences, and formal and informal surveys of current classroom textbooks, multiculturalism has inspired profound changes in the selection of literature for classroom study and in teaching strategies adopted for literature instruction. But the relation between these changes and the project of civic education remains virtually unexplored.

In some respects, the prevailing emphasis on the history/social studies curriculum is not surprising. Since the early decades of the twentieth century, civic education has been the official responsibility only of history and social studies teachers. Moreover, it is difficult to find English educators or literary critics who have seriously explored the role that a K–12 literature curriculum plays, or should play, in the formation of a specifically American identity and in the development of the attitudes and values needed for a form of self-government based on the primacy of individual rights and individual responsibilities.[1] My own essays on the possible anti-civic and antisocial effects of much contemporary American literature, and a 1992 essay by Peter Smagorinsky on ethical problems in teaching literature in a "multicultural" society, appear to be the first published efforts to raise questions about the influence of multiculturalism in the K–12 English language arts curriculum and its implications for civic education.[2]

Debates about the "canon" in the past decade have raised questions about the extent to which all students should be exposed to the seminal ideas in the history of Western civilization and thus to the political and economic concepts shaping citizenship in free and open societies. However, these debates have taken place almost solely at the college or university level, and often, though not exclusively, with reference to works of nonfiction. Moreover, they have rarely if ever focused on the significance, for the K–12 curriculum, of distinguishing American literature from non-American literature, whether composed in English or translated into English. As a consequence, they seem to have had little relevance for K–12 educators.

It has always been obvious that the literature students read can contribute to the development of their aesthetic and moral values – indeed, the nurturing of aesthetic and humanistic values has been a traditional goal of a literature curriculum. How school literature programs influence the development of our students' civic character and their identity as Americans has perhaps been less obvious. They do so by exposing students to historically significant works (such as Benjamin Franklin's *Autobiography*, Emerson's essays, or Thoreau's *Walden* and "Civil Disobedience") and to works of both fiction and nonfiction that portray the moral values, strengths, aspirations, myths, tensions, contradictions, and failings of our culture as reflected in the lives of its people, real or imagined. Yet as far as I can determine, only one literary critic has even implied that there may be a relationship between the particular works that Americans read and the development of those attitudes, concepts, and values required for the preservation of the American experiment in self-government.

In the preface to *Jeffersonianism and the American Novel* (1966), Howard Mumford Jones observed that in our political culture, the adult American is understood to be "a being capable of both rational and moral choice." Upon this assumption, he wrote, "the republic rests."[3] And yet, in his survey of American novels of the twentieth century, Jones found that this view of the individual as an autonomous moral being had been, if not obliterated, then seriously weakened. Although Jones's chief concern in this book was with the contemporary American novelist's lack of responsibility to the political republic (he had no quarrel with the contribution of contemporary novelists to the republic of letters), he was not unmindful of the unsolvable dilemma that an alienating and nihilistic literature presented to educators. What could the civically responsible literature teacher do who, understandably, taught contemporary American fiction? This question is all the more pertinent today, since the portion of the American literature curriculum devoted to twentieth-century works – including *The Great Gatsby*, *Death of a Salesman*, *To Kill a Mockingbird*, *The Glass Menagerie*, *The Grapes of Wrath*, *The Crucible*, *Black Boy*, *Of Mice and Men*, *Hiro-*

shima, and *A Streetcar Named Desire* – has expanded significantly in the past thirty years.

Though secondary school English teachers may not share Jones's views on the civic character needed for representative self-government, many do seem to share his views on the nature of the modern American novel. For example, John Cameron has noted the spirit of disillusionment, despair, and cynicism so often associated with the artistic achievement of our time, while Paula Burns has bemoaned the lack of good twentieth-century literature with at least one character of high moral standing.[4] Both Burns and Geraldine Vale have asked other teachers for help in finding more positive twentieth-century works for their students to read, although they have not suggested that the paucity of positive works has affected their students' civic attitudes.[5]

Today, it is quite possible that many secondary students encounter few adult or adolescent characters in the twentieth-century American fiction they are assigned to read who have a sense of social and intellectual purpose, moral principles, or a feeling of roots in any community. In addition to the novels and plays mentioned above, such works as *A Separate Peace, Catcher in the Rye, The Outsiders, The Chocolate War,* and *The Pigman* are also among the top thirty to forty titles taught in grades 7–12. These have been described by English educators as works that tend "to focus on the experience of adolescent male protagonists who are loners, separated from the influence of family and adult mentors, to reify adolescence as a state rather than show the successful passage of the young into adulthood, to idealize adolescence and adolescent characters at the expense of adults, and to emphasize depressing, negative conditions – confusion, alienation of the young, instability, irresponsibility, loneliness, and moral ambivalence."[6]

With the clear exception of *To Kill a Mockingbird,* the modern American works mentioned above are unlikely to inspire civic virtue in students or a sense of personal responsibility for their own behavior. Instead, they may imply that most Americans are driven by self-interest and greed or shaped by subconscious or external forces beyond their control. Thus, they may lead to negative judgments about the moral character of American society as a whole and to a cynicism about the capacity of the American people to sustain a representative form of self-government.

Jones voiced his fears about the influence of modern American fiction on the development of the moral and intellectual character he saw underlying this country's political institutions long before multiculturalism became a major force in education. But his concerns may be more relevant today than three decades ago in the context of the sharp criticisms of multiculturalism by Arthur Schlesinger[7] and others and their fears about its effects on the preservation of a democracy based on individual rights and responsibilities.

Why this might be so requires an examination of the reasons offered for including multicultural literature in the K–12 curriculum, the criteria frequently proposed for selecting or evaluating it, and the nature of some of the most highly recommended or frequently read multicultural texts. It is not, after all, immediately obvious why works recommended for increasing our students' awareness of this country's extraordinary ethnic and racial diversity and for enhancing their respect for each other regardless of ethnic or racial background should pose any problems for the development of their civic identity and sensibilities. Although the immediate purpose of this chapter is to suggest the range of complex questions that K–12 educators need to explore in selecting and teaching multicultural literature, its larger purpose is not to suggest that works by and about Americans as members of specific ethnic, racial, and other social groups do not warrant inclusion in the K–12 curriculum. They clearly do, for several reasons. To the contrary, its ultimate purpose is to suggest how multicultural texts can be included in the curriculum so that they do not negate or curtail the development of our students' civic identity and their sense of responsibility for each other as citizens of the same country.

MATTERS OF DEFINITION

In an essay suggesting the various dimensions along which controversy about multiculturalism can be located, Robert Fullinwider points out that the "core concepts and ideas in multiculturalism allow for quite divergent interpretation and development." "As a consequence," he continues, "very different programs and aims get called 'multicultural,' embracing quite different pedagogical strategies and theories, and supported by quite different educational and social diagnoses."[8] Unfortunately, the core concepts of multiculturalism are as vague and slippery in their application to literature programs as they are with respect to history and social studies curricula. Further, those who advocate multicultural literature or have designed multicultural reading lists or literary anthologies rarely if ever offer carefully worked-out definitions of the terms they use. Nor do they typically spell out the "cultural" attributes or differences they suggest students will find in their literary study of particular groups.

The root "culture" in "multicultural" seems to have a remarkably broad range of meanings. It may refer only to national groups like the French or Japanese – groups with specific customs, a distinct lan-

guage, an acknowledged national literature, certain religious and political values, and other distinguishing characteristics. Or, in addition,
it may refer to one of the many ethnic groups living in the United
States, Canada, or other countries with large numbers of immigrants
who retain only some of the customs and features of the original
group from which they derived. Or it may refer to social groups
defined primarily by other criteria such as gender, disability (e.g., the
deaf), sexual preference, or even geographical region (the inhabitants
of Appalachia, for example).

The term "culture" extends even to black Americans in this country
because of their racial differences from the majority and their historical origin as slaves. Yet while many distinguished black Americans,
such as the playwright August Wilson, see their group as possessing
a distinct culture, many others do not. And indeed, with respect to
language, religion, dress, and most customs, the majority of black
Americans are no different from most other Americans. Moreover, for
black Americans, as well as for immigrants from Asia, Africa, and
Latin America, race is not coterminous with culture. We need only
consider the differences among black Muslims, Ethiopian-Americans,
and Haitian-Americans in this country, and the persistence of many
distinct cultures in Africa itself.

Despite this range of meanings, however, literature programs designated as multicultural or multiethnic are intended in theory to reflect two broad principles: inclusiveness and the avoidance of stereotyping (or the deconstruction of assumed stereotypes). With respect
to ethnicity, inclusiveness refers to the curriculum's acknowledgment
of the existence of all self-identified ethnic/racial/religious groups in
this country through the assignment of literary works by or about
members of these groups. When designers of self-described multicultural programs choose to extend the meaning of culture to social
groups defined by gender, sexual orientation, or physical or mental
disability, then inclusiveness refers to the curriculum's acknowledgment of the existence of these groups as well. As a matter of practice,
curricular inclusiveness almost always refers to works by and about
females as well.

In professing its intent to avoid stereotypes, multiculturalism op-
poses the consistent characterization of people from any ethnic, racial, religious, or gender group in a way that is either unflattering,
demeaning, or limited. An unflattering stereotype of members of
specific ethnic or religious groups is created when works regularly
show, for example, Italians as members of the Mafia (Don Corleone in
The Godfather), or Jews as greedy or unscrupulous (Shylock in *The
Merchant of Venice*, Fagan in *Oliver Twist*). Some commentators see
demeaning or insulting stereotypes at work when black Americans

are portrayed as passive victims, either in slavery times or in contemporary society;[9] or when young American males are depicted chiefly as loners, confused social misfits, or morally depraved figures.[10] However, stereotypes are also created when members of particular groups are presented as capable of undertaking only a restricted range of activities, even if the activities are not negative in themselves – when women appear primarily in nurturing roles, for example, or when black Americans are presented only as gifted athletes.

THE RATIONALE FOR MULTICULTURAL
LITERATURE IN THE CURRICULUM

What are the reasons for including multicultural literature in the K–12 curriculum, whatever its specific nature may be? I offer here those that I have found or discerned in materials written primarily by educators, librarians, and journalists. There may be more, but these can at least help us see the contours of the intellectual and psychological terrain that multicultural literature may cover.

First, there seems to be universal agreement by its advocates that multicultural literature is needed because, as a 1991 *Newsweek* article put it, the "traditional fare . . . doesn't begin to reflect the complicated diverse world that children live in."[11] Nancy Shapiro, in a review of multicultural readers for college freshman composition courses, explains that many of the readers are designed for "culturally mainstream students who need their horizons expanded, who need to be exposed to the diversity of cultures and values in order to be able to function in today's world and help shape tomorrow's."[12] She sees mainstream students as students "who have lived a sheltered existence" and "need to learn about others in order to understand themselves." Aniece Kerr, a school librarian, asserts that "all Americans are members of an ethnic group. We need to help students become more ethnically literate and more sensitive to cultural differences."[13]

Multicultural literature is also judged to be important for egalitarian purposes. In 1990, a committee of the National Council of Teachers of English recommended that language-arts textbooks be "equity balanced," that is, "selected from a wide range of world cultures," so that students can learn to value "the cultural contributions of all groups in a pluralistic society."[14] Roberta Long, a professor of children's literature, explains that "if black children or Native Americans or Asians don't see themselves in books, they won't see themselves as important people. And we will be sending that message to white children, too."[15]

Most advocates seem to agree that a primary purpose of multicultural literature is to build the self-esteem of students whose social group has appeared infrequently, if at all, in the traditional curriculum. These students, it is argued, need to see that members of their group are an accepted part of the American national community. Proponents of multiculturalism tend to believe that self-esteem is a basic force motivating students to learn to read and to enjoy reading, and that the academic growth of non-mainstream students will be retarded or impeded if they do not see others like themselves in the literature they read. Thus, in another passage from her review essay, Nancy Shapiro discusses anthologies intended for "students on the margins – people of color, women, sexual minorities – who need to find some lifeline of connection to the academy, who need to be able to value their own personal and cultural identities, and who challenge the institution to expand its vision."[16]

Some educators believe that major curriculum changes are required in order to develop self-esteem in non-mainstream students. For example, Roseann Duenas Gonzalez writes:

> Token representations of the histories and literatures of culturally different children are inadequate attempts at engaging and inspiring students' participation in the educational process. One piece of literature or one chapter in American history cannot counter the negative perceptions that children of minority subcultures have of themselves or that society has of them. A significant proportion of the curriculum must be dedicated to positive ethnic histories and literatures and the many contributions that all groups have made to American life. Special emphasis should be placed on the predominant minority group of the school. Only when children perceive that they are accepted for who they are – both culturally and individually – can real learning begin.[17]

Both mainstream and non-mainstream students need exposure to multicultural literature, it is usually suggested, because it portrays non-mainstream students in ways that do not demean, damage, or stereotype them. The claim that multicultural literature offers healthy or positive portrayals of non-mainstream children, adults, and women in general often seems to imply that multicultural literature is a new literature, and that the existing literature offers only negative images or stereotypes of whatever groups the educator has in mind. For example, a second set of guidelines from NCTE, "Guidelines for a Gender-Balanced Curriculum in English, Grades 7–12,"[18] states that despite "significant changes in . . . fiction and nonfiction, women authors are still underrepresented and females are often stereotyped." The pamphlet goes on to stress that "balancing the curriculum" is important because it "allows all students to see themselves as doers and thinkers and as persistent and successful."

Multicultural literature, it is suggested, may also help students deal with issues of assimilation and acculturation. A high school English teacher, Linda Blair, reports that her English as a Second Language (ESL) students develop "strong, honest narrative voices" first by reading and discussing autobiographical narratives written primarily by authors whose second language is English, and then by writing their own autobiographies, modeled, in part, on the narratives. Blair believes that her use of this genre of "multicultural literature" as a prompt diminishes her students' "hesitancy, their inability to express themselves clearly in English," and helps them deal with the "issues central to immigrant students" from "multicultural backgrounds" – the issues of assimilation and acculturation which she sees grounded in alienation.[19] But although multicultural literature may help students deal with these issues, most if not all advocates believe that multicultural literature chiefly serves, and should chiefly serve, to help non-mainstream students preserve their particular social identities and social histories. Blair writes that reading autobiographies by people who faced issues of assimilation and acculturation helps us "reaffirm our ancestral struggles" and "reaffirm our own identities."[20]

According to some educators, multicultural literature can serve as a bridge to the mainstream literature that Americans see as part of the background of an educated person. At the 1991 fall conference of the National Council of Teachers of English, Connie Robinson and Randy Gingrich, two educators from the Cincinnati Public Schools, provided a lengthy handout on the rationale for using multicultural literature and on the particular program they have developed and used.[21] In this handout, Robinson and Gingrich assert that "alienation results from exposure to only the canon which is viewed as all male, all Western European, and usually dead." They recommend that students read authors who provide examples in their novels of the kind of conversational language the students may use (for example, such authors as Toni Morrison, Alice Walker, Gloria Naylor, and Langston Hughes). They argue that by reading such "multicultural" works as *The Color Purple*, *A Patch of Blue*, and *Kaffir Boy*, students will be better able and more motivated to read difficult "canonical" works, such as *Pride and Prejudice*, *Romeo and Juliet*, and *Othello*, and can then discover that "great literature speaks to all people." Gonzalez, too, suggests that "overt exploration and validation of the identity of minority students can serve as a bridge to successful learning experiences about people, places, ideas, and values that seem so different from their cultural understanding."[22] And Shapiro, in her analysis of cross-cultural anthologies for ESL students, discerns the expectation that "if students can feel comfortable with their own culture then they can more easily participate in mainstream American culture."[23]

Overall, there seem to be two very different audiences for multicultural literature, and thus two different sets of reasons for adopting it. Mainstream students are perceived as needing to read works about other cultures and the non-mainstream groups in this country in order to develop an understanding of their differences from mainstream culture and to see these other social groups as equal in value to their own. On the other hand, non-mainstream students are perceived as needing to see members of their ethnic or racial group in the literature they read for affirming and preserving their social identities, for raising their self-esteem, for motivating them to read literature at all, for facilitating their reading of mainstream works, and for facilitating their participation in public life because they see themselves as members of an accepted social group.

In short, it seems that, for the majority of students in this country, the responsibility of the schools is to broaden their educational experiences, while for the others it is to affirm the distinctive characteristics of members of their particular racial/ethnic group and to preserve their group identity even when they participate with the majority in the mainstream culture. What is not at all clear is whether non-mainstream parents are to be accorded the right to decide for themselves whether they want the public schools to label their children and focus on preserving their particular social identity as distinct from a mainstream American identity, thus perpetuating their minority or non-mainstream status, or whether they want the public schools to focus on what their children share in common with all other students as American citizens.

QUESTIONS ABOUT ASSUMPTIONS AND CRITERIA

A number of debatable assumptions seem to be embedded in the rationales for multicultural literature. For example, it is doubtful that all non-mainstream children suffer from lack of self-esteem, or that self-esteem generally precedes learning. Indeed, some non-mainstream groups have a great deal of self-esteem, to judge by their record of academic and economic achievement in this country, and the research evidence suggests with some consistency that learning and achievement precede the development of self-esteem.

The most debatable assumptions from both a literary and a civic perspective concern two related claims: that our traditional literature contains only stereotyped female characters and negative or stereotyped images of non-mainstream adults or children, and that non-mainstream students need to see only positive, non-stereotyped images of themselves in the literature they read. These related claims are particularly troubling for two reasons. They not only undergird the major criteria recommended by multiculturalists for selecting literature and for evaluating its appropriateness for the classroom, but they also seem to lead, however implicitly, to criteria for removing works already in the curriculum. And they do so whether or not the first of the two related claims is true.

It may seem difficult to evaluate the first claim fairly, since judgments about what is negative in our literature are always subjective. But surely critics who find traditional literature hopelessly pervaded by stereotypes have overlooked an abundance of counterexamples. For instance, my own reading of the Little Pear series as a child, or of Pearl Buck's *The Good Earth* as an adolescent, did not leave me with negative images of the Chinese. The central female characters in *The Merchant of Venice* and *Macbeth*, two major works read in almost all American high schools several decades ago, could hardly be described as passive or submissive. The few well-known works that have been frequently discussed as examples of racism or sexism, such as *Adventures of Huckleberry Finn, The Cay, Sounder, Charlie and the Chocolate Factory, Little Women*, and *Mary Poppins*, cannot be easily or simply dismissed with that charge. Nor do these works by any means constitute the whole corpus of works with female or non-mainstream characters that are frequently read by children or adolescents.

But even if a strong negative case could be made about our traditional literature, the multiculturalist injunction that students should read only positive ethnic literatures would appear to have serious negative effects on a teacher's professional freedom and the quality of the literary experience offered to students. To understand why, we need to look at the criteria that have been offered for selecting or evaluating multicultural literature.

At the 1991 NCTE Annual Conference, among the seven criteria for "Native American Literature" offered by Marsha and Tom Savage,[24] two university educators, were the following: "Are the Indian characters portrayed as individuals with their own thoughts, emotions and philosophies? The characters should not conform to stereotypes or be dehumanized." "Is offensive and degrading vocabulary used to describe the characters, their actions, their customs, or their lifestyles?" "Is the Indian culture respected, or is it presented as inferior to the white culture? Does the author believe the culture is worthy of preservation or that it should be abandoned? Must the Indian fit into an image acceptable to white characters in the story?" and "Are the illustrations realistic and authentic, or do they reinforce stereotypes or devalue the culture?" Among the six criteria for "Black Literature" are the following: "Has a black perspective been taken into consideration? There should be no stigma attached to being black; the characters should not conform to old stereotypes." "Is the black character a unique individual, or only representative of a group?" and "Does clothing or behavior perpetuate stereotypes of blacks as primitive or submissive?" Among the six criteria for "Asian-American Literature" are the following: "Does the book transcend stereotypes?" "Does the literature seek to rectify historical distortions and omissions?" and "Does the literature reflect an awareness of the changing status of women in society?" And among the eight criteria for "Hispanic Literature" are the following: "Are problems handled individually, allowing the main characters to use their own efforts to solve their problems? Or are all problems solved through the intervention of an Anglo American?" "Do the characters depict individuals, not stereotypes?" "Is the language free from derogatory terms or descriptions?" and "Is the culture treated with respect?" Similar guidelines have been formulated by other individuals or organizations in the name of promoting antiracist or anti-sexist curricula.

The American Library Association (ALA), in a resource book of multicultural materials and programs,[25] suggests only five broad criteria for inclusion of multicultural literature. The ALA recommends that librarians (1) look for a quality of reality that gives the reader a chance to experience something; (2) try to determine the author's commitment to portray cultural groups accurately; (3) avoid materials that sensationalize, enumerate unusual customs, or practice reversed stereotyping; (4) be sensitive to emphasis on cultural differences at the expense of similarities; and (5) whenever possible, use the same critical criteria appropriate for all types of literature – distinctive language and appropriate dialogue, style, relevance and potential interest, clear-cut plots, and believable characterizations. All these criteria, however, raise a number of practical questions for educators to consider.

Who decides on the answers to these questions? It is not at all clear who will serve as the authority for deciding on the answers to these criterial questions. Only members of the particular non-mainstream groups portrayed? Teachers or book reviewers who are not members of the group depicted in a particular book may be intimidated at the prospect of trying to offer a conscientious judgment. But if only members of the group in question can decide whether these criteria are satisfactorily addressed in the literary work under discussion, would that then constitute a kind of literary veto power? What happens if they reach no consensus? Or is there an assumption that members of all politically defined social groups think alike?

One might also wonder whether a scrupulous adherence to such criteria will leave us with many genuine works of literature, particularly because so many of these criteria are non-literary. How might they be weighted if a work seems to address certain criteria better than others, or some very well and others not at all? How can a disagreement about their weighting be handled? Perhaps some of the criteria might warrant intrinsically more weight than others. Again, who decides and how?

Do these criteria provide grounds for removing literature from the curriculum? Neither English educators nor advocates of multicultural literature have publicly discussed the basis on which currently studied works may be removed in order to make room for multicultural works. Normally, teachers gradually change their course offerings after they read new works and make judgments about their readability, literary merit, thematic relevance, and personal appeal for their students. But because of the guidelines recommended by multicultural educators or professional organizations such as NCTE, four factors may play a leading role in decisions about what works should be displaced: the age of the work, the gender of the author, the activities engaged in by the characters, and the language used in the work. Needless to say, all four factors bear no necessary relationship to literary merit, the moral import of a work, or its historical/cultural significance, which is why we should be as concerned about what leaves the curriculum as about what enters it.

Older works may be eliminated first, primarily because they are likely to display little ethnic or national diversity in their characters. What diversity exists may arise chiefly in the ranks of extremely minor characters. Works by males will undoubtedly be displaced in order to achieve a balance in gender. Finally, works judged to contain racist or sexist language – indeed, any language considered offensive by non-mainstream groups – will also be displaced, as will works judged to feature non-mainstream characters in "stereotyped" roles or engaging in "stereotyped" or demeaning behavior.

We have no studies indicating what works have been eliminated from the curriculum, or are being eliminated. But one wonders what might happen to many works of literature often read by secondary school students today that do not offer positive portrayals of non-mainstream characters, particularly male ones. Such works as *The Color Purple, Women of Brewster Place, Manchild in the Promised Land, Down These Mean Streets,* and even *West Side Story* come immediately to mind. Some of these are just beginning to become popular; others have been in the curriculum for a few years now. What might happen to works like these if the multiculturalist injunction that students should read only positive ethnic literatures is carried out? Should they be removed from the curriculum? Or aren't these texts the kind of works that the multiculturalist has in mind?

The research of Ann Trousdale clearly suggests one kind of work that may be dropped from the curriculum – books by white authors about the black experience.[26] Trousdale examined four prize-winning children's books about the black experience in America: *Amos Fortune, Free Man* by Elizabeth Yates; *Sounder* by William Armstrong; *Words by Heart* by Ouida Sebestyen; and *Roll of Thunder, Hear My Cry* by Mildred Taylor. The first three are by white authors, the fourth by a black author. Trousdale uses the fourth book as a "touchstone of authenticity against which the other three may be judged."[27] Comparing the religious beliefs imputed to black characters by the white authors with those attributed by the black author, Trousdale concludes that Yates, Armstrong, and Sebestyen "reflect, perhaps unconsciously portray, a white supremacist view of their black characters in emphasizing the benefits of white American civilization for African slaves, in prescribing a secondary role for blacks in American society, and in applauding behavior for their black characters that is docile, submissive toward whites, and accepting of injustice and oppression." On the other hand, the theology that informs the black characters' actions in Taylor's book, according to Trousdale, urges "resistance" and "action to lift racial oppression, to change the social order that perpetuates injustice."[28] Trousdale concludes that "if children's literature is to provide for children characters with whom it is healthy and meaningful to identify, if it is to provide a view of life which they recognize as authentic and one in which they can find possibilities for their own lives," such books as the three written by these white authors must be read with a "critical perspective." At the least, she believes, teachers need to be aware of the "limitations in perspective inherent in a writer's ethnic and cultural background."[29] Trousdale does not explicitly recommend removal of these books from the school curriculum, but it is not difficult to guess what teachers or compilers of anthologies will do when choices are to be made about which books on the black experience children should read.

In fact, one wonders how many older works, if any, in the "mainstream" culture will survive the kind of critical inspection that Trousdale suggests. Recently, the English department at a private school in the Boston area, with encouragement from a Multicultural Committee composed of parents and faculty, removed *Adventures of Huckleberry Finn* and *To Kill a Mockingbird* from its curriculum as part of an effort to improve multicultural education at the school. According to one parent, the former was dropped because the language in it was deemed offensive to the "children of color" in the school; the latter was dropped because class discussions of the central drama in the novel (the defense of a black man by a white lawyer) were considered "demeaning" to the "children of color" in the class. The parents who told me about this decision did not protest because they believed that they would be labeled racist or insensitive. Given similar circumstances, one wonders how many parents in any school would protest the removal from the curriculum of two of the most significant and popular works in the history of American literature. It is worth noting that they are works whose white characters powerfully illustrate the expression of principled thinking and individual conscience, a point we will return to later.

The internal censorship such criteria may stimulate is perhaps their most troubling implication. Internal censorship is a far more dangerous form of censorship than the kind stimulated by outside forces. It is not visible, as overt complaints are, and parents, students, or the public at large may never know what literary works have, in effect, been censored from the curriculum.

THE CRITERIA FOR INCLUSION

If the effort to organize a literature program must begin with consideration of the ethnicity, race, and gender of the characters in each work and how these characters are portrayed, and if these factors take precedence over such elements as theme, plot, setting, or appeal to students, a number of other crucial questions will arise in selecting multicultural works for the classroom. These questions further suggest the complexity of the decision-making process educators face if the selection of the literature that our students read concerns itself first with human beings not as individuals but as members of specific, politically defined social categories.

Which cultures should be selected? Given the finite nature of a course or curriculum, and assuming that a principled definition of "culture" can be agreed on, on what basis should cultures be chosen as "representative" of the ethnic and racial diversity in this country, or in the world at large? For example, if a choice of culture is to be made within the group called Native Americans, which one or ones should students read about? As Smagorinsky points out, within the state of Oklahoma alone, there are almost seventy different tribes, "many of which originate from different parts of the continent, speak different languages, have developed different cultures, and were continually at war with one another for centuries." Which tribes, he asks, "should speak for such a diverse race of people?"[30]

From a national perspective, should we choose those who regularly waged war on other Indian tribes, such as the Apaches or Oglala Sioux; those who lived peacefully with their neighbors, such as the Hopi; those who helped the white settlers, as did the Pawnee because they had been consistently victimized by the Sioux; or tribes from all these groups? As important as this general question is practically, I can find no discussion of the criteria one might use to decide which cultures should be part of the curriculum. Instead, it is assumed by almost all multicultural educators that literature about four groups of people should be included: "African-Americans," "Native Americans," "Asian-Americans," and "Hispanic-Americans." Beyond this obvious politically relevant set of categories, there is nothing to guide choices within or outside these groups.

What writers from a particular culture "represent" it? Even if there were agreement on what constitutes a distinct culture within this country, what writers who are members of that culture can be said to represent it? Will any writer from that culture be suitable, or do a whole host of specific considerations need to be addressed, such as the writer's gender, sexual preference, religion, political point of view, or social class? For example, if a high school literature class were restricted, for reasons of time, to a work by Edith Wharton or Willa Cather, whose work should represent female American writers in the early decades of the twentieth century? Since the members of most cultures, here or abroad, have never voted for literary "representatives," can any writer be eligible to represent that culture? Or is the term meaningless when taken out of its political context and applied to works of literature?

Must a writer be a member of the cultural group he or she portrays? With this question, we return to the issue of authenticity. Is it the case that literary works unequivocally reflect the ethnic or national identity of their authors? As Henry Louis Gates, Jr., has noted,[31] the battle of the books today is very much about the author, not the book. Thus the embarrassment when the author of *The Education of Little Tree*, a book purported to be the autobiography of a 10-year-old orphaned Indian boy raised by his Cherokee grandparents in Tennessee, was discovered to have been a Ku Klux Klan terrorist and speechwriter for Alabama Governor George Wallace. The book had received much critical praise from Indians and book critics, has sold more than six million copies, and is in classrooms everywhere. Should the book be withdrawn, or can fake writers of a particular culture also "represent" that culture? The private school near Boston that removed *Huckleberry Finn* and *To Kill a Mockingbird* from its curriculum also removed *The Education of Little Tree*, perhaps because its presence would have served as a continual reminder of the praise the book received for its authenticity and thus mock the philosophical thrust of the ongoing "antiracist" training sessions for parents, students, and faculty conducted by its Multicultural Committee on the principle that what we think or say expresses not our individuality but our "affinity group" – a group defined by race, ethnicity, or gender. (Incidentally, those parents who refuse to take or have not yet taken part in these training sessions are called "non-folk" – not a far cry from Orwell's "non-persons.")

If the demand for authenticity is extended to the categories of gender or sexual preference as well as race and ethnicity, it becomes even more dubious. Certainly women have been known to write successfully about men, and men to write successfully about women. Further, it is not at all clear that readers cannot identify with characters of the opposite sex. While some theorists claim that students identify with characters of their own gender, there is no research suggesting that this is necessarily the case and that the opposite is not possible. In view of the many writers who have been able to fake their social identities so successfully that members of the group portrayed by the major characters cannot detect the writer's inauthenticity, there appear to be no valid criteria for determining which writers represent a particular culture for a multicultural literature program. As Gates concludes, "segregation . . . is as difficult to maintain in the literary realm as it is in the civic one."

What constitutes equitable representation for all distinctly identifiable groups? If all national and ethnic groups can themselves be broken down into social subgroups with distinct identifying features, does equity demand that these subgroups also be represented within the literature curriculum? In arranging for literary selections about, say, the Cherokees or the English, must equal representation be offered to subgroups defined by gender (male and female Cherokees, for example), or religion (English Catholics and Protestants), or other significant features? If so, the number of potential groups with a claim to inclusion in a multicultural literature program could increase geometrically. Given the vast number of cultural groups and subgroups that might be deemed eligible for representation in a multicultural literature curriculum, decisions would clearly have to be made about the proportion of the total selections that should be allocated to multicultural selections and the proportion that should reflect mainstream culture.

Gonzalez suggests that the number of non-mainstream students in a particular school system should be the determining factor; the more non-mainstream students, the larger the number of non-mainstream selections. Conversely, in a school with few non-mainstream students, one might expect a small number of multicultural selections. In that event, however, the mainstream students might not be exposed to the diversity that it is claimed they need. We may therefore assume that with the growth of multicultural curricula, a large proportion of the literature that all students read might well be non-mainstream. This in turn leads to a further consideration: if the mainstream culture is "represented" by only a few literary works, and the vast majority of the literary selections are about non-mainstream groups, can the works "representing" the mainstream culture still be said to be mainstream?

Who decides? As useful as it would be to have criteria proposed for the other questions, it would be even more useful to have criteria for determining the make-up of the selection committee. The following questions are an extension of those concerning the particular people who would decide whether a specific work met the criteria for acceptability as a multicultural work. Who should decide what writers represent a particular culture – assuming that we can agree on some boundary lines for a distinct culture and come up with an extensive list of potential nominees to represent that culture in the literary world? Should spokespeople of voluntarily organized members of that group have the major voice in deciding who represents them? For example, should only officials of the National Organization for Women or an NCTE Committee on Gender Equity decide what writers or works should represent women? Should literary critics? Should the minister of education in the country whose culture is under consideration? Should the editors and publishers of an anthology or book? Should a group of teachers whose students will be the audience for that writer? And if there is disagreement among members or officials of these various groups, on what basis can a decision be made?[32]

QUESTIONS WARRANTING RESEARCH

I have suggested that practical questions about the selection of multicultural literature have not yet received the attention they deserve. By the same token, additional questions raised by self-designated multicultural literary texts, the instructional practices associated with their use, and a number of recommended reading lists have yet to be extensively addressed. This second set of questions warrants systematic research because of the serious civic consequences the answers may entail.

How prevalent is reverse cultural stereotyping? Unfortunately, one can find many instances of reverse cultural stereotyping – often to the point of mean-spirited caricature – in recently composed texts deemed multicultural. Smagorinsky calls literary works exhibiting reverse cultural stereotyping "didactic texts written from a particular cultural perspective," works that "pit race against race, culture against culture, . . . elevating the values of one culture above those of the other."[33] In discussing the example of the captivity tale, Smagorinsky cites a researcher who found that

> many recent ones are from the Amazon and are usually told in terms of an ecological/save the rainforest interpretive frame. The film *The Emerald Forest*, for example, is based on the true story of a young boy abducted by Amazonian Indians. His father, an American engineer engaged in building a dam on the Amazon, searches for his son for 10

years. When he finally locates his child, he discovers that the boy has "gone native." This story and other modern tales twist the traditional frame so that the Indians are represented as heroes, living at one with nature, and the white man becomes the savage destroyer of a Rousseauistic idyll.[34]

As another example of reverse cultural stereotyping, Smagorinsky offers "Chee's Daughter," a frequently anthologized story[35] which features a clash between Chee, a Navajo "who lives according to the traditional ways of his culture, and his in-laws, who have attempted to adopt Western capitalistic ways." According to Smagorinsky, "Chee's wife has died, and tradition has decreed that their daughter be raised by the in-laws. This potentially compelling story deteriorates into caricature, with the in-laws becoming one-dimensional figures embodying the worst of Western ways."[36] The following passages illustrate the caricature.

> As his father-in-law walked heavily across the gravelled lot, Chee was reminded of a statement his mother sometimes made: "When you see a fat Navaho, you see one who hasn't worked for what he has."
> Old Man Fat was fattest in the middle. There was indolence in his walk even though he seemed to hurry, indolence in his cheeks so plump they made his eyes squint, eyes now smoldering with anger.
> Some of the tourists were getting into their cars and driving away. The old man said belligerently to Chee, "Why do you come here? To spoil our business? To drive people away?"
> . . . Chee's dark eyes surveyed the land along the highway as the old man continued to brag about being "progressive." He no longer was tied to the land. He and his wife made money easily and could buy all the things they wanted. Chee realized too late that he had stumbled into the old argument between himself and his wife's parents. They had never understood his feeling about the land – that a man took care of his land and it in turn took care of him. Old Man Fat and his wife scoffed at him, called him a Pueblo farmer, all during that summer when he planted and weeded and harvested. Yet they ate the green corn in their mutton stews, and the chili paste from the fresh ripe chilis, and the tortillas from the cornmeal his wife ground. None of this working and sweating in the sun for Old Man Fat, who talked proudly of his easy way of living – collecting money from the trader who rented this strip of land beside the highway, collecting money from the tourists.

At the end of the story, Smagorinsky continues, "a new highway diverts traffic away from Old Man Fat's business and he and his family have become destitute. Meanwhile, Chee has had an exceptional harvest and brings his in-laws some of his bounteous produce to help them out. The food will get the in-laws through the winter, but not with the baby to feed as well; and with that realization 'the Little

One ceased to be their daughter's daughter and became just another mouth to feed.' They promptly trade their granddaughter for food, and Chee and his daughter ride off to live the traditional Navajo life in communal serendipity while the in-laws are presumably left to rot in the seething swamp of capitalism."

"Chee's Daughter" is not a rare example in the curriculum. Reverse cultural stereotyping appears in many other frequently assigned multicultural works, such as *Farewell to Manzanar*, by Jeanne Wakatsuki Houston and James D. Houston, Toni Morrison's *The Bluest Eye*, and Laurence Yep's *Dragonwings*. I have discussed the issues posed by *Dragonwings* more fully elsewhere;[37] here I provide two short passages to illustrate the reverse cultural stereotyping that pervades this highly recommended novel for the middle grades.

The novel is about a personable young Chinese boy who comes to America to live with his father in San Francisco's Chinatown in the first decade of this century. The novel, which is narrated in the first person by the young boy, begins with the following paragraph:

> Ever since I can remember, I had wanted to know about the Land of the Golden Mountain, but my mother had never wanted to talk about it. All I knew was that a few months before I was born, my father had left our home in the Middle Kingdom, or China, as the white demons call it, and traveled over the sea to work in the demon land. There was plenty of money to be made among the demons, but it was also dangerous. My own grandfather had been lynched about thirty years before by a mob of white demons almost the moment he had set foot on their shores.[38]

A negative view of this country pervades the story from beginning to end. All Americans are consistently referred to as demons, white demons, or white demonesses. Aside from the Chinese boy's young American friend and her aunt, there are no positive portraits of Americans in this novel, and in fact no others have any individual character. Moreover, even the Chinese boy's young American friend does not escape unflattering touches. After reporting her enjoyment of E. Nesbit's children's stories, the narrator goes on to reveal her real tastes in literature:

> *"I've got some of these, too,"* the demon girl pretended to say casually. She slipped some dime novels from behind her back. . . . There were *Ned Buntline* specials about the adventures of *Buffalo Bill* in the wild, wild West (to me it was east, though, since I judged things geographically in relation to the Middle Kingdom). There were others about *Jesse James* and how he tortured his robbery victims. But her pride and joy were the *Nick Carter* detective stories, with a dead body on almost every page, as she boasted.[39]

Clearly, this portrait of the "demon girl" is not very appealing, implying as it does that even young American girls (not just adults or boys)
are inclined to sadism and violence.

In a three-page afterword to the original hardcover edition, Laurence Yep explains why he wrote the novel: "It has been my aim to
counter various stereotypes as presented in the media. Dr. Fu Man-
chu and his yellow hordes, Charlie Chan and his fortune-cookie wisdom, the laundrymen and cooks of the movie and television West-
erns, and the houseboys of various comedies present an image of
Chinese not as they really are but as they exist in the mind of White
America."[40] And yet, given that Yep's book was published in 1975, a
reader might wonder whether the stereotypes that Yep believes most
Americans hold really do exist in the minds of the children for whom
this book was written.

While works like *Dragonwings* and "Chee's Daughter" may serve to
break down the stereotypes that multiculturalists believe Americans
have of certain ethnic groups (the Indian as savage or lazy, the Chinese as cook, laundryman, or houseboy), the broad-scale cultural
stereotypes that they in turn deliberately play up (all Americans or Europeans as violent, prejudiced, selfish, inhumane; all non-Americans
or non-Europeans as virtuous and/or victims) may be at least as damaging, to both white and non-white Americans, as those they claim to
be fighting against. They may be more harmful, in fact, if such broad-
scale cultural stereotypes are pervasive in the multicultural works
students are required to read. The presence of a reverse stereotype
here and there is not a problem. The question is how pervasive these
stereotypes are. Without systematic research, however, we cannot
tell.

If it should turn out that reverse stereotypes are widespread, there
are several grounds for concern from a civic perspective.

First, such works clearly do not teach mutual respect and understanding. At a time when we are supposed to be concerned about
improving race relations, reverse cultural stereotyping amounting to
a blanket condemnation of a whole group or race of people (and the
elevation to sainthood of all the others) is no more morally acceptable
than the original stereotypes we are attempting to redress. But more
important, pervasive reverse cultural stereotypes may have several
unhealthy effects on white Americans. They may at first elicit guilt
about the racism, environmental destruction, immorality, and greed
that have characterized many white Americans and Europeans
throughout their history. But guilt is rarely a stable or healthy psychological mechanism for motivating good deeds. Inevitably pervasive
reverse stereotyping arouses anger and then indifference or an attempt to point out the same flaws in others, especially when it is

obvious from real-world information and experience that the suggested cultural dichotomy between the virtuous and the vicious, here and abroad, is a false one. Further, the presence and acceptance of reverse cultural stereotypes suggests a double standard – that it is acceptable to stereotype white Americans and Europeans in general, but not others. The writers of such works (and those who promote their use) thus invite charges of hypocrisy and dishonesty. Ultimately the moral stature of those who have been, and may still be, the victims of the earlier stereotypes is degraded, and sympathy lost.

Such works may also leave both white and non-white American readers indifferent to or actively opposed to the needs of our civic communities. Why should readers of many different literary versions of *Dragonwings* want to be honest, taxpaying and socially responsible citizens of this country if they believe that white Americans almost without exception have been and remain irreparably racist, environmentally destructive, and morally depraved? Indeed, if they come to believe from their school curriculum, their literary and artistic culture, and the media that all political, intellectual, and moral values associated with the West are tainted, that a society based on individual rights and responsibilities is incapable of social justice, they may well believe those who claim that social justice would be better advanced by the elevation of group rights over individual rights, by a cultural democracy that preempts self-definition and genuine individual choice, and by a race-based multicultural curriculum, such as the one proposed by James Banks and adopted by the Board of Directors of the National Council for the Social Studies, in which students are taught according to someone's notion of their race's "learning style."[41]

Do works featuring reverse cultural stereotyping enjoy a suspension of critical judgment? Dragonwings received a Newbery Honor Award when it was first published. The reviews cited on the paperback edition indicate that it was acclaimed as a "fine, sensitive novel written with grace" (ALA *Booklist*) and as an "exquisitely written poem of praise to the courage and industry of the Chinese-American people" (the *New York Times*), while *Publishers Weekly* found "Yep's images and perspectives breathtakingly original."[42] No elementary teacher, reading such glowing reviews, would suspect that the novel is little more than a vehicle for the author's animus and a subtle piece of propaganda. Why do children's book critics fail to note Yep's crude manipulation of his young readers' feelings against white Americans (as well as his less than graceful prose)? If a so-called literary work portrays a non-white character positively, does nothing else matter? Or are the anti-white stereotypes not to be noted? It is not hard to imagine that the kind of criteria proposed for multicultural works can place subtle pressures on literary award-giving committees and book reviewers and perhaps even on would-be authors of books containing characters from particular social groups.

Similarly, Smagorinsky suggests that the presence of "Chee's Daughter" in high school "raises some important questions about an unexamined attempt to include multicultural materials in the literature curriculum." He suggests that if didactic texts such as "Chee's Daughter" have a place in the classroom, "that they be used as examples of manipulative, propagandistic texts whose message has distorted their medium."[43]

I do not wish to imply that all literary texts deemed multicultural are propaganda or that texts showing all white characters as unpleasant are necessarily degraded pieces of literature. One recent list of middle-grade children's books by and about black Americans addresses the question of whether the "European-descended characters" in each book are "supportive" or "non-supportive." Of the fifteen titles, eight have no "supportive" white characters. Some of these titles, however, such as *The Bluest Eye*, are of unquestioned literary merit.[44]

Nevertheless, in light of the professed interest by prominent educators and national educational organizations in eliminating literary stereotypes of non-mainstream groups, the unremarked-upon presence of hostile stereotypes of whites, Americans, or people of European descent in much of the recently composed multicultural literature available in or recommended for the classroom is at the least ironic. Nor is this phenomenon restricted to literature or to multicultural curricula. Such movies as *Driving Miss Daisy* reflect the same all-encompassing reverse stereotyping; all the black characters are portrayed as virtuous, while all southern white Christians are portrayed as mean, bigoted, or violent. And I have read no review calling attention to that fact.[45]

Do multicultural texts focus obsessively on capitalistic greed and racism in this country (or in the West)? Newsweek's 1991 article on multiculturalism in children's literature is only one of many that raise this question. "Long gone are the books that condescendingly introduced children to the quaint customs of our little friends from foreign lands," writes reporter Malcolm Jones, Jr. "Instead, there is 'The Last Princess' . . . a biography of Princess Ka'iulani, who tried in vain to prevent American businessmen from taking over Hawaii in the late 19th century." Jones goes on to say that by "Using the trademarks of children's publishing, including cheerful formats and sumptuous artwork, artists and writers are introducing children to some of the world's harsher realities."[46] Although a naive teacher might well be forgiven for thinking that all books about the customs of other peoples should qualify as multicultural, Jones suggests that multicultural literature for children should be a junior version of "oppression studies." The point, of course, is not that children shouldn't read books about prejudice or greed. Of course they should. The question is how often the term "multicultural" serves as a code word for works that seem intended not so much to inform about a non-mainstream culture, or simply to entertain, but rather to demonize the mainstream culture. It is exceedingly difficult, for example, to find a recommended multicultural text that touches upon greed, racism, or religious bigotry (or the existence of slavery or forced labor) in China, India, Japan, or any Islamic country.

To what extent do questionable classroom activities accompany the study of multicultural works? A number of such questionable classroom activities have come to my attention. For example, consider a set of assignments from *Literature for Us All*, a guide to multicultural literature instruction prepared by high school teachers participating in the California Literature Project. For a unit entitled "The Search for Justice and Dignity," students are asked to read Arthur Miller's *Death of a Salesman*, Maya Angelou's *I Know Why the Caged Bird Sings*, and *Farewell to Manzanar* (a true story about the internment of Japanese-Americans during World War II), as well as Shelley's poem "Ozymandias." According to the unit outline, reprinted in an *English Journal* article by Patricia Simmons Taylor of UCLA,[47] one purpose of reading the Miller play is "to study the struggle of the individual to find personal dignity in a materialistic society." Similarly, the purpose of studying *Farewell to Manzanar* is "to show how the members of the Wakatsuki family struggled to maintain dignity in an unjust society" and "to investigate that time in American history, seemingly at odds with the spirit of democracy, when Americans were imprisoned by Americans – when, how, why."

As preparation for reading Maya Angelou's work, the outline suggests that students attempt to define discrimination, and then write in journals about a time when "they felt discriminated against." To prepare for reading *Farewell to Manzanar*, students are to "interview parents or grandparents to determine their ancestry and report on any injustices perpetrated upon their ancestors." After they have finished reading the book, two of the suggested follow-up activities are to "Conduct a mock trial of our government's policy of internment during WW II" and "Write persuasive letters to the legislators regarding reparations for those who were interned." Some of these assignments fall under the rubric "Ways Beyond Literature" and are suggested as a means of helping students make connections between literature and real-world experience. But the likely effects of the assignments are to stimulate students' feelings of victimization by others, to foster interethnic animosity, and to encourage negative feelings toward their own government and, by implication, their own society.

Classroom projects of this kind are far from unique; I have discussed other examples, and the ethical problems they raise, elsewhere.[48] If teachers invite students to recount acts of prejudice directed against them or their families as members of a particular social group, such assignments of necessity reinforce group stereotypes. They may also create an unhealthy sense of moral superiority in those students who can claim victimhood for themselves or their ancestors, and encourage equally unhealthy feelings of envy or hatred in those who can't claim the privileged status of victim. These effects are especially likely if students are given no opportunity to discuss the social changes that have taken place or the political reforms that have been enacted to reduce discriminatory behavior. If teachers find a compelling reason to ask students about prejudice directed against them, they should *also* invite these students to think about acts of friendship displayed toward them by members of the same group to which the prejudiced persons belong. But I have yet to find such an assignment.

Are students being exposed to the full range of ethnic groups in this country? In surveying syllabi or teacher-made curriculum materials for multicultural literature courses, one cannot help but be struck by the limited range of ethnic groups that are "represented" by the authors on their required or recommended reading lists. It is extremely difficult to find works by American authors who come from one of the many European ethnic groups in this country or who write about them. Only Blair's recommended list of fictional or true autobiographies of American immigrants contains authors of European ethnic background: five out of fifteen. But in the extensive handouts that Nonie Ripley, a teacher from Houston, provided at the 1991 NCTE Fall Conference, not one of the few non-black, non-Hispanic, non-Indian, and non-Asian authors on her list of recommended readings for her multicultural unit, entitled "Red and Yellow, Black and White and Brown: Minds Across Five Cultures," was a non-Anglo-American author or even a European author.[49] In the handouts on multicultural literacy provided by Robinson and Gingrich, the two educators in the Cincinnati Public Schools, the "canonical" works of literature they discussed are all by British authors, while the American writers are almost all black Americans, with the exception of some Appalachian poets. A "Multicultural Literature Reading List in Progress," distributed at a multicultural workshop at the 1991 NCTE Spring Conference, included more than fifty works, almost all by black, Indian, and Hispanic authors. At this workshop, I asked the person chairing the session, a graduate student at Michigan State University, why few or no European ethnic groups are represented on multicultural reading lists; she replied that they aren't there "because they have assimilated and achieved the American Dream." Apparently, they have been disqualified from the literature class because they no longer experience prejudice, discrimination, or exploitation. Possibly, also, because so many members of these ethnic groups have written about their experiences in this country as liberating and personally fulfilling despite prejudice, discrimination, and exploitation. Unfortunately, if the history of European ethnic groups is ignored in literature courses, it becomes much easier to create monolithic anti-white stereotypes and to cast prejudice and discrimination in racial terms.

CONCLUSIONS AND SUGGESTIONS

The introduction of multicultural literature into the school curriculum represents an overdue and well-intentioned effort to integrate works by or about social groups that have until recently been absent or inadequately presented. It would indeed be unfortunate if the sincere effort by many, perhaps most, teachers to expose all American students to the full range of ethnic and racial groups in this country, to undo any stereotypes that may have been stimulated by older works, and to give all students a genuine sense of belonging to this country were to lead, whether unintentionally or not, to the negative stereotyping of mainstream Americans, to the exclusion of certain groups, and to a curriculum that reflects in the eyes of some observers the spirit of premodern tribalism.

Literature teachers have a clear professional responsibility to incorporate into their programs the best and most illuminating literature from the entire range of ethnic and other social communities in this country, regardless of the author's feelings about European cultures, this country, or the majority of its citizens. In seeking to include newer or possibly neglected works that will correct the bias perceived in traditional curricula, teachers cannot help but exclude some older works. They should also want to include newer works featuring admirable characters who demonstrate clear thinking and understandable anger about the injustices their group may have endured. In doing so, however, teachers also have a professional obligation to consider whether their literature programs may be inadvertently fostering interracial and interethnic hostility and undermining the psychological basis for civic participation in a multiethnic and multiracial society. If the potential for a negative influence on race relations exists, teachers need to discuss how their literature programs can best promote understanding and tolerance of social differences without at the same time fostering social divisiveness or excluding works that still present important values to today's students.

The civic aim of multicultural education, Robert Fullinwider has written, is to "create the grounds for mutual respect among students by teaching them to understand and appreciate their different cultures and histories."[50] There are at least four ways in which educators can pursue this aim, while promoting their traditional goal of preparing students for responsible citizenship, and for American citizenship in particular.

First, public school literature programs should be designed so that all students, regardless of ethnic or racial background, are exposed to the full range of ethnic and racial diversity in this country. However, the shaping or promotion of children's cultural or religious identity should not be undertaken by the public schools. If parents want their children to embrace a particular cultural or religious identity, they are free to enroll the children in after-school programs or in religious schools which define their mission in these terms. As a nation, we would benefit as much from the separation of ethnicity and state as we have from the separation of church and state. Ethnic interests should be allowed to flourish on a voluntary basis without the stultifying control of government bureaucracies. Apparently, this is what many parents want, if only their voices could be heard by scholars, educators, and public officials. In the most extensive effort to measure Hispanic attitudes to date, "an overwhelming majority of those surveyed who call themselves American citizens said that the goal of bilingual education should be to teach English or both languages rather than to preserve the Spanish language and culture among Hispanic young people."[51]

Parents and children should also be offered a completely free choice about how they wish to identify themselves. Parents who consider themselves and their children simply as American citizens and who want their children to be educated as individuals, not as stereotyped members of specific ethnic or racial groups, should not be classified and referred to by teachers and official school documents by group designations they have not chosen for themselves.

Second, teachers should ensure that a curriculum including works by or about a variety of social groups is not chiefly "white guilt" (or white male guilt) literature, as typified by works such as *The Bluest Eye*, *Farewell to Manzanar*, and Leslie Marmon Silko's *Ceremony*.[52] No student or group will benefit from a fairy-tale curriculum in which all non-white (or female) characters are virtuous and all white (or male) characters are bigoted, hateful, morally confused, alienated, or nihilistic. Inevitably, a plethora of such literature breeds contempt for the literature and a lack of sympathy for the "virtuous" groups.

From a civic perspective, teachers have the responsibility to consider the moral, or rhetorical, effects of a work of literature on their students. This does not mean excluding works by or about non-white groups. There are many literary works by and about members of minority groups that are realistic yet do not show most if not all white characters as bigoted or deeply flawed in other ways. Such works as *Nisei Daughter*, by Monica Sone, or *Journey to Topaz*, by Yoshiko Uchida (stories based on the authors' experiences in internment camps for Japanese-Americans during World War II); *In the Year of the Boar and Jackie Robinson*, by Bette Bao Lord (a story about a young Chinese girl as an immigrant to Brooklyn in the 1940s); and *Maggie's American Dream*, by James Comer (a true account of a tough-minded black mother in an intact family whose four children all became successful professionals despite racial discrimination), can easily substitute for *Farewell to Manzanar*, *Dragonwings*, and *Women of Brewster Place*, by Gloria Naylor, a bleak novel about mainly single mothers and their children in a housing project – and a novel that is increasingly finding its way into high school classes. From a civic perspective, teachers also need to make sure that all students read some books that portray whites as well as non-whites as strong moral human beings – that works like *Huckleberry Finn* and *To Kill a Mockingbird* stay in the curriculum and are not removed for spurious reasons.

Third, public school educators should consider offering a label-free literature curriculum in which works are judged chiefly on their merits, regardless of the religion, gender, and ethnicity of the author, and integrated within our national literature simply as the works of American writers. Educators would have to let publishers know that they did not want our literature anthologies to reflect an explicit division of this country into five spurious racial groups, as current fashion dictates. Instituting a label-free curriculum would mean that not every ethnic group would have to be represented at every grade level so long as students were exposed over a period of years to a rough balance between works about Americans as members of ethnic groups and works about Americans as Americans. A label-free curriculum would also mean that works by Mexican-Americans, Irish-Americans, Chinese-Americans, and so on, were presented as part of our national literary tradition, rather than simply as works belonging to a non-mainstream or non-dominant group. If such works as Rudolfo Anaya's *Bless Me, Ultima* or Lorraine Hansberry's *Raisin in the Sun* are seen only as the products of a particular ethnic or cultural group, and not as an integral part of our national literature, then teachers will appear to be suggesting that these works are by marginalized people and represent marginal literature. To designate a work as a text by a Mexican-American, Latino, Jewish-American, Korean-American, or female writer (or by a European-American writer, whatever that label is intended to mean) inescapably seems to marginalize it: to designate it as a text by an American writer does not. Recent attempts by some academic scholars and public officials to marginalize the mainstream itself by the label "European-American," when the vast majority of immigrants want to become part of the mainstream for academic and economic advancement, may ultimately damage minority children's academic development and their opportunity to advance economically, both nationally and internationally.

Finally, and perhaps most important of all, the curriculum must maintain a distinction between American and non-American literature and make sure that the vast majority of literary works studied in grades K–12 are by and about Americans, whatever their racial or ethnic background might be. Our literature programs also need to expose all students to those works or authors within the body of American literature that will help them make coherent intellectual connections between our culture's past and present. Although students need exposure to some world literature through all grades, literature programs in American public schools have an obligation to provide students with as full an acquaintance as they can with American literature (and all the many social groups its best literature may reflect). American educators are under no obligation to strive for equity in representing all the thousands of different national or regional cultures around the world, especially if this would mean giving short shrift to our own multiethnic culture.

The importance of this suggestion cannot be overestimated. If students are to understand how unique the American national experience has been and what American writers think we are – for good or for bad – then they must become thoroughly familiar with works expressing what Howard Mumford Jones has called "the American imagination." This is true whatever the students' racial or ethnic backgrounds, and whatever the backgrounds of the writers themselves.

The distinction between an American literature, composed by writers born or raised in this country or by writers who adopt and then write about this country, and a non-American literature is a critical one for literature instruction today. In the attempt to undo what they claim is a Eurocentric bias, many English educators seem prepared to change what is now a chiefly American-centered literature curriculum into one dominated by authors from other countries. At the present time, the great majority of the literary works studied by American students, especially the top forty or so major titles, are by American authors.[53] But this has not been the case for most of American history. Since the beginning of the century, there has been a gradual shift from a predominantly British literary curriculum to an American one, and this process accelerated after World War II.[54] In a 1907 survey, only 9 of the top 40 authors studied in 67 Midwestern high schools were Americans; by 1989, almost 75 percent of the authors studied were American. If the charge of Eurocentrism is intended to mean that most of the titles high school students read today are by European authors, it is clearly untrue; British works have been largely displaced, and few works translated from French, German, Russian, and other European countries have ever been a regular part of American high school literature programs. If the charge is intended to mean that the majority of works in most secondary schools are by American authors of European descent, with no consideration of how many years the families of these authors have lived in this country, then what we are dealing with is simply a crude political attempt to fudge the vast cultural differences between a Mark Twain or a Willa Cather and a Thomas Hardy or a Virginia Woolf, that is, to deny that American culture as a whole is a different culture from British (or European) culture.

The growing attempt to change what is now a chiefly American-centered literature curriculum into one dominated once again by non-American authors is by no means an attempt to reinstate British culture. Rather, it seems to be an effort to transform the literature curriculum of the public schools into a conglomeration of world cultures. This new curriculum would include works from countries in much of the Western Hemisphere, on the grounds that their varied literatures can all be referred to as "American." It would also include works in English from countries which are part of the British Commonwealth or former colonies of the British Empire. In an article on the "globalization" of English, Miles Myers, the executive director of NCTE, writes that whereas "we have traditionally defined 'English literature' as literature from Great Britain, some scholars have suggested that the term should be replaced with 'literature in English.' This shift would presumably open our booklists and courses to the exceptional literature in English from India (Raja Rao), from Africa (Chinua Achebe), from around the world."[55] This is already happening. In addition, translations of works by Central and South American authors have also been rapidly entering the curriculum. Certainly, students should be exposed to some of these works. But if we want to develop our students' civic identity and, hence, the basic bond supporting their sense of social responsibility to each other despite racial, ethnic, and religious differences, we need to preserve the American-centered literature curriculum it took us two hundred years to achieve.

NOTES

1. E. D. Hirsch, Jr., seems to be the only prominent scholar in the field of English who has addressed even a part of this question. He has proposed

that the ability to participate fully in American political, economic, and cultural life is in large part a function of cultural literacy, and he continues to work on the elements of a common core curriculum for grades K–8 at his Core Knowledge Foundation in Charlottesville, Virginia, even though he has been almost totally excoriated and shunned by the English language arts establishment for his efforts.

2. Peter Smagorinsky, "Towards a Civic Education in a Multicultural Society: Ethical Problems in Teaching Literature," *English Education* (December 1992): 212–28; Sandra Stotsky with Barbara Hardy Beierl, "Teaching Contemporary American Literature: A Professional Dilemma," in *Connecting Civic Education and Language Education: The Contemporary Challenge,* ed. Sandra Stotsky (New York: Teachers College Press, 1991); Sandra Stotsky, "The Changing Literature Curriculum in K–12," *Academic Questions* 7 (1) (Winter 1993–94): 53–62.
3. Howard Mumford Jones, *Jeffersonianism and the American Novel* (New York: Teachers College Press, 1966), p. xi.
4. Paula Burns, "Desperate in Peoria," *English Journal* 74 (February 1985): 76–7; John Cameron, "Reclaiming Our Humanity in Twentieth Century Literature: An Annotated Reading List for High School and College Teachers," in *Connecting Civic Education and Language Education,* ed. Stotsky, pp. 91–8.
5. Geraldine Vale, "Mollified in Madison: Optimism in Contemporary American Literature," *English Journal* 78 (April 1989): 19–24.
6. Ben Nelms, "Holden's Reading," *English Journal* 78 (1989): 13.
7. Arthur M. Schlesinger, Jr., *The Disuniting of America: Reflections on a Multicultural Society* (New York: W. W. Norton, 1992).
8. Robert K. Fullinwider, "Multicultural Education," *Report from the Institute for Philosophy and Public Policy* 11 (3) (Summer 1991): 12.
9. Ann Trousdale, "A Submission Theology for Black Americans: Religion and Social Action in Prize-Winning Children's Books about the Black Experience in America," *Research in the Teaching of English* 24 (1990): 117–41.
10. Nelms, "Holden's Reading," p. 13.
11. Malcolm Jones, Jr., "It's a Not So Small World," *Newsweek,* September 9, 1991, pp. 64–5.
12. Nancy Shapiro, "Review of Five Cross-Cultural or Multicultural Readers," *College Composition and Communication* 42 (December 1991): 524–30.
13. Aniece Kerr, "Great Advances in Children's Literature," *Brookline Citizen,* February 20, 1992, p. 5.
14. Committee on Elementary Language Arts Textbooks, "Guidelines for Judging and Selecting Elementary Language Arts Textbooks" (Urbana, Ill.: National Council of Teachers of English, July 1990).
15. Quoted by Malcolm Jones, Jr., "It's a Not So Small World," p. 64.
16. Shapiro, "Review," p. 524.
17. Roseann Duenas Gonzalez, "When Minority Becomes Majority: The Changing Face of English Classrooms," *English Journal* 79 (January 1990): 16–23.
18. NCTE Committee on Women in the Profession, "Guidelines for a Gender-

Balanced Curriculum in English Grades 7–12" (Urbana, Ill.: National Council of Teachers of English, 1990).

19. Linda Blair, "Developing Student Voices with Multicultural Literature," *English Journal* 80 (December 1991): 24–8.
20. Ibid., p. 28.
21. Connie Robinson and Randy Gingrich, "Multicultural Literacy," unpublished materials handed out at the National Council of Teachers of English Fall Conference, Seattle, Washington, November 1991.
22. Gonzalez, "When Minority Becomes Majority," p. 19.
23. Shapiro, "Review," p. 525.
24. Marcia K. Savage and Tom V. Savage, "Exploring Ethnic Diversity Through Children's and Youth Adult Literature," *Oregon English Journal* 14 (3) (Spring 1992): 7–11.
25. Carla Hayden, ed., *Venture into Cultures: A Resource Book of Multicultural Materials and Programs* (Chicago: American Library Association, 1992), p. vi.
26. Trousdale, "A Submission Theology for Black Americans," pp. 117–41.
27. Ibid., p. 119.
28. Ibid., p. 137.
29. Ibid., p. 139.
30. Smagorinsky, "Towards a Civic Education," p. 22.
31. Henry Louis Gates, Jr., "'Authenticity,' or the Lesson of Little Tree," *New York Times Book Review*, November 24, 1991, p. 1.
32. See Sandra Stotsky, "Multicultural Education in the Brookline Public Schools: The Deconstruction of an Academic Curriculum," *News & Views* 10 (October 1991): 29–34. To judge from the composition of a newly formed curriculum advisory committee in Brookline, Mass., that has been charged with revising the high school's social studies program, who selects the community members of an advisory group and what criteria are used in their selection may be the most crucial questions of all. In a town like Brookline, one might ordinarily expect community members of such a committee to be selected on the basis of their knowledge of the field, diverse educational interests and academic points of view, and the public recognition that being a "community representative" implies. Yet, after using the local newspapers to encourage applications from parents and other citizens for the community positions on the faculty-run advisory committee, the chairman of the high school social studies department – one whose politically biased curriculum has received a great deal of publicity – selected two blacks, two Hispanics, and one Asian, all locally unknown; one white female known publicly for her extreme views on multiculturalism; and one white male known for his concerns about the academic orientation of the current curriculum, whom the chairperson had to choose if he wished to avoid negative publicity and the accusation of censorship right from the start.

If these seven had been the only people to apply for membership, there would be no issue. But after obtaining a ruling from the town counsel that all applications were public information, I discovered that five other people had applied and been rejected. Of these five, who were all white, two were retired history/social studies professors who had innocently volunteered for the committee, thinking their expertise would be welcome, while another was co-president of the local League of Women Voters. I also discovered that the Asian member had never applied to be on the committee; the chairman had asked him to serve "in order to have the 'Asian' constituency in Brookline represented." It is difficult not to conclude that race or ethnicity was the major criterion for membership on this committee.

Although there are many situations in which race or ethnicity warrants consideration, it should not be the only criterion for membership on any curriculum committee, no matter whether a community is chiefly black and Hispanic or, as is Brookline, over 70 percent "white." Such a criterion leaves out the most relevant constituencies for any school – those parents or community members with concerns for particular groups of students, such as the non-college-bound, and those who do volunteer work in the schools and have a demonstrated interest in its functioning – all constituencies that cross racial and ethnic lines.

33. Smagorinsky, "Towards a Civic Education," p. 16.
34. The researcher, Gary Ebersole, is quoted by Debra Shore, "Our Captors, Our Selves," *University of Chicago Magazine* 83 (5) (1991): 28–32.
35. Juanita Platero and Siyowin Miller, "Chee's Daughter," in *Literature & Language, Grade 10* (Evanston, Ill.: McDougal, Littel, 1992), pp. 528–38. The story also appears in *Prentice Hall Literature, Grade 10* (Englewood Cliffs, N.J., 1994), pp. 77–87.
36. Smagorinsky, "Towards a Civic Education," p. 18.
37. See Sandra Stotsky, *Connecting Civic Education and Language Education*.
38. Laurence Yep, *Dragonwings* (New York: Harper & Row, 1975), p. 1.
39. Ibid., p. 127.
40. Ibid., pp. 247–8.
41. James Banks, "Curriculum Guidelines for Multicultural Education," *Social Education* (September 1992): 274–88. These guidelines provide an example of a contradiction common among multiculturalists. Banks emphatically urges educators to treat students as individuals; yet at the same time, he wants a racial and ethnic cast to all aspects of the curriculum. In practice, the latter would inevitably tend to cancel out the former.
42. The *New York Times* education section for February 19, 1992, provided a short "multicultural" reading list to help teachers teach the topic of "prejudice and how some groups have mistreated others throughout history." *Dragonwings* was one of the seven "well-written and historically valid" books on the list, all described by the *Times* education editor as "informative, unbiased and intriguing to children."
43. Smagorinsky, "Towards a Civic Education," p. 29.
44. Debra Ridley, "Annotated Bibliography of African-American, Hispanic American, Native American Indian Books, for K–6, that Portray European Characters in Supportive and Non-Supportive Roles" (Indianapolis: Free to Read – The African-American Child's Book Club, December 27, 1990; personal communication).

45. The practice of reverse stereotyping has been examined in the history and social studies curriculum. In a study first published in 1986, Paul Vitz, a psychologist at New York University, looked at the content of elementary social studies textbooks and basal readers to determine "what social and moral values animate the books generally used in the public schools." For his study of basal readers (the instructional texts used for teaching reading in grades 1 to 6), Vitz categorized the stories and articles in all the grade 3 and grade 6 readers of eleven publishers. He found, among other things, many instances of what he called role reversals, such as dragon-slaying princesses, but no examples of princes slaying dragons or of men even attempting to rescue women. Stories showing competition, especially physical competition between girls and boys, almost always had the girl winning. There were frequent stories of female successes in traditionally male activities, such as stories about women fliers like Amelia Earhart and Harriet Quimby, but only one page-long story on the Wright brothers and nothing on Charles Lindbergh or other male aviation pioneers. In addition, Vitz found many stories that rewrote or misrepresented history by referring to women judges, merchants, and soldiers "at times and places where, in fact, no women performed such labors." In sum, Vitz's findings suggest that the cultural and historical integrity of leading elementary school readers has also eroded. See Paul Vitz, "Censor at Work: (Anti)Family Values in Public School Textbooks," *The Family in America* 5 (1991): 2–7.

46. Jones, "It's a Not So Small World," p. 65.

47. Patricia Simmons Taylor, "None of Us Is Smarter than All of Us: The Reform in California's Curriculum," *English Journal* 77 (December 1988): 14–19.

48. See Sandra Stotsky, "Ethical Guidelines for Writing Assignments," in *Social Issues in the English Classroom*, ed. C. M. Hurlbert and S. Totten (Urbana, Ill.: National Council of Teachers of English, 1992), pp. 283–303.

49. Nonie Ripley, "Red and Yellow, Black and White and Brown: Minds Across Five Cultures," unpublished materials handed out at the National Council of Teachers of English Spring Conference, Indianapolis, Ind., March 1991.

50. Robert Fullinwider, "Multicultural Education," *University of Chicago Legal Forum* (1991): 80.

51. Roberto Suro, "Hispanic Pragmatism Seen in Survey," *New York Times*, December 15, 1992, p. A20.

52. I have briefly discussed the teaching of "white-guilt literature" in "*EJ* Forum: Reader-Response Criticism and Classroom Imperatives," *English Journal* 82 (March 1993), pp. 20–1, in response to the editor's invitation to comment on an article by a high school teacher describing her students' reactions to *The Bluest Eye*.

53. See Arthur N. Applebee, *Literature in the Secondary School: Studies of Curriculum and Instruction in the United States* (Urbana, Ill.: National Council of Teachers of English, 1993); Sandra Stotsky and Philip Anderson, "Variety

and Individualism in the English Class: Teacher-Recommended Lists for Grades 7–12," *The Leaflet* 89 (1990): 1–11.

54. Sandra Stotsky, "Whose Literature? America's!" *Educational Leadership* 49 (December 1991/January 1992): 53–6.

55. Miles Myers, "The Globalization of English," *Council-Grams* 54 (November/December 1990): 8.

Chapter 11

Teaching American literary history

ARTHUR EVENCHIK

In an essay he published a century ago in the *North American Review*, Mark Twain attempted to describe how the life of a people finds expression in its literature. The occasion for his reflections was the appearance of a travel book by a Frenchman named Paul Bourget, who had come to the United States for an extended visit two years before. Some reviewers had praised Bourget for the acuity and fairness he brought to his portrayal of America. Yet it seemed to Twain that he had been an oddly credulous tourist, taking every stranger at his word and putting too much faith in the validity of his own impressions. Moreover, once Bourget had drawn what he called "a bundle of sketches from life," he made the mistake of trying to generalize about the "national character." Not content to provide an account of American arts and manners, his real hope was to pass beyond them and to capture something he described as "the American soul."[1]

Quests of this kind were not all that unusual among nineteenth-century literary tourists; Mark Twain, who was a travel writer himself, knew this as well as anyone. Nonetheless, he felt somewhat provoked by what he saw as the effrontery of Bourget's enterprise. A visitor to a foreign land, he noted with some asperity, cannot through observation alone gain access to a nation's inner life; such an achievement requires years of "unconscious absorption" by those who are born to that life. Moreover, even a native writer would never presume to have captured, by force of knowledge or imagination, any such abstraction as the American soul:

> Does the native novelist try to generalize the nation? No, he lays plainly before you the ways and speech and life of a few people grouped in a certain place – his own place – and that is one book. In time he and his brethren will report to you the life and the people of the whole nation – the life of a group in a New England village; in a New York village; in a Texan village; in an Oregon village; in villages in fifty states and territo-

ries; then the farm-life in fifty states and territories; a hundred patches of life and groups of people in a dozen widely separated cities. And the Indians will be attended to; and the cowboys; and the gold and silver miners; and the negroes; and the Idiots and Congressmen; and the Irish, the Germans, the Italians, the Swedes, the French, the Chinamen, the Greasers; and the Catholics, the Methodists, the Presbyterians, the Congregationalists, the Baptists, the Spiritualists, the Mormons, the Shakers, the Quakers, the Jews, the Campbellites, the infidels, the Christian Scientists, the Mind-Curists, the Faith-Curists, the train-robbers, the White Caps, the Moonshiners. And when a thousand able novels have been written, *there* you have the soul of the people, the life of the people, the speech of the people; and not anywhere else can these be had. And the shadings of character, manners, feelings, ambitions, will be infinite.[2]

It is no surprise that Twain should have launched his inventory by noting the writer's fidelity to "a certain place." The impulse to generalize the nation has often been resisted on grounds of regionalist sentiment. In 1906, the frontier historian Frederick Jackson Turner called for the North, South, and West to retain their distinctive characteristics in the new century, arguing that in doing so they would refute the idea that national unity implied national uniformity.[3] During the 1920s and 1930s, the Southern founders of the Fugitive and Agrarian literary movements – including Robert Penn Warren, Allen Tate, and John Crowe Ransom – defended their inherited culture as a bulwark against the standardizing pressures of the modern industrial age.[4] Mark Twain participates in the regionalist tradition when he observes that there is no American village per se, no farm-life or city-life uninflected by local differences. In the first half of the passage, the only collective identity he recognizes in America – apart from the brotherhood of writers – is that of people "grouped in a certain place," and the only common life he imagines is the "life of a group."

And yet, as Twain proceeds with his catalogue of American communities, there are points at which his exuberance carries a certain ironic force. When he juxtaposes Idiots and Congressmen, for example, or when he allows the various religious sects to proliferate, he derives a comic effect from the perception that these ostensibly separate groups are not as different as they imagine – a point they could grasp for themselves if they were not so insistent on the superior virtue of their members or the singular merit of their respective doctrines. The Mind-Curists and the Faith-Curists will never agree about the path to physical and spiritual healing, yet from Twain's point of view they are under the sway of kindred delusions. The infidels refuse their allegiance to every sect, but once Twain has blithely mixed them in among the others, they seem to *constitute* a sect. And of course the pieties of group identification receive a final blow when

Twain brings the train-robbers and Moonshiners into his picture, knowing full well that the seekers after the "soul" of a people are usually inclined to leave them out.

We can hear, then, at least two voices in the passage – one that is generously aware of a "hundred patches of life," and one that takes a wryly diligent inventory of the more bemusing examples. This second voice may caution us against regarding difference as valuable for its own sake. But it also gives Twain's closing affirmation a greater resonance than it might otherwise have achieved. Unprepared for the sudden earnestness of the conclusion, we are more easily moved to accept its assertion of literature's power to embody a nation's existence: "And when a thousand able novels have been written, *there* you have the soul of the people, the life of the people, the speech of the people; and not anywhere else can these be had." This national literature will possess a greater scope and inclusiveness than any single observer or traveler can claim. It will acknowledge realities that we have failed to incorporate into our prevailing self-definitions and our customary language. When Twain speaks of "the people," we are to understand that he refers to a multiplicity: what he means by their "life" and "soul" and "speech" is not what the generalizer means, for he knows that "the shadings of character, manners, feelings, ambitions, will be infinite." And this last sentence reminds us that multiplicity exists not only within a nation, but also within its constitutive groups and then, once we reach the level of feelings and ambitions, within individual human beings.

THE MIRROR OF OUR IDEALS

When Twain proposed this conception of a national literature, he was looking ahead to a literary canon – "a thousand able novels" – that had not yet been created. Within a few years, however, a generation of scholars was looking to the past and trying to define the literary tradition that America had already produced. Unlike Twain, these historians did not write as if there were forms of experience and ways of life still to be incorporated within an expansive national literature. Indeed, as Nina Baym explains, their enterprise was in some ways a flight *from* experience. Until the Civil War, the study of history had been the primary means by which schools imparted a sense of American identity. But since "history had been overcast by the shadow of the Civil War, a new subject was needed as the centerpiece. American belles lettres emerged as its substitute."[5]

The literary histories that Baym examines from this period all celebrated the creation of a distinctively American literary culture – a culture, they agreed, that had originated in New England and that retained the distinguishing features of a Puritan spirituality. Today it is often assumed that the early literary histories were created by and for a relatively homogeneous citizenry – an America of the same racial and ethnic stock as that of the major figures they identified and honored. But the common schools for which many of the first literary histories were written had largely been founded for the benefit of non-English immigrants, who had begun to arrive in the United States in significant numbers in the 1830s. The major educational reforms of the late nineteenth century, including the expansion of compulsory schooling, were attempts to address the "specters of cultural chaos and social violence accompanying mass immigration and industrialization."[6] And the teaching of a national literature was viewed as one means of promoting assimilation and inculcating spiritual values in a potentially restive population.

This context may help to explain why some of the histories were so careful to identify what was truly "native" to the American tradition. Barrett Wendell and Chester Noyes Greenough, writing about Walt Whitman in *A History of Literature in America* (1907), assert that his "conception of equality, utterly ignoring values, is not that of American democracy, but rather that of European. His democracy, in short, is the least native which has ever found voice in our country."[7] The sharp rhetorical distinction between "His democracy" and "our country" has the effect of denaturalizing the poet who had proclaimed himself the supreme representative of an emerging national tradition. Such a gesture has profound implications if one believes, as many literary historians of the period did, that a writer's place in the canon is contingent upon his fidelity to authentic American principles. The historian Richard Burton professes this belief unequivocally in *Literary Leaders of America* (1903), when he writes that American literature is "valuable to the young student and future citizen of the Republic just in proportion as it seems to mirror our American ideals and as it shall have a tendency to build up the reader into a worthy citizenship."[8]

PROPAGANDISTS AND CHAMPIONS

Thus we find, appearing around the turn of the century, two ambitious conceptions of a national literature, conceptions that in many ways anticipate views adopted in contemporary debates about multicultural education.[9] Mark Twain's conception, which we may designate as "pluralist," emphasizes the descriptive value of literature: the aim of the native novelists is to capture the infinite shadings of American life. The historians' conception, which defines literary study as a component of civic education, requires the national literature to "mir-

ror our American ideals." With its prescriptive emphasis, this conception would probably exclude from the canon some of the "thousand
able novels" that Twain would have readily admitted.

This is not to say that pluralism and civic education are inherently
in conflict. A civic educator may find American ideals embodied in
works from a variety of regions or ethnic communities. A pluralist
may find that an inclusive national literature performs a civic function
by making citizens of different backgrounds more familiar, or more
fully imaginable, to one another. But instead of attempting to reconcile the two conceptions here, I propose instead to subject them both
to a measure of critical scrutiny. Ultimately, I want to argue that they
can be of only partial use to the teacher of American literature, that
the sense they give of the origins and purposes of literature is inadequate and sometimes misguided. Let us, then, examine the two conceptions separately, beginning with the one that regards literature
primarily as a vehicle of civic education.

The first difficulty with the civic conception is that it makes the
literary historian or teacher the arbiter of what is genuinely American.
We see this in Wendell and Greenough's assertion that Whitman's
idea of equality is oblivious to values and thus "the least native that
has ever found voice in our country." It is clear that the writers are not
merely remarking upon Whitman's intellectual lineage; they are also
declaring his idea of equality inferior to "ours." But in their apparent
certainty that they *know* the native conception better than Whitman
did, they close themselves off from one of his central lessons: that the
democratic ideal still awaits its adequate expression, that it must be
endlessly rediscovered rather than merely affirmed. George Kateb,
who calls Whitman "perhaps the greatest philosopher of the culture
of democracy," articulates this lesson when he observes that the theory of democratic individualism

> is such a strange idea, and so untypical of past human experience, that
> those who live it and live by it – even though imperfectly – have to
> keep remembering, or keep learning as if they never knew, both the
> basic meaning and the farther implications of what they profess and
> enact.[10]

Whitman himself, in his late prose, declares that the highest vision of
democracy "has yet few or no realizers and believers. I do not see,
either, that it owes any serious thanks to noted propagandists or
champions, or has been essentially help'd, though often harm'd, by
them."[11] No wonder the historians called him inauthentic.

The second difficulty with the civic conception is closely related to
the first. If we take seriously the civic criteria for literary value that
Burton proposes, then a major portion of our literature will always

appear suspect unless we disguise it with tendentious and evasive readings. This is at least as true of the canonical texts as it is of anything admitted into the curriculum under the banner of multi-cultural education. Thoreau writes in *Walden:* "wherever a man goes, men will pursue and paw him with their dirty institutions, and, if they can, constrain him to belong to their desperate odd-fellow society."[12] Now a reader may justly feel that this is a thoroughly American sentiment, but for the civic educator that is not the issue: whatever Burton may reasonably be taken to mean by "worthy citizenship," Thoreau's words do nothing to foster or advance it. Nor does classic American fiction typically honor the Jeffersonian ideal of the citizen as "a being capable of both rational and moral choice."[13] "If I had a yaller dog that didn't know no more than a person's conscience does," declares Huck Finn, "I would pison him."[14] On one level, this is an obvious joke on Twain's part; but Huck is in earnest. When he makes his momentous decision to rescue Jim from slavery, he is prompted not by any rational judgment or moral conviction, but by affection and loyalty; whatever conscience he has is only the "de-structive morality implanted by a slave society."[15] Thus, as Lionel Trilling observed in an influential preface to the novel, "Ideas or ide-als can be of no help to him," and at last "he consents to be damned for a personal devotion, never questioning the justice of the punish-ment he has incurred."[16] This fact alone may not disconcert the civic educator; we cannot expect Huck Finn to display the same rationality and moral clarity we would expect from an adult American. But Tril-ling went on to argue that for the serious reader, Huck's experience provokes an enduring skepticism, a permanent revolution of con-sciousness that the civic educator might well find troubling:

> [N]o one who reads thoughtfully the dialectic of Huck's great moral crisis will ever again be wholly able to accept without some question and some irony the assumptions of the respectable morality by which he lives, nor will ever again be certain that what he considers the clear dictates of moral reason are not merely the engrained customary beliefs of his time and place.[17]

It was because Trilling recognized this aspect of the novel that he harbored a certain respect for its early censors – all those scandalized librarians and indignant school boards. *Huckleberry Finn*, he remarked in partial tribute to their judgment, "is indeed a subversive book."[18] His most profound disagreement was not with them, but with those who failed to notice the subversiveness of the novel, either because they did not see the significance of Huck's dilemma or because they wishfully regarded him as an exemplar of principled resistance to evil.

Another influential reading of the novel, from Harold Kaplan's book *Democratic Humanism and American Literature*, may seem more congenial to the civic educator. Kaplan agrees with Trilling that *Huckleberry Finn* exposes the corruptions of a democratic society – "the evil the people do, and can always do." Yet he argues that Twain's satire cannot be "revolutionary and absolute," because the writer knows that he cannot place his hopes "in the intervention of a better sort of people, nor in the intervention of good rulers, nor of God."[19] Twain does not deny our failings, but his comic vision manages to preserve us from a disabling self-distrust. This interpretation of the novel is less "subversive" than Trilling's, in that it assures us that Twain's skepticism has its limits. However, the democratic faith that Kaplan discerns in *Huckleberry Finn* is explicitly non-religious. It trusts in the people, having forsaken all other illusions; it does not trust in God. To the literary historians at the turn of the century, this would certainly have been an unwelcome interpretation, since it finds the novel rejecting the spirituality they perceived as central to the American literary tradition.

Finally, the civic conception of literature raises difficulties because it exaggerates the role that civic identity can or ought to have in our students' experience as readers. Here we might look for guidance to a brief reminiscence by Eudora Welty. As a young woman in Mississippi in the 1930s, "reading at my own will and as pleasure led me," Welty happened to discover Virginia Woolf's *To the Lighthouse*. "Blessed with luck and innocence," she writes, "I fell upon the novel that once and forever opened the door of imaginative fiction for me, and read it cold, in all its wonder and magnitude."[20] It was not as an American that Welty passed through that door. She did not read with the idea that Virginia Woolf belonged to a culture separate from her own, and that Woolf's characters were significantly remote from her because they were British subjects. The truth of the novel, as she rightly saw, was not a truth of nationality: "Set down here in the surround of the sea, on the spinning earth, caught up in the mysteries and the threat of time, the characters in their separate ways are absorbed in the wresting of order and sequence out of chaos, of shape out of what shifts and changes or vanishes before their eyes."[21] What happens in *To the Lighthouse* occurs not simply in the Isles of Skye, in the surround of the sea, but "on the spinning earth." The characters are caught up not only in a summer holiday preceding the First World War, but also in "the mysteries and the threat of time."

It may be a product of luck and innocence thus to respond to literature. Welty's interpretation may seem suspiciously transcendent, in an era when criticism is so vitally and fruitfully concerned with literature's specific social and historical dimensions. But sometimes, when our students are reading Chekhov or Shakespeare, Dickinson or Welty or Rita Dove, they do respond in this way. It is one of the signs that they are *becoming* readers. The language of civic education, however, is impoverished before this experience; it neglects those qualities of intellect and sensibility out of which literature arises and to which it speaks.

ANCESTRAL TRADITIONS AND
ARBITRARY ENCLOSURES

In some respects, the pluralism that Mark Twain articulates in his essay from 1895 is quite different from the civic understanding of literature that we have been considering. In his culminating sentence, Twain speaks of "character, manners, feelings, ambitions," but not of values or ideals. This will surprise no one, in light of the famous warning at the start of *Huckleberry Finn*: "Persons attempting to find a motive in this narrative will be prosecuted; persons attempting to find a moral in it will be banished; persons attempting to find a plot in it will be shot."[22] That reading is a morally freighted experience, that books can exert ethical influence, is indisputable; that the duty of the reader is to extract "a moral" from books is a notion that Twain rejected as sanctimonious and oppressive.

Furthermore, when Twain speaks of literature as encompassing the soul and life and speech of the people, he insists that "not anywhere else can these be had." This suggests that we cannot anticipate or determine what we will learn of ourselves from the pages of a national literature. In contrast, the civic conception seeks an avowal of what it already knows about American ideals and, by implication, American reality. In David Bromwich's words, such a conception assumes that "one is supposed to come to the right books with a received image of one's culture; the books are then used as primary documents to confirm that image." For books to work in this way, however, "one must have been finding in them only what one was expected to find. A curriculum used like this becomes a machine for coming of age in a culture."[23]

The pluralist view of literature, however, is open to objections that are often reminiscent of those that the civic conception inspires. For instance, if the civic educator defines readers and writers with too much regard for their nationality, the pluralist may be no less restrictive in his emphasis on the importance of ethnic or regional identity. Here again, we can look to Eudora Welty for guidance. To a pluralist who reads in the spirit of Twain's 1895 essay, the most notable fact about Welty is likely to be her sense of place, her skill in representing the life and speech she came to know growing up in Mississippi. And certainly there is much in her work to invite this understanding of her achievement – enough so that one would be skeptical of a critical approach that made light of her identity as a Southerner. (When my students write about Welty's stories, they occasionally misquote them, unconsciously adapting her phrasing to the idiom of their own part of the country. They have failed to hear the writer's voice; and a lesson in style follows as they discover what has been lost in their translations.) On the other hand, the abiding interest and value of Welty's writing cannot be said to lie chiefly in its regional characteristics. There is, in the first place, much debate as to what actually constitutes "Southern writing"; and Welty herself, in her reviews and essays, has shown strikingly little interest even in addressing the question. "It may be," Carol Shields suggests, "that she despaired of defining so slippery an essence as regionalism." It is equally plausible that she was unwilling to see her own work, or that of any other writer, confined within such "arbitrary enclosures."[24]

Welty is not alone in this resistance. The contemporary dramatist Horton Foote, who grew up in Wharton, Texas, and who sets many of his plays in a fictional version of his hometown, recently spoke of his artistic aims in language remarkably close to Welty's in her description of *To the Lighthouse:*

> I've never thought of myself as a regionalist. I don't lean on place, but on what transcends time or place. Essentially, people don't change. Fashion changes; crops change; they drive cars now instead of buggies. There are different moral climates and social attitudes. But you strip all that away and there is the same search for dignity, the search for meaning to life. How to bring order out of this chaos.[25]

The temptation for the literary pluralist is to "lean on" place or time or group identity, and thus to mistake these aspects of a writer's vision for its heart.

There is a second way in which the pluralist conception may force writers into arbitrary enclosures. It does so by creating segregated literary histories, in which a given author is understood mainly in relation to others belonging to the same ascriptive group. Werner Sollors has argued that such histories often assert connections between writers "who may have little in common except so-called ethnic roots," while neglecting other "obvious and important literary and cultural connections. . . . James T. Farrell may thus be discussed as a pure Irish-American writer, without any hint that he got interested in writing ethnic literature after reading and meeting Abraham Cahan, and that his first stories were set in Polish-America – not to mention his interest in Russian and French writing or in Chicago sociology."[26] In general, Sollors writes, our literature is a product of the "polyethnic mixings" of American culture, and those who ignore this fact will invent an oddly constricted set of literary genealogies:

> Do we have to believe in a filiation from Mark Twain to Ernest Hemingway, but not to Ralph Ellison (who is supposedly descended from James Weldon Johnson and Richard Wright)? Can Gertrude Stein be discussed with Richard Wright or only with white women expatriate German-Jewish writers? Is there a link from the autobiography of Benjamin Franklin to those of Frederick Douglass and Mary Antin, or must we see Douglass exclusively as a version of Olaudah Equiano and a precursor to Malcolm X? Is Zora Neale Hurston only Alice Walker's foremother? In general, is the question of influence, of who came first, more interesting than the investigation of the constellation in which ideas, styles, themes, and forms travel?[27]

Because Sollors is so intent on establishing the cosmopolitan nature of American literary culture, he tends to slight the degree to which ideas, styles, and so on, also travel and are sustained *within* particular racial or ethnic traditions. Of course, Zora Neale Hurston is not "only" Alice Walker's foremother, nor is she "exclusively" of interest to black women writers. Yet it was Walker who in the 1980s reclaimed Hurston's writings from the oblivion to which our literary culture had largely consigned them.[28] Gerald Early, who is no less intrigued than Sollors by the larger "constellation" of American literature, nonetheless observes that black writers "surely write books as a kind of ongoing dialogue with other books by blacks."[29] Henry Louis Gates, Jr., while emphasizing the "hybridity" of African-American culture, draws attention to "the formal relationships that obtain among texts in the black tradition . . . [and] the vernacular roots of the tradition."[30] Still, Sollors is right to warn that an "ethnic literary history" may overlook the migration across group boundaries of "ideas, styles, themes, and forms," all of which are as necessary to the creation of literature as the native writer's unconscious absorption of a people's inner life.

There is a final difficulty with the pluralist conception. When Mark Twain declared that the novelist refuses to "generalize the nation," he seemed to say that the native writer has no interest in defining, or even speculating about, the nature of American identity. In his account, what writers create is an able depiction of their respective communities. But the critic Constance Rourke, in her classic book on American humor, observed that the imagination of American writers is "perennially engaged by the problem of the national type."[31] However elusive and complex that identity might be, they feel compelled to say something about it, and not simply to record the particularities of the groups into which they were born.

Rourke's account of American literary history received an especially strong endorsement from Ralph Ellison. In an essay from 1957, he agreed that one of the "enduring functions" of the American novel

> is that of defining the national type as it evolves in the turbulence of change, and of giving the American experience, as it unfolds in its diverse parts and regions, imaginative integration and moral continuity. Thus it is bound up with the problem of nationhood. During the nineteenth century it was clearly recognized by those writers who speak meaningfully to us today, and it comes through novels which in their own times went, like *Moby-Dick*, unread. *Moby-Dick, The Adventures of Huckleberry Finn, The Bostonians,* and so on, are all "regional" novels, and each simultaneously projects an image of a specific phase of American life, and each is concerned with the moral predicament of the nation.[32]

Ellison is careful to say that "the national type" is evolving rather than stable, unfolding and not yet fully realized. He knows, too, that the "imaginative integration" that the writer achieves may have less to do with the discovery of shared purposes and ideals than with the exploration of a common "moral predicament." Nonetheless, he does not dismiss, as Twain did in 1895, the idea that American literature is engaged in a project of national self-definition. Indeed, Ellison places Twain among the writers committed to that project, and his claim makes undeniable sense. Though we are free to call *Huckleberry Finn* a "regional" novel, and though the Library of America has included it in a volume of Twain's work entitled *Mississippi Writings*, no one believes that these designations take us very far in understanding the novel. A book may be regional and, simultaneously, concerned with the "moral continuity" of the American experience. The life it describes may be meaningful not just as an expression of group identity, but also as a "specific phase of American life." Though the native writer may not exactly wish to "generalize the nation," the nation may be his inescapable subject.

ALTERNATIVE VISIONS

To some modern-day civic educators or literary pluralists, the doubts I have raised about earlier attempts to articulate a conception of the national literature may seem inapplicable to their own ideas and purposes. For example, many contemporary pluralists do not assume that the work of a writer from a particular community is inspired only by that community's life and cultural tradition. Moreover, they are fully aware, just as Ellison was, that a writer "reveals a larger segment of life than that of the specific milieu which engaged his attention."[33] Teachers in "multicultural" literature programs see this truth confirmed all the time. An Asian-American child in a California class-room reads Chaim Potok's *The Chosen* and discovers that, in many respects, the story of a Chasidic youth in Brooklyn fifty years ago is *her* story.[34] And finally, contemporary pluralists often agree that the books they teach are concerned with larger questions of American identity and the "moral predicament of the nation." It is for just this reason, they say, that introducing minority authors into the curriculum is sometimes controversial. These are the authors who make our moral predicament *visible;* they do not merely provide exotic detail about particular subcultures.

For their part, civic educators do not uniformly adopt the view that American literature is valuable only as a means of promoting citizenship, and the curriculum they select may be much more diverse than that of the literary historians who preceded them. Far from believing that literature must simply reflect "our American ideals," they may welcome writers who explore tensions among our ideals, as Whitman did when he asked how a commitment to individual freedom was to be reconciled with the imperatives of national unity. They may also acknowledge that one of the traditional aims of literature is to point up discrepancies between "asserted ideals and daily practices."[35] For these educators, American literary culture assumes civic importance not because it provides a mirror for established beliefs, but because within that culture individuals have continually reformulated the idea of democracy, sought to renew its prophetic force, and traced its fate within a complex and sometimes recalcitrant social reality.

Clearly, then, no single form of the civic or pluralist conception – whether from the turn of the century or from the 1990s – can be taken as definitive. Scholars and teachers continue to develop their own variants of these ideas, and in doing so they address the kinds of issues we have examined here. They ask how closely each conception accords with their best understanding of literature itself. They call attention to moral, aesthetic, and intellectual dimensions of the reading experience that any theory narrowly pursued will always dismiss or overlook.

Unfortunately, when debates over reading lists or pedagogical methods become too contentious, people often allow their theories to become enemies of thought. They slight the importance of traditions they know little about, and fail to persuade us that they comprehend the ones they ostensibly favor. At such times, hardly anyone thinks to ask what writers themselves have had to say about the functions of literature. Indeed, the debates can be so politically charged that they virtually leave literature behind.

English teachers, as it happens, are well acquainted with this last phenomenon. We have all had students who wanted nothing more than to shift each day's discussion from literature to something more exciting; the idea is to get the teacher "off the subject." But in the classroom, we know that it is usually best to resist such distractions. We do this not out of a sense of duty, but because we have a conviction that whatever book we are teaching is among the most interesting objects in the world. It remains a bit mysterious to us, no matter how often we have read it. It may help us understand our own experiences, or it may draw us out of our prescribed and customary selves. When our heated conversations about the teaching of literature neglect these possibilities, they are off the subject. We would do well to lead the discussion back.

NOTES

1. Paul Bourget, *Outre-Mer: Impressions of America* (New York: Charles Scribner's Sons, 1895), pp. 5, 44. Apparently Mark Twain read a serialization of Bourget's travel book in the *New York Herald*. There are minor differences between the newspaper translation and the one in the Scribner's edition: for example, where the newspaper has Bourget referring to "the American soul," the book has him referring to "the American spirit." Since Twain responded to the former phrase, I have quoted it here.
2. Mark Twain, "What Paul Bourget Thinks of Us," in *The Complete Essays of Mark Twain*, ed. Charles Neider (Garden City, N.Y.: Doubleday, 1963), p. 169.
3. John Higham, *Send These to Me: Immigrants in Urban America*, rev. ed. (Baltimore: The Johns Hopkins University Press, 1984), pp. 203–4. Higham observes, however, that with regard to ethnicity, Turner was an assimilationist.
4. For a contemporary novelist's reflections on the Southern Agrarians, see Mary Louise Weaks, "An Interview with Madison Smartt Bell," *Southern Review* (Winter 1994):1–12.
5. Nina Baym, *Feminism and American Literary History* (New Brunswick, N.J.: Rutgers University Press, 1992), p. 83.
6. Ibid.
7. Quoted in Baym, p. 95.
8. Quoted in Baym, p. 81.
9. Recently a number of writers have examined historical precedents and sources for the arguments advanced in the "culture wars." See, for example, Toni Marie Massaro, *Constitutional Literacy: A Core Curriculum for a Multicultural Nation* (Durham, N.C.: Duke University Press, 1993), and Russell Jacoby, *Dogmatic Wisdom: How the Culture Wars Divert Education and Distract America* (New York: Doubleday, 1994).
10. George Kateb, *The Inner Ocean: Individualism and Democratic Culture* (Ithaca, N.Y.: Cornell University Press, 1992), pp. 240, 241.
11. Walt Whitman, *Democratic Vistas*, in *Complete Poetry and Collected Prose*, ed. Justin Kaplan (New York: Library of America, 1982), p. 956.

12. Henry David Thoreau, *Walden*, in *A Week on the Concord and Merrimack Rivers, Walden, The Maine Woods, and Cape Cod*, ed. Robert F. Sayre (New York: Library of America, 1985), chap. 8, p. 459.

13. Howard Mumford Jones, *Jeffersonianism and the American Novel* (New York: Teachers College Press, 1966), p. xi. Quoted in Sandra Stotsky, "Multicultural literature and civic education," Chapter 10, this volume.

14. Mark Twain, *Adventures of Huckleberry Finn*, in *Mississippi Writings*, ed. Guy Cardwell (New York: Library of America, 1982), chap. 33, p. 851.

15. Wayne C. Booth, *The Company We Keep: An Ethics of Fiction* (Berkeley: University of California Press, 1988), p. 460.

16. Lionel Trilling, "Huckleberry Finn," in *The Liberal Imagination*, uniform ed. (Oxford: Oxford University Press, 1981), pp. 107–8.

17. Ibid., p. 108.

18. Ibid.

19. Harold Kaplan, *Democratic Humanism and American Literature* (Chicago: University of Chicago Press, 1972), p. 251.

20. Eudora Welty, "Foreword," in Virginia Woolf, *To the Lighthouse* (New York: Harcourt Brace Jovanovich, 1981), p. vii.

21. Ibid., p. xi.

22. *Adventures of Huckleberry Finn*, "Notice," p. 619.

23. David Bromwich, *Politics by Other Means: Higher Education and Group Thinking* (New Haven, Conn.: Yale University Press, 1992), p. 193.

24. Carol Shields, "Wafts of the South," *Times Literary Supplement*, August 12, 1994, p. 20.

25. Quoted in Wilborn Hampton, "For This Father, Daughter Knows Best," *New York Times*, November 6, 1994, p. 6.

26. Werner Sollors, "A Critique of Pure Pluralism," in *Reconstructing American Literary History*, Harvard English Studies 13, ed. Sacvan Berkovitch (Cambridge: Harvard University Press, 1986), pp. 255–6.

27. Ibid., p. 257.

28. See Alice Walker, *In Search of Our Mothers' Gardens* (San Diego: Harcourt Brace Jovanovich, 1983).

29. Gerald Early, "Introduction," in *Lure and Loathing: Essays on Race, Identity, and the Ambivalence of Assimilation*, ed. Gerald Early (New York: Penguin Books, 1994), p. xiv.

30. Henry Louis Gates, Jr., *Loose Canons: Notes on the Culture Wars* (New York: Oxford University Press, 1992), pp. xvi, 33.

31. See Constance Rourke, *American Humor: A Study of the National Character* (New York: Harcourt Brace, 1931). Quoted in Ralph Ellison, "Society, Morality, and the Novel," in *Going to the Territory* (New York: Random House, 1986), p. 250.

32. Ellison, "Society, Morality, and the Novel," p. 250.

33. Ralph Ellison, "A Very Stern Discipline," in *Going to the Territory*, p. 303.

34. Author's interview with Marilyn Colyar, English teacher at San Marino High School, June 20, 1994.

35. I take this phrase from James Alan McPherson, "Junior and John Doe," in *Lure and Loathing*, ed. Early, p. 178.

Index